PUNK
FOOTBALL

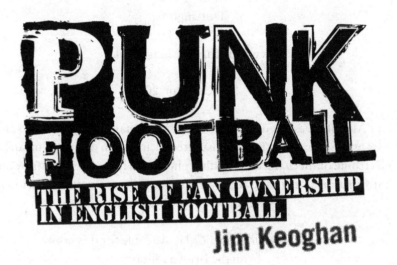

PUNK FOOTBALL

THE RISE OF FAN OWNERSHIP IN ENGLISH FOOTBALL

Jim Keoghan

First published by Pitch Publishing, 2014
Pitch Publishing
A2 Yeoman Gate
Yeoman Way
Durrington
BN13 3QZ
www.pitchpublishing.co.uk

A CIP catalogue record is available for this book
from the British Library.

ISBN 978 1-90962-636-2

Typesetting and origination by Pitch Publishing
Printed in Great Britain

Contents

Contents

Acknowledgments

FIRST I would like to say a big thank you to everyone who agreed to be interviewed. Each person featured in this book has been exceptionally generous with their time and I hope that they're satisfied with the outcome.

Special thanks need to go to Kevin Rye at Supporters Direct for not only giving me a wealth of information about supporters trusts but for also patiently answering the many, many questions I have asked him over the past year. And also to Daniel Geey, who took the time to explain the intricacies of football finance regulation, much of which initially bamboozled me.

Several publishers have been kind enough to allow me to reproduce their work for which I would like to say thanks. These are *The Guardian* (interview with John Armstrong-Holmes) and *Vision Sports Publishing* (extract from Dick Knight's autobiography *Madman*). I'm grateful to Pitch Publishing for giving me this opportunity and would like to thank all those involved with the creation of the book. On a personal level, Emma and Jamie have proven to be a distraction that has been sorely needed, and one that I am eternally appreciative.

Most importantly though I save my biggest thanks for Nicky, without whom there would be no book. Not only have you read and re-read a subject area upon which you have no interest, you have also corrected my many spelling mistakes, supported me, and when necessary given me a much deserved kick up the arse (although a few more cups-of-tea wouldn't have gone amiss).

Introduction

GROWING up in Liverpool, it's generally the norm that young kids choose one of two options when it comes to picking a team to support. To begin with, it was Liverpool who held attraction for me. Like lots of young lads, I was drawn to the colour red and at the age of four, that's pretty much all that matters. Coming from a family of die-hard Evertonians though, this was never likely to last. And sure enough, not long before the Christmas of 1980, I was pulled aside by my mum on one cold December night and calmly informed that Father Christmas doesn't visit Kopites. What child could remain loyal to their club in the face of such a horrifying truth? Certainly not me. I metaphorically crossed Stanley Park and switched teams immediately.

On the morning of the 25th I awoke to see the heap of presents at the end of my bed and felt not excitement but relief. I had been forgiven for my earlier transgressions and my mum's timely intervention had saved me from a lifetime of miserable Christmases.

Much later I of course learned that all this was a lie. Not only did Father Christmas hold no footballing prejudices, he was also a fictitious construct. From that point on the only morbidly obese, bearded alcoholic I would see at Christmas would be my Uncle Peter.

By the time I had realised the deceit it was too late. My attachment to Everton had become entrenched, the affiliation coinciding with an upsurge in my interest in the game and cemented by those all-important first experiences of live matches at Goodison. The dye had been cast and I was stuck with them, come hell or Mike Walker.

But what is the nature of this attachment? Through the writing of this book, I've been pondering what it means to be a supporter. There is a great quote about fandom in Ken Loach's 2009 masterpiece *Looking for Eric*. Delivered during an argument between two Manchester United supporters, one of whom has semi-abandoned Old Trafford in favour of the city's supporter-owned club FC United of Manchester, the quote goes, 'You can change your wife, change your politics, change your religion but you can never, never change your favourite football team.'

Is that always the case? I have certainly met plenty of people who have switched allegiances or, more depressingly, supported more than one club. But I suppose that for many fans the singular uniqueness of following a team for life does hold true.

Objectively though, it doesn't really make sense. As an Evertonian, as my dad never tires of telling me, I was a very lucky blue during my early years of following the club. Before the age of 12 I had seen Everton win two First Division titles, one FA Cup, one European Cup Winners' Cup and a handful of Charity Shields (the latter still mattered back then). I was there for Everton's Golden Age, witnessing more success in those first eight years of support than some fans of other clubs enjoy in their entire lives.

After the age of 12 though, all that luck seemed to dissipate. I was there instead for the mediocrity of the early 1990s, the horror of our flirtation with relegation during the middle part of the decade and the return of mediocrity as the century ended and the new millennium began. I have now followed the club for 33 years and during the last 18 Everton have managed just one piece of silverware. And yet my love for the club hasn't ebbed. On a Saturday afternoon I care just as much about the result today as I did all those decades ago. It is why I was at Goodison when we clinched the league title against QPR in 1985 but also why I was there when we almost went down against Wimbledon in 1994 and again against Coventry in 1998.

But why should this degree of loyalty be the case? In every other walk of life people are changeable. We go off friends, we split from partners and we alter our perspective on issues that once mattered so much to us. But not when it comes to football. We also use our leisure time to do things we enjoy. If a film is crap, we don't watch it again. If we go out to a restaurant and the food is indigestible slop then there'll be no return visit. If you went on holiday and found not an idyllic villa with a sea view (as promised in the brochure) but instead a half-finished shack with views of the local dump then it's unlikely that you'll be going back there anytime soon.

Football supporters commit to disappointment, pay to watch crap and forego the opportunity to enjoy happiness elsewhere. And they do this year-in-year-out, repeating the same cycle like an imprisoned zoo animal. As fans, if we were all rational consumers then every one of us would follow Manchester United, reasoning that such a choice represents the best shot at long-term happiness. But while thousands of people have done this (including many who probably shouldn't), most don't. The reality is that most of us who choose to follow a team, do so in the knowledge that success will be rare. I moan about Everton winning just the one piece of silverware in recent memory but for the followers of many clubs, that would be more than enough.

In the course of writing this book I have met supporters from across the leagues. Some, like the followers of Liverpool, Arsenal and Manchester United, have known success at the very highest level. Whereas others, like those of York City, Stockport County and Brentford, have had little to shout about during their long histories. But whether a glory-drenched supporter of a big club or trophy-less follower of a lesser light, the commitment I've encountered is as dogged at the bottom as it is at the top.

But for much of football's history in England, this dogged dedication never extended to supporters wanting to become involved in the running of the clubs they followed. Unlike in other parts of the world, such as Spain and Germany, the average fan in this country was happy to see him or herself as little more than a customer, albeit one whose loyalty verged on the pathological.

Whereas our continental cousins immersed themselves in their clubs by becoming stakeholders, members with a say in how matters were run, over here supporters were content to pay their money at the gate, watch the game and go home, without any thought to getting involved behind the scenes. Punters might have 'lived and died' for their team and chipped in money now and then to get the club through hard times but that didn't mean they ever wanted to run it.

Over the past few decades though, things have begun to change. No longer content to merely be enthusiastic customers, some football supporters in England have started to view their relationship with the club differently. Although the initial stirrings of change were first felt back in the late 1980s, it was from 1992, when a handful of fans of Northampton Town bandied together to form England's first football supporters' trust, that the redefining of what it means to be a 'fan' in this country began in earnest.

The aim of those pioneering fans was simple, to unite the collective strength of the supporters to raise as much money as they could to help the club out financially. Fans across the country had been doing this off-and-on for decades but this time it was different. This time the supporters wanted something in return. This time they wanted a share in the club. That they got one proved that together supporters could be something more than customers. It was a lesson that more and more fans began to heed and over the decades that followed the supporters' trust movement blossomed.

It is a movement that's adopted the catchy moniker 'punk football'. But its adherents don't have mohicans, lacerate their clobber with safety pins or gob on people. And you won't see the fans of AFC Wimbledon, FC United of Manchester or Exeter City hanging around the King's Road attempting to subvert the system by slightly unsettling passers-by. In fact, punk football only shares one thing in common with the music scene from which it derives its name; and that's the embracing of the 'do it yourself' aesthetic.

Above all else, beyond the fashion, the songs and the effin 'n' jeffin on live TV, what set punk apart from the rest of the music world (a quality that would inspire musicians for years to come) was the scene's DIY approach. Eschewing the established music industry system, punk bands produced their own albums, distributed and promoted their works independently and put out their own merchandise.

And it's this DIY ethos that lies at the heart of punk football; ordinary fans eschewing the established system and deciding that there is nothing stopping them from getting together to run the clubs they support or to establish new clubs of their own. Over the past few decades, right across football, from AFC Liverpool in the North West Counties Football League to Swansea City in the Premier League, ever increasing numbers of fans have been bandying together to do things themselves. And through this growth, punk football has redefined what it now means to be a supporter. No longer is fandom confined to the terraces. In English football today dogged devotion can take supporters all the way to the boardroom.

Looking back it's easy to see 1992 as a watershed in the domestic game. It was the year when the Premier League first kicked off. Since then the story of what's happened at the top has been told again and again, to the point where the tale of the Premier League's impact has woven itself seamlessly into the tapestry of the game's history. But the revolution that started at Northampton Town has often been overlooked. The tale might not have the glitz or the glamour of the Premier League but the rise of supporter power and that change in what it now means to be a 'fan' is still a story that needs to be told.

1

In the Beginning

MOST supporters have a picture that comes to mind when people talk about football club owners. For those, like me, whose formative years were the 1970s and 1980s, it's the old-school stereotype that pops into our head: the cigar-chewing, sheepy-wearing, local boy made good; a member of the city or town's glitterati who wants to bring the hard-nosed lessons he learned in the business world to the club that he supported as a boy. But if that all seems horribly archaic and you're more of a child of the Premier League era, then the images that come to mind are probably of the game's new generation of owners, like the Russian oligarch, the Middle Eastern sheikh, or the passionless, dead-eyed, American automaton.

It seems that as long as the game has been around, it's men (and it is largely men) like those above who have been in charge of the clubs that we follow and the relationship between English football and the business world appears to be as old as the game itself. Tales of boardroom disagreements between the manager and the owner and the times when the 'Gaffer' is given the full support of the board just days before he is given the elbow, form part of the collective memory of most fans. Along with the many managers and players who come and go over the years, the names of chairmen and owners also stick in supporters' minds, so important are they to the functioning of the clubs we love.

But how did it happen? How did English football become like this? Because it wasn't always this way; there was a time when clubs were the preserve of the players and the fans, with little room for the involvement of the local brewer or carpet magnate. To find out how it happened we have to go on a journey, back in time to the primordial swamps of football's beginnings, when the game as we know it was first starting to take shape.

Football in England has a long (and occasionally exceptionally violent) history. The earliest known reference to some form of the game taking place appears in an account of London life, written around 1175 by William Fitzstephen, biographer of Thomas Becket. Writing on the various festivities and entertainments that took place in the capital on each Shrove Tuesday, Fitzstephen describes how in the afternoon the youth of the time would head off to a patch of ground (likely near Smithfield) just outside the city for the 'famous game of ball'. This was a regular occurrence and one that even attracted spectators, who were usually those too old to play.

The game that was played then and for many centuries afterwards was so disorganised and brutal, it would be unrecognisable to us today (even to Joey Barton). Medieval football was essentially a massive kick-off, a poorly-defined contest between crowds of young lads, played in a disorganised fashion through the towns of England. There might have been opposing 'goals' to aim the ball towards but the way in which teams could do this allowed for pretty much anything. This licence for lawlessness created a game in which violence and personal injury (even sometimes resulting in death) became the norm. These were riotous affairs that would make the most bad-tempered of Old Firm head-to-heads look tame by comparison.

Despite attempts by the authorities to outlaw football (they were troubled by the social upheaval that occasionally accompanied games), the sport gradually weaved its way into the fabric of English life, becoming an essential part of the folk customs of this country by the Middle Ages. Although enjoyed by all classes, in its primitive form football primarily belonged to the lowest level of society, where its riotous nature found a more receptive audience. But this popularity among the lower classes proved to be something of a handicap as it made football vulnerable to any social changes that were occurring within the lives of working men. And during the 18th and 19th centuries these came thick and fast.

For much of the early existence of football working-class life changed very little. The country was agrarian and most ordinary men had a job that was in some way tied to the land. But this relationship underwent a radical transformation with the advent of the industrial revolution in the late 18th century. As the factories and mills grew in size, and the cities started to expand outward into the countryside, more and more workers found themselves drawn into the industrial workforce. Leisure time became limited, as Scrooge-like employers often restricted holidays to Christmas and Easter. Even Sunday, the traditional English day of leisure, was sacrificed to the rapacious appetite of the expanding economy.

Although by no means uniform, with examples of traditional football surviving in several working-class communities in the north, the ancient traditions of the game were scarcely evident among the vast majority of industrial workers during the first half of the 19th century. The people simply no longer had time for the 'people's game'. And it's possible that football would have disappeared completely had it not been for the saving presence of the most improbable group in society that you would ever imagine riding to the rescue of the game; the pupils and masters of the English public school system.

Despite working-class dominance of early football, the sport had also found its way into the country's public schools. Once there, it quickly evolved, with each institution developing its own version. Like much early football, what was played in the public schools during the 17th and 18th centuries bore little resemblance to the game we know today. The game remained fairly anarchic, with scrums still evident, forward passing often forbidden and at Eton it was even illegal to turn your back on a charging player, as this was considered ungentlemanly (although apparently it was perfectly 'gentlemanly' to kick the shit out of your opponent at the same time).

Key to the game becoming more recognisable to our modern eyes was the revolution that took place in the public school system during the mid-19th century. Prior to this, aside from a sprinkling of Latin and Greek, pupils had largely been left to their own devices; leading to a culture of unruliness in schools (several even suffered mutinies). A reform movement, led by the educator, historian and headmaster of Rugby, Thomas Arnold, began to initiate change during the early Victorian years. This was complemented by the arrival of more middle-class students in the schools, whose parents demanded something more for their children than a smattering of Latin and Greek and the occasional beating. In time, greater emphasis was placed on education and discipline, the latter underwritten by the prefect system.

As an integral and wildly popular part of student life, football was pulled into this wider effort to bring order to the schools. The game began to get greater support from headmasters who thought that a better structured, organised and less anarchic sport would be a valuable tool in their efforts to instil a stronger sense of discipline among their pupils.

To satisfy the desire to bring greater structure to football, and also eliminate anomalies, written rules governing the sport first began to appear in the 1840s. Through this process of codification, public school men from different institutions were able to recognise the common features of football played elsewhere, a process that would ultimately lead to matches taking place between schools and not just within them.

Preserving and then modernising the game within the public school system was all well and good but this didn't really benefit the rest of society for whom football remained a pastime associated with a long-lost age. This would soon change. As the sport became a more entrenched part of public school life (often becoming a compulsory activity) old-boys began playing the game after they had left. What started as just a handful of them founding clubs linked to their former school, such as the Old Harrovians and the Old Rugbeians, quickly spread as more and more established new clubs of their own.

But old-boys could only fill so many of the positions within these new teams so increasingly the men behind the clubs turned to the communities they settled in. In Lancashire for example, two of the county's earliest football clubs, Turton FC and Darwen FC, were established by former pupils of Harrow, who having returned from school imbued with a love of the game, set about recruiting local lads into the sport. This was the beginning of a trend that would start to see the working-classes reacquainted with football, albeit in a revolutionised form to that which had existed prior to the 18th century, one with far fewer numbers of players, a more codified set of rules and less chance of its participants being maimed.

Along with those simply seeking local working men to join their newly-formed teams, the working-classes were also encouraged to take up football by members of the middle-class, such as charity workers and church clerics, who were living or working in poorer communities. During the latter half of the 19th century working men gradually began to acquire more leisure time, a change attributable to the efforts of political reformers and trade unions. There existed a vein of thought among many interested in the welfare of the working-classes that if left to their own devices, working men might not use this extra time productively, instead squandering their hard-earned time off on drinking, gambling and other unsavoury, yet thoroughly enjoyable pursuits.

For these concerned citizens, football appeared to be the answer, the perfect way to occupy idle hands. The Church in particular pursued this approach and it's telling that by the

1880s around a quarter of the football clubs that had been established in England had originated from a local church. In Liverpool, which quickly became the footballing epicentre of England, by the mid-1880s 25 of the 112 football clubs in the city had religious connections, the most famous of which, Everton, originated from St Domingo's Methodist Church in Kirkdale in 1878.

Part of the reason why football was so readily embraced by working men was because the game lent itself easily to urban life. It needed no equipment other than a ball and could be played by anyone, regardless of size, skill or strength. It was simple to play, easy to understand, and could take place under most conditions and on most surfaces.

The spread in the popularity of football was also assisted by the founding of the Football Association (FA) in 1863. On 26 October, representatives from several of the recently established football clubs such as Forest, Blackheath and War Office met together to establish an association that could clarify the rules of the game. Those that were ultimately agreed upon removed any overlap between football and rugby, by for example outlawing the handling of the ball and the legality of just kicking someone if they were faster or better than you. The establishment of codified rules meant that it was now simpler for teams to play against each other, something that acted as a catalyst for a rapid growth in fixtures during the latter half of the 19th century.

Working-class interest combined with the organisational structure that the FA also provided ensured that football expanded swiftly between 1870 and the turn of the century. In 1867 the FA had just ten clubs affiliated to it. By 1888 this had risen to 1,000. Fast-forward to 1905 and the figure stood at a mightily impressive 10,000.

But what were these clubs? What were the differences and similarities to the football clubs, both league and non-league, that we know today?

To begin with they were simply members' clubs, with those who joined paying a subscription to do so. Although initially dependent upon the organising efforts of former public school boys, as time passed clubs were established by ordinary working men too. Many of these originated within workplaces, the railways proving a particularly effective midwife to several teams. One such club, Newton Heath FC, was formed in 1878 by workers from the Carriage and Wagon Department of the Lancashire and Yorkshire Railway depot in Newton Heath, southern Manchester. This was a club that would, after a name-change and relocation, eventually morph into that footballing behemoth Manchester United.

Such was the popularity of the game among the working-classes that eventually fixtures started to attract crowds, bringing into existence the 'football supporter' for the first time. To begin with, these early supporters would have been those members of the club that weren't playing, ex-players who still had an interest in the team and friends and family of those involved. In many instances, these supporters also paid a membership fee, which would act as a season ticket; one that would also provide them with a say in how the club was run.

This latter aspect of membership was important. When football first became popularised, most clubs were run as democratic entities, owned and controlled by the players and members. These were clubs like Aston Villa and Woolwich Arsenal. By the late 1880s the former was run by a nine-man management committee, with each position elected by the club's 382 members. A few hundred miles further south, Woolwich Arsenal, which had been established by employees of the Royal Arsenal in 1886, represented an interesting example of working-class organisation. During the early years of its existence a management committee of working men, elected by a membership dominated by working men, ran every aspect of the club.

In the very early days of football, when businessmen were involved it was usually because there was a connection with a place of work. At Thames Ironworks in East London, the owner Arnold F Hills helped establish a club with his works foreman Dave Taylor. Although this organisation, which would eventually sever its ties with both Hill and the Works and become West Ham United, was run by its members, Hill provided it with a stadium (one of the most impressive in England at the time) and established a sports committee that insured the players against loss of wages resulting from injury.

Alongside these more formal relationships, there were also occasional instances of local businessmen with an interest in the game throwing a club a few quid, such as Lancashire industrialist Sydney Yates. In 1883, his local club Blackburn Olympic had a great season, culminating with them reaching that year's FA Cup Final. During the closing ties of the competition, Yates provided the club with £100 to help undergo special training in the luxurious setting of Blackpool.

That the nature of this limited and often ad hoc involvement ultimately changed, a process that saw businessmen drawn into the game, was attributable to the growing sophistication in the way football was organised during the closing decades of the 19th century.

Key to this was the arrival of the professional footballer in the 1880s. Professionalism had long been an anathema to many of those involved in the sport. Players were amateurs and the view, predominant among the old-boys who dominated football in its infancy, was this is how it should stay. These were men who believed that the game should be played for the sake of enjoyment, that players should remain respectful towards the opposition in victory or defeat and that at all times the notion of fair play had to be upheld.

But as anyone who has played or followed football can attest, such ideals often wither in the face of competitive hunger. And for those imbued with this, one way to satisfy its rapacious appetite was to pay for the best talent available. At first, professionalism was a 'behind-closed-doors' affair. Along with 'under-the-table' payments, players were brought to clubs and given financial inducements to sign, or should it be a works team, a cushy job in the company.

Probably the first known person to play football solely for financial reasons in England was a one-eyed Glaswegian shipyard worker called James Lang, who came south to play for Sheffield's The Wednesday in 1876. Although Lang was given a position at a local knife factory, his time was chiefly taken up by playing football and reading the paper (which is coincidently my dream job).

Despite efforts by the FA to uphold the amateur ethos, including the fining or suspending of any clubs who were caught offering players financial reward, in 1885 professionalism was eventually legalised. The impetus for this change throughout had come from teams of the north-west, specifically those based in Lancashire. Clubs like Preston North End and Burnley were among the first to flout the FA's prohibition against professionalism and the most vocal in their support for it to be legalised. They were also two among several northern clubs who had threatened to break away from the FA and form their own rival football authority should their demand not be met.

Once legalised, professionalism grew rapidly. Amateurism, and the clubs that still adhered to that principle, declined in response to professional teams who were simply better. Prior to legalisation, the encroachment of professionalism had already weakened the supremacy once enjoyed by the public school clubs anyway (the kind that were most strongly identified with the cause of amateurism). Teams like Wanderers, Old Etonians and Oxford University had dominated the FA Cup during its early years, and for the first decade of the tournament's existence, no working-class club even managed to reach the final. This started to change in the early 1880s, and as the decade progressed, more professionally organised clubs like Blackburn Rovers, West Bromwich Albion and Aston Villa started to eclipse their amateur rivals, a switch that was subsequently never reversed.

But although they might have lost the debate, that didn't mean that those who valued amateurism were necessarily in the wrong or that their arguments weren't valid. One of the fears stated by those who resisted the legalisation of professionalism was the belief that its introduction would bring the demand for more cash into the game, and by doing so change the nature of football forever. And in this, they were right on the money. Professionalism was the catalyst for the creation of the game as we know it in England today (warts and all).

For those clubs with access to money, the potential was now there to buy the best team possible. When it came to raising finance for wages, transfer fees and the improvement of facilities, the first area of recourse for any club to turn to was the fans and members. From being a sport watched by a handful of people in the 1860s, by the turn of the century the popularity of football had grown enormously. In 1875 only two games had pulled in crowds of more than 10,000 people. Within a decade that had increased to 18. But the most dramatic rise in attendances occurred in the 1890s, following on from the establishment of the Football League in 1888. During the league's first season 602,000 people watched the matches between the country's 12 leading clubs. By the eve of the First World War the figure had reached 9 million. Football was fast becoming the national sport.

The rise in number of spectators gave clubs much-needed income to pursue the dream of building teams that could compete. Initially, the fans who turned up to watch these games stood on man-made earth embankments overlooking the pitch or, for a limited number of lucky individuals following the more affluent clubs, on simple, uncovered terraces that could hold a small number of supporters. It was the kind of salubrious setting that brings to mind the unlamented away end at Roker Park on a Saturday afternoon.

Aware that demand for the sport was growing exponentially and that the greater the number of supporters that could be accommodated, the greater the income a club could enjoy, between 1890 and the outbreak of the First World War, football clubs began to construct purpose-built stadiums, the first example being Everton's Goodison Park, which was built during 1892.

The sums involved in constructing stands and stadiums were often beyond anything that a members' club could achieve through gate receipts, cash donations or subscriptions alone, leading many clubs to seek additional levels of finance. One of the simplest ways to do this was to turn into a joint-stock company. For these nascent professional sides there were numerous advantages to this move. Aside from the fact that a club could now issue shares which could pay a dividend, these companies also enjoyed limited liability; meaning that if the business became insolvent shareholders would not be liable for any of the debts (a legal protection that would make would-be investors more willing to part with their cash).

Small Heath (who would later morph into Birmingham City) became the first club to travel down this path in 1888. Over the following decades more and more clubs followed suit and by 1921, 84 out of the Football League's 86 clubs had converted to private companies. But this shouldn't necessarily have meant that it was businessmen that would come to dominate the clubs that we love. After all, when shares are issued, they are done so to all and not necessarily just to the wealthy.

And in the early days of the game there *were* many examples of working-class supporters investing in the clubs they followed. At Woolwich Arsenal, that paragon of working-class organisation, in 1893 the club incorporated with a nominal capital of 4,000 shares, each priced at £1 each. From this, around 1,500 were allotted to 860 people, the vast majority of whom were working men living in the Plumstead and Woolwich areas and likely employed at the Arsenal.

But although working men and working-class supporters did buy shares across football, they tended to be very much in the minority. Part of the problem was that share prices were often too high for the average supporter to afford. But even when clubs went out of their way to offer shares at a low price and specifically target working-class supporters, which is what Croydon Common, Dartford FC and Southport FC did around the turn of the century these efforts often met with little success.

In reality, shareholding never really took hold among working-class supporters. And even when a number of them did make the effort to invest, they could rarely buy in volume. By contrast, local businessmen and professionals from the middle-classes could buy shares by the bucketload, giving them the opportunity to gain influence at a club in a way that an ordinary working-class shareholder never could. This is why positions on the board at English football clubs tended to be dominated by this section of the local community. Directorships were largely gobbled up by big shareholders, not someone who had managed to rustle up enough cash to buy a tiny stake. At Liverpool FC at the turn of the century, just a decade after the club's establishment, 60 per cent of voting shares were owned by the club's eight directors. Liverpool were fairly representative of the industry at the time in the professional game and perfectly illustrate how power in football became concentrated in the hands of the better-off.

But it was as true of football back in the late Victorian and Edwardian period as it is today, that the game was a lousy one to get involved with if you want to earn a few quid. Back then, although some of the more successful league clubs like Everton, Chelsea and Liverpool were capable of making profits, there were many more that did not. During the 1898/99 season, things got so bad that the Football League had to issue a circular asking clubs to contribute to a common fund which would be used to bail out fellow league members who were on the bones of their arse. Few shareholders, large or small, ever received a dividend from their club, a reality perfectly illustrated during the 1908/09 season when only six out of 62 prominent clubs paid out to their shareholders. Of those that did, this was limited to five per cent of the share's face value, following the issuing of the FA 34; a statute designed to ensure that profits went back into the game and not into the pockets of speculators.

For a hard-nosed businessman, what allure did football hold then? What reason was there for them to invest so much cash in an enterprise so unlikely to offer a decent return, if any at all?

For some, there were profits to be made if you looked beyond the accounts of the club itself. Several brewers became involved, using the game as a way to market what they produced. Products were advertised at grounds and players, both past and present, were given pubs to run in the hope that it would increase custom. Manchester City became known as the 'brewers club' because so many early benefactors, such as local beer magnate Stephen Chester Thompson, were involved in the trade.

But for many other individuals that became owners, major shareholders and directors there were often motivations for involvement beyond what could be done for their bank balances. Some simply loved the game and were avid supporters of the clubs they became connected with. Others already had an association with the club, having served on the management committee prior to incorporation. Involvement as a director was also something that was passed down through families, motivating those affected via a sense of familial obligation. The descendants of Chelsea's founder Gus Mears continued to be involved with the club after his death in 1912, maintaining ownership until 1982, when they sold up to Ken Bates.

Another motivation for involvement, one that might seem quaint by today's standards, was a sense of civic duty. The game's huge popularity meant that clubs quickly evolved into important institutions within the cities and towns of Victorian and Edwardian England, becoming an indelible part of their civic tapestry. The concept of serving your community and enhancing civic pride was something much valued among the middle-classes of the time. Investing in a club and becoming chairman or a director could be seen as part of this public service ethos. It's possibly why so many leading philanthropic figures of the various towns and cities that boasted professional football clubs, men such as John H. Davies at Manchester United, a man who supported many sports and charitable causes in the local area, became investors.

But whatever the reasons for involvement, by the eve of the First World War the reality was that ownership had become dominated by the richer elements of local society. What's more, the model that had emerged during the 1890s, a private company with limited liability, had also achieved complete dominance in the professional game. Democratically run members' clubs (the model that had prospered during football's infancy) were consigned to the margins.

And for much of the past 100 years very little has changed. Although local businessmen have sometimes been replaced by Arab sheikhs or Eastern European petrochemical billionaires and the presence of the 'single owner' has become more common, in terms of how clubs are owned and organised English football today differs very little fundamentally to that which existed a century ago. But despite the resilience of the private model, in recent years changes to the game have started to challenge its apparent infallibility. As the following chapter reveals, just because something has trundled along successfully for some time, doesn't mean that it will remain untroubled forever.

2

Drowning in a
Sea of Debt

WITH all the tales that we hear today of debt, insolvencies and football clubs being minutes away from folding, it's hard to believe that for much of its history, professional football in England was, in financial terms at least, a relatively sedate affair. Between 1900 and 1980 only a handful of professional Football League sides went out of business because they could no longer balance the books; clubs like New Brighton Tower FC (1901), Wigan Borough FC (1931) and Accrington Stanley FC (1966).

When you take into account how much economic and social turmoil took place during those 80 years it's remarkable how many clubs survived.

In their riveting book *Soccernomics* authors Stefan Szymanski and Simon Kuper illustrate this point through the work of the economic historian Les Hannah. A few years ago, Hannah made a list of the top British companies in 1912 and researched what had become of them by the mid-1990s. He found that nearly half of these giants had simply disappeared, succumbing to a mixture of bankruptcy, nationalisation and takeovers. Among those that had survived, many had gone into new sectors, meaning that very few had managed to prosper within their original industry.

Considering that the time-span that Hannah chose to look at included several recessions, a couple of depressions and the two World Wars, the fact that so many companies had suffered should probably not come as a massive surprise.

But over roughly the same period it would seem that the vicissitudes of the economic world didn't apply to English football. In 1923 the Football League consisted of 88 teams organised in four divisions. In the 2007/08 season, 85 of these still existed, 75 of them remaining in the top four divisions. Football seemed able to shrug off recessions, depressions and World Wars in a way that no other industry could, as though the ebb and flow of market forces were of little consequence to the game.

There are many reasons for the uniqueness of football as an industry; the technology of the sport can never become outmoded, rivals from abroad are forbidden from entering a league and undercutting domestic clubs and a team which fails to keep up with the competition can always survive in a lower league.

The customers are different too. Put simply, supporters aren't 'normal' punters. When the business is failing and the team underperforming, most fans don't desert their club en masse. It is a form of brand loyalty that companies like Tesco and Asda must look on with a sense of awestruck envy.

But these factors only go part of the way to explaining why so few clubs went under. After all, those same factors exist today and yet no one could claim that English football is a world characterised by financial sanity. The reality is that the long period of relative stability, one that stretched from the First World War until the early 1980s, also rested in part upon several peculiarities of the English professional game, the most important of which was the imposition by the Football League of the maximum wage.

In an era when Cristiano Ronaldo can earn more in a week than the average UK worker will earn in a decade, it seems amazing to think that there was a time when footballers' wages were little higher than those of the average working man or woman. First mooted during the early 1890s, the thinking behind the idea of regulated wages was to prevent rich clubs from poaching talent from their less financially endowed rivals. After all, the lure of moving to Everton, Villa or Liverpool might not be so great if you could earn just as much by staying put at Bury. Despite objections from some of the richer clubs, who believed that a maximum wage would hold them back, the Football League introduced it at the beginning of the 1901/02 season, stating that no player could earn more than £4 per week.

Over the next 60 years, the amount a player could bring home edged up to the point where, in 1961, a footballer was able to earn as much as £20 per week (although the vast majority didn't make as much as this). Despite the increase, this was hardly a sum that placed them in the higher echelons of wage earners. In fact, during the course of the maximum wage's lifespan, footballers as a whole ended up becoming relatively *worse* off when compared to other working-class professions. When the cap was introduced it represented a comfortable living wage, double the norm enjoyed by the average industrial worker. By 1960, the maximum wage of £20 was only £5 higher than that brought home by the average man working in industry.

This was part of the reason why English football was losing talent to clubs elsewhere in the world. Men like Neil Franklin (Stoke City to Independiente Santa Fe in 1951), Billy Higgins (Everton to Millonarios in 1951) and John Charles (Leeds to Juventus in 1957) were part of a small but growing trend that saw players move to countries without wage regulation.

The drain of talent and a general level of discontent among footballers towards their relatively meagre wages meant that eventually something had to give, and that something came in the surprising form of Jimmy Hill. Back in the early 1960s, prior to his brief managerial career and before his time as a broadcaster, Hill forged a name as a trade union firebrand. The union in question was the Professional Footballers' Association (PFA) and Hill earned his reputation during his time as chairman when he organised a campaign for the abolition of the maximum wage.

Hostility towards the cap among professional footballers had blossomed during the post-war years when clubs, despite enjoying a financial bonanza provided by record attendances, had been reluctant to work with the Football League to increase the level of players' earnings by much. The cap had helped ensure that most clubs got by financially, protecting them from paying the true value of what their players were worth.

Hill's genius was in devising the popular argument against the maximum wage, presenting the cap as an anachronism for three reasons. First, he argued, footballers should not be paid less than the people coming to watch them on a Saturday afternoon. Second, he reasoned that it was wrong to compare footballers with members of the working-class because they were not akin to labourers in a factory but instead comparable to professionals in the entertainment business, people who tended to earn much more than £20 per week. And lastly, Hill believed that footballers had the right, just like any other employee, to have the freedom to negotiate how much they were paid.

This three-pronged argument, straightforward enough to gain traction among footballers, fans and the media, was then backed up by Hill's organisation of a player strike on the issue (a tactic that received huge support among PFA members). Media and public support for the players' cause, combined with the growing realisation that the PFA was intent on carrying through its threat, led the Football League to cave in. On 18 January 1961, not long before the strike was due to come into effect, they capitulated to the PFA's demands and the maximum wage, one of the central pillars of English football, was no more.

Although this was great for the players, and much deserved, the immediate effect of the abolition was ballooning wage inflation. The most publicised example of this was the experience of Fulham and England captain Johnny Haynes, who not long after the cap was lifted managed to get his wages increased to £100 per week, representing the kind of inflation you would expect in Weimar Germany, and not Craven Cottage. As spectacular as this was, Haynes represented the extreme end of the trend and most players didn't enjoy anywhere near such a stratospheric rise in income (some tight-arsed clubs, such as Liverpool and Manchester United, even attempted to continue their own 'unofficial' cap for a few years after the abolition).

But despite Haynes being something of a statistical outlier, his footballing comrades were still a lot better off in the years that immediately followed the demise of the cap. According to research by Szymanski and Kupers the inflation-adjusted increase in wages during the 1950s for clubs with complete financial records was less than ten per cent. For those same clubs, between 1961 and 1974, the corresponding inflation-adjusted rise was 90 per cent (an increase only partly offset by growth in revenues).

Although the increase had slowed by the late 1970s, as football began to adjust to the new regime, many clubs were finding it difficult to function in an era of unregulated wages. The maximum wage had protected them for decades and without it life was becoming tough.

It was a harsh reality that was compounded by the problem of falling attendances. During the post-war years, English football became massively popular. Parental tales of grounds packed to the rafters, of young lads being separated from their mates via the ebb and flow of the crowd, of pubs and city centres becoming deserted on Saturday afternoons as men and boys in their tens of thousands flocked to the home games, were rooted in fact and not just rose-tinted nostalgia. This surge in people going to the match reached its apex in the 1948/49 season when aggregate league attendances hit just north of 41 million.

But the boom proved short-lived, and what occurred over the following four decades was a slow decline. There are plenty of reasons why crowd numbers waned in England over this period. Social habits changed as higher earnings and a wider array of leisure pursuits became available to the average punter. The grounds themselves, due to decades of underinvestment, became pretty dilapidated, with several remaining roofless, which on a rainy Saturday afternoon could be fairly unappealing to those now accustomed to a more luxurious way of life.

These factors were then exacerbated in the 1970s and 1980s by the rise of hooliganism, which tarnished football's reputation, putting existing fans off going to the game and ensuring that a younger generation of supporters coming through were also less inclined to take to the terraces. By the 1985/86 season the trend reached its nadir, with aggregate attendances that year standing at an abjectly low 16.5 million.

With fewer punters left to milk and wage bills now reflecting the true value of players, clubs began to look at other ways to increase their revenues. One of these was sponsorship, which took off in earnest during the 1980s. It was this need to balance falling attendances with rising wages that we can thank for the corporate logos that currently spread themselves unappealingly across the kits of the clubs we follow.

Although Kettering Town had been the first English club to head down this path, with the glamorous adoption of Kettering Tyres as their kit sponsor, they had done so in 1976, one year before the FA had legalised such a move. Because of this, the title of first 'official' shirt sponsor has to go to Liverpool, who struck a deal with the Japanese electronics giant Hitachi to have their name emblazoned upon their iconic kits in 1979.

Another idea, although one that emerged solely from the higher echelons of league football, was a call for home teams to keep all of the matchday gate receipts. Until 1981 these had been shared, with 20 per cent of what was taken by the home team given to the opposition. The system had been introduced as a means by which wealthy clubs could subsidise poorer ones.

When wages had been capped and tens of millions of punters were pouring through the turnstiles, gate sharing had been begrudgingly tolerated by the bigger clubs. But with attendances falling and wages prey to the mercies of the free market, the big clubs were less inclined to be so kind-hearted. Using the threat of breaking away to form their own 'super league', independent from the rules and regulations of the Football League (a tactic of intimidation that the big clubs used regularly throughout the 1980s) they were able to force their will and have this redistributive mechanism abolished.

These changes made the 1980s a difficult time for many clubs. Sponsorship and greater commercial sophistication (such as the opening of club shops) could only go so far. Losses started to grow and debt ratcheted upwards. At times this debt could reach untenable levels, and the prospect of a club going out of business began to haunt English football.

In his exhaustive history of league football between 1888 and 1988, the writer Simon Inglis made the effort to flick through the 1981/82 season's *Rothmans Football Yearbook*, which provided an insight into the extent of the financial crisis hitting English football during that season. According to the book, many clubs were haemorrhaging money at the time, with the likes of Bristol City and Chester City losing thousands per week. Others such as Darlington and Rochdale United spent most of the campaign on the verge of collapse. And some, like Hull City, even went into receivership, so dire was the financial situation at the club.

The methods employed to avoid going under varied from club to club. Most trimmed the staff and cut wages, others appealed to supporters' clubs and directors to provide loans or donations. If they were lucky enough to have any, there were also clubs that sold land for redevelopment, such as Hull City, Crystal Palace and Bolton Wanderers (supermarkets), AFC Bournemouth and Brentford (houses and flats) and Tranmere Rovers (a pub). Some more adventurous clubs even developed their own land, including Notts County (sports centre) Bristol City (bowling green) and Aston Villa (conference suite).

But with so many financial factors working against them, occasions arose when it was beyond an individual club's capabilities to cope and in the early 1980s the prospect of teams going out of business started to appear in the game on a regular basis, with several like Bristol City, Wolves and Derby County all coming close to folding.

In the case of Bristol City, who found themselves in a deep mess during 1982, survival was only achieved by the controversial practice of phoenixing. Wealthy backers from among the fans formed a new company called BCFC PLC (1982) to replace the old company Bristol City Football Club PLC. BCFC PLC then arranged to buy the club's ground off the receiver and asked the Football League if they could take the old club's share in the Fourth Division. In reality the new company was exactly the same as its predecessor, with the crucial difference that they hadn't taken on the debts or any of the expensive players. Although popular among the fans, this was hardly a move that endeared the club to the numerous creditors, who lost out following this legal sleight of hand.

Throughout the 1980s and into the 1990s, even when attendances began to slowly improve from their 1986 nadir, losses and debt remained a constant problem across football. For the big clubs the solution seemed obvious, television. Football had been a regular part of the TV schedule since the mid-1960s following the BBC's launching of *Match of the Day* (MOTD) in 1964. During the 1970s and 1980s, both MOTD and ITV's *The Big Match* (later called simply *The Match*) were the main sources of football on TV. I can still recall the hush of expectation that fell over my house on a Sunday afternoon when the first bars of 'Goal Crazy' by Rod Argent piped up, heralding the promise of *The Match*'s televisual football feast.

Since TV had first arrived in the world of football, revenues had been shared equally across all four leagues, an element of democracy that seems unbelievable from today's vantage point. This all changed in 1988 when, following threats by the top-flight clubs that they would break away from the Football League, a new dividing structure was established that saw 50 per cent of the £44m four-year deal with ITV awarded to the First Division clubs, 25 per cent to the Second Division, and 25 per cent to be shared between the Third and Fourth. TV was fast becoming one of the easiest ways for clubs to increase their revenue. And it was one that would only prove more lucrative as the years wore on and satellite television entered the market, bringing with it mind-boggling amounts of cash.

The early 1990s was a transformative time for English football. Grounds were redeveloped after the publication of the *Taylor Report*, which recommended the removal of many of the terraces that were once such an integral part of the matchday experience. Following years of threats, the top flight did eventually break away from the rest of the Football League, creating the Premier League in the process. And BSkyB managed to wrestle control of televised football from its terrestrial competitors, in the process providing the Premier League with more money than it could ever have imagined. The first deal struck by Sky to televise top-flight football in 1992 cost the company £305m for a five-year contract. When the agreement was renewed in 1997, the figure had more than doubled to £670m. During 2013, both Sky and BT won the rights to broadcast Premier League football in a three-year deal worth £3bn, an insane escalation in cost that shows just how important TV money has become.

But despite this massive influx of cash, the problem of clubs haemorrhaging money and borrowing to cover losses hasn't gone away. If anything it's worsened. In the top flight (the league which has benefited most from TV's bounty) during the 2011/12 season a combined total of £2.4bn was made by the Premier League's 20 clubs. Although very impressive, and a figure that dwarfs that made in other major European leagues, over the course of that season those same 20 clubs made a combined net loss of £205m. From these, only eight registered a profit. Of those that made losses before tax, several reported figures that were pretty hefty, such as Manchester City (£99m), Liverpool (£41m) and Sunderland (£32m).

This continued profligacy has resulted today in only two Premier League clubs, Norwich City and Swansea City, being debt-free. As of 2012, the remainder have net debts that range from the modest (Fulham's £4m) through to the fairly big (Everton's £46m) and finally encompassing the truly massive (Newcastle United's £129m). Although not all of this is caused by operational losses, plenty of it is. At Liverpool during the 2011/12 financial year, the club's £41m loss (on the back of a £49m loss the year before) has been a big contributory factor to the club's net debt of £87m.

Elsewhere in the football pyramid, the situation is hardly better. In the Championship, during the 2009/10 season the league made a record loss of £133m and 14 clubs each shipped more than £5m. Overall, Championship clubs were spending £4 for every £3 they generated in revenue. In the same season, League 1 clubs collectively made a record loss of £52m, and League 2 clubs one of £8m. As of 2013, the 72 clubs that make up the Football League carry a collective debt of £1bn, much of it attributable to continued losses.

The failure to overcome this problem has created a period of unrivalled instability in modern football. Between 1982 and 2010, there were 67 cases of formal insolvency proceedings affecting clubs in the top four English divisions. The majority of these have taken place in recent memory, illustrated by the fact that if we just took the period 2002–2011 the figure for total insolvencies in the Football League stands at 36. For some of the clubs affected there have also been repeat events, seeing the likes of Darlington, Swindon Town and Rotherham United coming close to folding on more than one occasion over the past 30 years.

Key to this has been the inability of English football to accommodate the problem of rising wages. It is a trend most keenly felt in the Premier League, which between 1992 and 2010 saw a total wage increase of 1,508 per cent. At the same time, players in the Football League also enjoyed sizeable rises too, if not quite as impressive, with earnings expanding by 518 per cent, 306 per cent and 233 per cent respectively for the next three divisions. As a dispiriting comparison, over that same period the average worker has seen his or her pay go up by a mere 186 per cent.

This would be fine if income was able to keep up, but despite clubs earning more than ever before it hasn't been the case. Back in 1997, the average Premier League club spent 47 per cent of their turnover on player salaries. By 2012, this figure had risen to an average of 70 per cent. Within this there were some clubs, such as Villa and Blackburn that were paying almost their entire turnover on wages (90 per cent and 86 per cent respectively) and even one club, Manchester City, shelling out more than 100 per cent.

And it wasn't just a trend confined to the Premier League. During 2010/11, clubs in the Championship were forking out 88 per cent of their turnover on wages, a figure higher than any other European league. And just like the division above, within this some clubs such as Bristol City (157 per cent of turnover) Leicester (130 per cent) and Southampton (125 per cent) were splashing out incredible amounts on players' salaries.

At a very basic level the end of the maximum wage made this possible. With the cap removed, wages were free to rise, letting footballers earn what they were truly worth. But the removal of the maximum wage alone can't explain the wage inflation that has occurred in the game, specifically the eye-popping increases of the past 20 years.

One contributory factor has been the Bosman ruling, delivered by the European Court of Justice in 1995, which declared that at the end of his contract any player is now free to move to a club of his choosing. Bosman had two inflationary impacts. First, it put players in a much stronger position when it came to bargaining for higher wages because clubs could sign them at the end of their contract without having to pay a transfer fee. And secondly, during the course of their careers players now have fewer contracts, as clubs seek to protect themselves by tying players into longer and longer deals. As a result, top players have looked to sign more lucrative deals to maximise their career earnings.

But as important as this is, Rob Wilson, football finance expert at Sheffield Hallam University, feels that of more significance than the impact of Bosman has been the massive amount of money that has flooded into football.

He says, 'Foreign investment into the game, from the likes of Roman Abramovich and Sheikh Mansour, people with personal fortunes that reach into the billions, has certainly contributed to the huge amounts of cash that have been sloshing around English football in recent years. A generation ago, you didn't have these kinds of owners. Clubs, even in the early days of the Premier League, were still mainly owned by "local-boys-made-good", people whose personal wealth was more modest.'

At the same time, the money being pumped into the game by satellite broadcasting has continued to grow, which Rob feels has only accentuated the impact of people like Roman Abramovich.

He continues, 'Prior to the age of Sky, terrestrial broadcasters weren't paying that much for the rights to show games. That all changed in 1992. Since then, Sky has put billions into the game, specifically into the pockets of Premier League owners. And over the past decade the figures we're talking about have just got bigger and bigger. Combined with the arrival of a new generation of billionaire owners, what's happened has been a simple case of supply and demand. With a finite number of players out there we've had a classic example of excess money chasing a limited resource, which was always going to lead the cost of luring that resource to a club and then keeping it there to rocket.'

This mismatch between supply and demand has not just impacted upon wages. There has also been a corresponding explosion in the cost of buying players. According to the website Pay As You Play, which is packed full of all kinds of statistical goodies about modern football, back at the dawn of the Premier League, the average player transfer cost was

£594,000. By the end of the 2010/11 season that same figure had risen to an almighty £4.83m. This represents a level of cumulative inflation of 730 per cent. Over the same period of time the Bank of England's cumulative Consumer Price Index has been just 77.1 per cent.

'And although this has been most keenly felt in the Premier League, wage pressure and transfer cost increases have fed down into the lower leagues,' argues Rob.

Championship clubs want to recruit the best talent in order to challenge for promotion and access the financial bonanza that awaits them in the Premier League. To do this often means paying Premier League level costs, which themselves are massively inflated. Lower down the pyramid, League 1 clubs want to get into the Championship, which means paying Championship level costs, which as we know have been inflated.

'This goes on and on, a cost spiral infecting the entire game,' continues Rob. 'And it's one aggravated by the parachute payments provided to clubs who are relegated. When it comes to leaving the Premier League, these payments can be as high as £60m over four seasons.'

But what can clubs do? This is the market that has been created and if you want to succeed then playing along seems to be the price that has to be paid. What's more, according to *Soccernomics*, when it comes to wages, all the evidence points to the fact that the more you spend then the better a club will do.

Between 1978 and 1997 the authors looked at 40 football clubs in England and found that if you took their spending on salaries for the entire period, then a massive 92 per cent of variation in league position was entirely attributable to the amount they paid out. And this correlation shows little sign of weakening. The authors also looked at clubs playing in the Premier League and the Championship between 1998 and 2007, finding that the degree of correlation remained high, standing at 89 per cent.

But before we let owners (and managers) off the hook too quickly, it's worth bearing in mind that despite the strong relationship between wages and league position, Szymanski and Kuper found a much weaker correlation between net transfer spending and success. Keeping a good player costs money but buying one is always a gamble. There is probably not a fan alive that can't immediately bring to mind three expensive transfers who turned out to be an unmitigated disaster. As an Evertonian, my three personal favourites are:

Alex Nyarko
Bought for £4.5m from Lens in 2000, Nyarko played 33 times in four seasons, scored one goal and was the subject of a protest by a fan who ran on to the pitch to essentially tell the player how shit he was.

Ibrahima Bakayoko
Dubbed 'Baka-joke-o' by the Goodison faithful, this £4.5m forward arrived from Montpellier during the wilderness of the Walter Smith years. Just four goals in one season and some appallingly lacklustre performances ensured that he was soon shown the door.

Per Krøldrup
This was possibly one of the worst transfers in the history of the English game. Krøldrup moved to Everton from Udinese for £5m in 2005 and played just one match. At £5m per game it makes Per one of the most expensive players to ever feature in the Premier League.

The need to shell out millions in wages and the temptation to do the same with transfers has created an environment in which most clubs, small and big, have spent much of the past two decades living beyond their means, a decision that tends to leave them at the mercy of soft loans (those with a below-market rate of interest) provided by financial backers, over-dependent upon other external sources of revenue (such as television money) and reliant on maintaining their league position.

'The risk inherent within this model is revealed once a change occurs, such as an owner walking away from the club, the collapse of a lucrative TV deal, or a team suffering relegation. Indebted clubs, already stretched beyond their means, inevitably have a greater propensity to slide towards financial ruin in these circumstances,' says Professor Tom Cannon, a member of the University of Liverpool's Football Industry Group.

The sorry tale of Bradford City provides a perfect illustration of what can happen when the desire for success, or in this instance the desire to maintain residency in a certain league at any cost, pushes the club too far.

When Geoffrey Richmond took control of Bradford in 1994 he found a club that was in the doldrums. Mired in the Second Division, struggling with debt and facing several winding-up petitions, this was not a club that you could imagine storming into the Premier League within a few years. Yet that's exactly what happened. Richmond's commercial nous, the canny appointment of Paul Jewell as manager and the recruitment of some cheap but experienced senior pros conspired to produce something of a perfect storm. Bradford inched their way up the pyramid and at the beginning of the 1999/2000 season lined up with the likes of Manchester United, Arsenal and Chelsea in that year's Premier League campaign.

Contrary to what would occur later, Richmond was financially cautious during the club's inaugural season in the top flight. And it was an approach that paid off. Despite hanging around the relegation zone for much of the season, the club managed to avoid going down when, on the final day of the campaign Bradford beat Liverpool 1-0 at home, a win that helped them to sneak into the safety of 17th place.

The fans were ecstatic to say the least. Bradford had been written off by the pundits virtually from the moment they had earned promotion. But here they were, one of the game's minnows, taking on the big clubs and surviving, proving the pundits wrong in the process.

But sadly for the Bradford faithful it would be some time until the fans would ever enjoy a level of elation even remotely close to that experienced when they defeated Liverpool. Buoyed by their improbable survival and keen to establish the club as a permanent fixture in the top flight, Richmond then changed tack in the summer of 2000. What followed was later described by the owner as 'six weeks of madness'. Financial prudence was shown the door and a mini-age of profligacy established at Valley Parade. A spending splurge saw a raft of expensive signings arrive, such as David Hopkin (£2.5m from Leeds), Ashley Ward (£1.5m from Blackburn), Dan Petrescu (£1m from Chelsea) and Italian striker Benito Carbone (who came on a free transfer but with a wage bill of £40,000 per week, proper big-boy money).

Despite Richmond's high hopes, his spending splurge was in vain and during the campaign that followed Bradford were mired in the bottom three and eventually relegated, finishing the season with just 26 points.

A drop in attendances (something exacerbated by the team's poor performances in the First Division during the following season) and the loss of much of their Sky money all conspired to greatly weaken Bradford's income. Along with this, the club were also unfortunate to enter the Football League just as the ITV Digital catastrophe was beginning to hit clubs.

Back in 2000, the digital broadcaster (a consortium of Carlton Television, Granada and BSkyB) brokered a £315m, three-year deal with the Football League to broadcast its games. The hope was to use the perceived limitless appetite for televised football to boost the company's revenues. Sadly for ITV Digital, it was an appetite whose capacity had been misjudged, mainly because watching Stockport County v Grimsby Town didn't have the same draw for the average punter as Manchester United v Liverpool or Chelsea v Arsenal.

Subscriber numbers remained well below their predictions and in the March of 2002, with losses mounting by the day, the broadcaster entered administration. For many owners, several of whom had been basing their spending upon the predicted income from the deal, the fact the company went bust while still owing Football League clubs around £179m came as a devastating blow. Despite a subsequent link-up with Sky netting the Football League £95m over four years, it still meant a big readjustment to the television revenues received.

At the same time as revenues were declining, Bradford were also still saddled with the hangover from Richmond's 'six weeks of madness' as the club struggled to fund both the debt taken on to pay for the new acquisitions and the Premier League level wages the arrivals commanded.

At the end of that first season in the second tier, during which the club finished an underwhelming 15th, debts became unsustainable and in May 2002 Bradford entered administration. At the time every tangible asset at Valley Parade had a debt of some description secured against it. Required to sell their best players and unable to afford adequate replacements, the club tumbled down the football pyramid and by 2007 were competing in League 2, enduring another period of administration along the way for good measure.

From one perspective you could argue that this could all be attributable to bad luck, as relegation coincided with the collapse of ITV Digital. The club also lost Paul Jewell at the beginning of the second season in the Premier League, a man whose presence might have averted such a disastrous campaign. But from another more realistic perspective it's difficult to deny that Bradford's problems originated from financial mismanagement while in the top flight. Without the revenue stream that Premier League football provided, accommodating the debt and wage structure that had been created was always going to be a struggle.

Not every story of a football club enduring financial problems is as dramatic as Bradford's. Their rapid decent down the pyramid is pretty rare. But the tale does illustrate how the problems of excessive wages and acquisition of debt combined with a need to maintain the status quo on the revenue side can create real problems. What happened to Bradford City might have been extreme, but it was also part of a trend evident right across football as clubs, regardless of whether putting together multi-million pound sides or creating squads on modest budgets continued to spend more than they should on players and pay them more than they could afford.

'The problem,' argues Professor Cannon, 'is that the current system encourages risk. Aside from the ever-present expectations of fans, the financial rewards on offer as a club progresses up the football pyramid are extremely hard to resist.'

The Championship play-off final is a great example of this. It is estimated that this one game is worth £120m to the victors, a sum made up of television money, potential parachute payments and an associated rise in commercial revenue. This makes it the most profitable match in world football. With so much to potentially gain you can appreciate why some owners take risks to vie for promotion.

For most clubs, the financial problems that have come to characterise football over the past two decades have been troublesome but just about manageable. White knights ready with soft loans, banks that are willing to provide generous overdrafts and creditors who accept a pittance rather than nothing are just some of the many factors which conspire to ensure that England's professional clubs continue to remain in business. But sometimes there are no white knights to come to the rescue. Sometimes, the bank is in no mood to play nice. Sometimes, the creditors are so numerous and the debts so large that even the repayment of a pittance is beyond the means of a club. These occasions, which have grown in number during the past 15 years, have called out for a new solution. And that solution has arrived in the form of punk football and the way in which it has initiated a radical transformation in what it now means to be a supporter.

3

Apathy to Activism (The Rise of Punk Football Part One)

WHAT is a football fan? Well, that probably depends who you ask. For some, fandom is all about commitment, about buying a season ticket, going to away games, acquiring merchandise with the fervour of a 1990s Newcastle supporter; essentially giving everything you can for the club. For others it is a looser affiliation, something you wear with pride but not something that necessarily commands your unwavering attention. There are even some (and this information may shock you to your very foundations) who contravene that most vital of football maxims and follow two teams not one, splitting their allegiance in a way that must horrify traditionalists everywhere.

But whatever your approach to the game, what remains true is that if you choose to follow a club then automatically a relationship is formed. But what is this relationship? Are you merely an exceptionally loyal customer, a source of income to be endlessly milked by the board? Or are you a stakeholder, a vital element in the community of the club with a voice that demands to be heard? In England, for most of the game's history, fans were largely seen by owners as residing very much in the former camp.

Once the structure of English football clubs had settled into a model that we recognise today, the role of fans reverted mainly to one of customers. The days of supporters being members who had a say in the club's business were consigned to the past (at least in the professional game). The only fan organisations that did emerge during the early decades of the 20th century were supporters' clubs and these principally arose as a way for fans to get together socially with like-minded souls.

Although it was never the intention for these organisations to become involved with ownership, they still developed a close financial relationship with their football clubs, as Dr Rogan Taylor, director of Liverpool University's Football Industry Group, explains, 'As time passed, supporters' clubs became an important source of cash for many football clubs. They ran lotteries (something the FA forbade football clubs to do), organised "penny-on-the-ball" competitions and put on whist drives, smoking concerts and Saturday dances. Along with this direct provision of cash, supporters' clubs also offered assistance in other ways, such as members giving up their time to provide free labour for stewarding, maintenance and the production and distribution of matchday programmes.'

Although much of what was provided year-on-year was quite modest, some supporters' clubs gave assistance that was at times pretty extraordinary. At Luton Town during the 1930s, the supporters there did almost as much as the club to improve the facilities at Kenilworth Road. Along with raising some of the funds to for the redevelopment of the 'Bobber's Stand', members also helped clear away tons of soil with spades and wheelbarrows when the stand was being excavated prior to its renovation.

To today's fan, one conditioned by the modern reality that supporters don't give out without getting something back, we would expect the clubs to give a little in return. But the rich and powerful men who ran the game didn't become rich and powerful men by sharing and playing nice. In the overwhelming majority of cases what the supporters got in return for helping out was precisely nowt.

There were some exceptions, such as at Southampton where in 1934 the fans were given a representative on the board in recognition for the pivotal role they had played in assisting the club through a tricky financial crisis during the early 1930s. And at Aldershot, where the supporters' club had been effectively underwriting the club for over a decade, the chairman appointed a supporter-director in 1967. But these, and a tiny handful of others, were the exceptions to the rule. For the clubs, supporter organisations were primarily seen as a fundraising arm, there to provide financial assistance for the good of the club and in return they got little more than a pat on the head.

In the defence of owners and chairmen, this was how most supporters wanted the relationship to be. It is easy for us, accustomed as we are to an age of supporter protests and a belief that the clubs we follow should heed the opinion of the fans, to look at the behaviour and attitudes of owners with disdain. But back then supporters weren't like us, they didn't feel that it was their 'right' to have a say in how their football club was run.

The attitude of the overwhelming majority of those involved in supporter organisations was best exemplified in the motto of the National Federation of Football Supporters' Clubs (NFFSC), which had been established in 1926. For it, the aim of both the national organisation and its constituent members was to 'Help and not to Hinder'. This was the linguistic embodiment of the passivity that dominated the thinking of fans for much of the 20th century. It was a passivity rooted in a parental relationship, one which placed the club as the parent and the supporters' club as the child. The parent knew what was for the best and the child should keep its opinions to itself.

This isn't to say that fans always agreed with the club, it's just that the only medium for supporter organisation at the time (and the only medium through which supporters could have exerted any influence over their clubs) was exceptionally conservative in nature. Individual members might have had a problem with the status quo, but these views were always in the minority among fan organisations and also unrepresentative of supporters as a whole.

But this benign environment wasn't to last. And the seeds of change were sown through the development of a new kind of supporter organisation, one that would start to appear in the 1960s and then blossom and expand during the 1970s and 1980s. It was a model of organisation that shared the same indifference towards fan representation as the supporters' clubs but which through its actions would ultimately precipitate the beginnings of supporter activism as we know it today.

Although regarded as a problem that is largely associated with the 1970s and 1980s, violence at football games actually has a much longer history. The occasional bit of trouble between rival fans was evident in the early decades of the game. During professional football's infancy, followers of Preston North End were particularly renowned for their propensity for a 'kick-off' and were in many ways the Millwall of their day. There are reports of Preston fans knocking railway officials unconscious at Wigan station in 1881, being involved in an attack against Bolton Wanderers players and supporters at the end of a game in 1884 and as the instigators of a massive fight with Queen's Park (Glasgow) fans in 1886.

In a sport that attracts huge amounts of people and where partisan tensions run high it's perhaps unsurprising that periodic bouts of crowd violence should occasionally erupt. But until the 1960s, this was never on a large scale or thought to be a threat to either the game or society in general. It is telling that for decades the men who ran football grounds never made any effort to segregate those attending the match. This modern reality, something that fans of all colours have come to regard as perfectly normal, only started to happen during the 1960s when hooliganism first began to become a problem.

Although plenty of the violence that took place was disorganised and ad hoc, gangs of young lads charging through a town or invading the opposition 'end' during a game, lots of it wasn't. At many clubs, fans formed themselves into hooligan 'firms', small groups of well-organised supporters whose sole purpose of travelling to a match was to do battle against opposition supporters. These highly disciplined, hierarchical groups, who often applied military ranks, like 'general' and 'lieutenant' to their members also adopted catchy monikers, such as the Leeds United Service Crew, the Inter-City Firm (West Ham) and the Chelsea Headhunters, becoming infamous in the process among both the press and their peers.

Although certainly a break from the deferential conservatism of the supporters' club, the football hooligan movement was hardly a step forward for the cause of fan activism. The small minority who participated in the violence had no interest in establishing a dialogue with the club or in having their views appreciated by the board. In fact, it's debatable whether they even cared about the game itself. All that seemed to matter to these 'supporters' was kicking heads and dressing in the very best leisurewear that money could buy. Or failing that anything made by Fila.

By the mid-1980s, hooliganism had become endemic within the game both at club level and a national level too, playing a special role in what was to become something of an *annus horribilis* for English football. The 1984/85 season has long been seen as a nadir for the national game, marred as it was by dramatically poor attendances, escalating levels of supporter violence and, worst of all, the tragic deaths of several fans. And yet, 1985 would also be the year from which punk football can trace its origins.

The three incidents that are most closely associated with that season are the death of a young Birmingham City fan at a home game against Leeds United, the devastating fire that ripped through the main stand at Bradford City's ground, Valley Parade, and lastly, the Heysel Stadium disaster, during which rampaging Liverpool fans contributed to the deaths of 39 Juventus supporters prior to the kick-off of that season's European Cup Final.

These events, one of which (Bradford) was attributable to chronic underinvestment and poor safety standards and the other two caused by crowd violence, contributed to a perception in the press, in government and abroad that English football was in a state of decay. The reputation of supporters in particular reached a new low. Not only were English teams subsequently banned from European competitions after Heysel but the Conservative government, led by Margaret Thatcher, demanded tougher policing inside and outside of games and began to discuss bringing in draconian measures to tackle the problem of hooliganism, such as the introduction of ID cards for supporters.

At the time of the Heysel disaster, lifelong Liverpudlian Rogan Taylor had just completed a PhD, in the non-football-related subject of *Shamanism, Faust and Psychoanalysis.*

He said, 'I was devastated by Heysel, just sickened by what had happened. To have the club you love associated with something so horrific was like getting a stiletto heel to the gut. But what struck me in the immediate post-Heysel period was that amid the acres of newsprint and comment on the subject, most of which looked at why what had happened had happened, no one was asking what it all meant?

'This interested me because a lot of my research had involved the study of meaning. So I thought I would write something of a provoke-piece, looking at this question and then send it in to one of the national newspapers "on-spec".'

Through his appraisal of the meaning of Heysel, Rogan came to the conclusion that the network of relationships within English football, the vascular system upon which the game depended upon for survival, had broken down. For him, Heysel was a warning, an alert that a massive heart attack was on its way, one from which the already sickly patient might never recover.

He continued, 'As part of the piece, I was writing about Liverpool's game against Inter Milan in the 1965 European Cup. I was including something about the ref who was rumoured to have been on the take and rang a mate of mine, Pete Garrett, to ask him who that was. I mentioned what I was working on and he asked to have a look at it. The next day I got a knock on my door and Pete, a few other reds I knew and some local Evertonians were on the doorstep. They'd read what I'd written and thought I was on to something. But Pete suggested that we go further. He thought that it was incumbent upon the fans to do something to solve this problem too. It wasn't enough just to diagnose the patient as sick, we had to provide a remedy.'

Their remedy turned out to be the Football Supporters' Association (FSA), an organisation created by fans to campaign on issues that mattered to them.

'Although that wasn't its first name,' laughs Rogan. 'Pete came up with the idea to call it the Football Supporters' Union. Keeping in mind that this was the mid-1980s, a time when trade unionism was becoming a byword for "militancy" and that we were all citizens of the country's most politically militant city, after some reflection we thought that perhaps "association" has a less aggressive tone to it. So that became the name that we signed the letter/article off with when it was sent into *The Guardian*, stating that this would be an organisation that would give fans a voice and start to work towards rebuilding the national game.'

None of those behind the new-born organisation had any expectations as to what the response would be like. As it was, the FSA was an immediate hit. Within two weeks, thousands of fans of all colours had written to Rogan and Pete, praising and supporting what they were doing.

Rogan said, 'The overwhelming tone of the letters was that it was about time something like this existed. It seems weird now, but back then the only time you ever saw a football supporter on TV, he was probably being carted off the pitch by the police. And when football was ever debated in the papers or on TV, there was never a fan representative, never anyone there to articulate what the fans thought. Unbeknownst to us, out there in the big wide world, there were a proportion of supporters who had just been waiting for something like our organisation to come along and represent their views.'

And it wasn't long before the FSA had capitalised on this and turned itself into a national organisation, one that would over the years that followed provide supporters with a voice to campaign on a wide range of issues, such as policing, ticket provision and travel arrangements to away games.

Although the FSA was the first concrete sign that fans were becoming more activist, it was soon followed by a wave of club-level activity which appeared to show that beyond the confines of the boardroom and supporters' clubs, ordinary fans were now organising themselves and this time with any notion of deference towards the parent club clearly cast aside.

This was most evident with the rise of fanzine culture. Fanzines had been part of the music scene since the beginnings of punk back in the mid-1970s. Home-produced with glue and Sellotape, and then photocopied and stapled for circulation, fanzines were never the slickest of publications. But what they lacked in sophistication they more than made up for in wit, commentary and passion. This was not the view of the conventional music press, filtered through the eyes of a dispassionate editor; this was the perspective of the fan, the person who was living and breathing everything that punk was about.

For the early pioneers of the football fanzine movement things were no different. Anyone who ever took the time to flick through the pages of an official club programme in the 1980s will understand what a joyless experience this could be. Alongside an anodyne perspective from the manager, some pieces about the youth system and a section on the opposition, club programmes were largely made up of padding and adverts.

So boring were these publications that the only way even two rabidly obsessed Evertonians such as my brother and I could squeeze any enjoyment out of them was to invent a game called Answer Bingo. Every edition of the Everton programme would carry an interview with one of the squad's players, usually pictured at home with their wife and two lovely Alsatians. The interviews, which asked such probing questions as 'What is your perfect meal?', 'Who is your favourite musician?' and 'What do you do when you're not playing football?' often elicited that same array of blandly predictable answers (steak and chips, Phil Collins, play golf). In Answer Bingo you got a point for every answer that was correctly predicted. The scores were always high, right up until we came across the mercurially-minded Pat Nevin, whose left-field leanings were the sole highlight of over a decade of reading that insipid publication.

When fanzines arrived, they made the average supporter realise just how unremittingly dour the matchday programme was. With their emotive explorations into the nature of fandom, their witty yet incisive commentary on the state of the club and their willingness to criticise the manager, the players and the owners, they provided fans with a medium that was independent from the machinery of the club.

What's more, according to Martyn McFadden, founder of Sunderland's long-standing fanzine *A Love Supreme*, along with giving fans somewhere to vent their frustrations, these publications could also act as a unifying point, a rallying medium through which supporters could begin to challenge the club.

He says, 'Fanzines like mine represented an alternative voice for the fans. For years, individual supporters obviously had views that differed from those held by the club but the problem was that there was nowhere for these views to go. Supporters' clubs were never much use, so fans were left feeling a bit impotent. Fanzines changed all that. If you felt strongly about something you could write an article. And depending upon that response, that article could show you that you weren't alone in your opinion. It could also provoke debate and maybe make other supporters question aspects of the club's behaviour.

'Those of us involved with the fanzine found that, once the publication had reached a certain level of popularity, there was also the opportunity to organise supporters to protest against the club. I'm not sure whether publications like mine made football fans more political or whether we were symptomatic of a new generation of fans who were generally less deferential and more activist but fanzines were definitely part of a trend that saw the relationship between fan and club undergo a transformation.'

Another part of the game that saw supporters become more active concerned the issue of racism. It might be less of an issue than it once was, specifically in the Premier League, but racism was once a common feature on the terraces. At many grounds abuse directed at black players was not just a regular part of football's culture but also ignored by clubs too. And one club with a particularly poor reputation when it came to this issue was Leeds United.

The casual racism evident among supporters at Elland Road was given extra impetus by the presence of far-right organisations at the ground. Following on from early attempts at infiltration and agitation in the 1970s, by the 1980s the National Front (NF) and the British National Party (BNP) had established a visible presence at Elland Road (along with several other football grounds around the country) and it would not be an uncommon sight at Leeds to see NF and BNP members freely selling their newspapers outside the stadium on a Saturday afternoon.

To some Leeds fans the culture of tolerated racism, allied to the visible presence of fascist groups among supporters, proved too unpleasant to tolerate. In 1987, a fan-led, anti-racist initiative was launched by Leeds supporters who were already involved in wider anti-racist work. Under the banner of Leeds Fans United Against Racism and Fascism, the group challenged the racist culture at Elland Road by leafleting and distributing anti-racist stickers outside the ground and through the publication of their own anti-racist fanzine, *Marching Altogether*.

Previous efforts to tackle racism at the ground, which had been sporadically taking place since the 1970s, had always originated from outside groups such as the Anti-Nazi League or the Socialist Workers Party. According to Dr Paul Thomas, one of those behind the founding of Leeds Fans United Against Racism and Fascism, while laudable, this outsider approach always came with limitations.

He says, 'For anti-racist campaigns to make progress in the long term at Leeds United or any other club, the campaigners had to have credibility, had to be, and be seen to be, a fellow fan who actually went to games regularly and knew what they were on about. In the 1970s and 1980s there were plenty of people in the media and politics stereotyping all football fans, so there was a natural suspicion that campaigners were another group there to criticise them. It hadn't helped that previous anti-racist campaigners like the Anti-Nazi League mostly hadn't been fans (although we salute their efforts), and had left before kick-off after leafleting. We were determined that this time around, things would be different.'

Leeds supporters were not the only ones to tackle racism in the game. Other fan campaigns, such as Geordies are Black and White at Newcastle United and efforts by the 200-strong fanzine movement, which was predominantly and actively non-racist, to tackle this issue illustrated that supporters were becoming organised and political in a way like never before.

For those who had long desired to see football fans become more activist, the growth of fanzines, the establishment of the FSA and the campaigns against racism were all encouraging signs. But what these developments failed to provide was a way for supporters to independently and constructively engage with their club at a grass-roots level. And as time passed this is what fans were increasingly demanding.

Football in the 1990s was undergoing tremendous change. The terraces were disappearing at many grounds, ticket prices were rising and the arrival of Sky was transforming the game into a very different animal. At the same time, the arrival of debt as a serious issue was undermining the sense of permanence that had once underpinned the game. With more clubs facing winding-up orders and the prospect of folding, the feeling that your team would be there for you come hell or high water was becoming less guaranteed. As the 1990s wore on, these changes would inspire supporters to become more radical and act in ways that would have seemed inconceivable to the generation that preceded them.

4

From the Terraces to the Boardroom (Supporter Power Part Two)

IF, for some reason, you had spent the last 20 years living in a cave, cut off from the rest of humanity and, to stretch this a bit, you were also a hermit who had previously possessed a long-standing passion for football, should you choose this season to re-engage with the sport you would be struck by how unrecognisable it had become. And this wouldn't be just in terms of appearance, such as the fact that the game was more ethnically diverse, that the moustache is now dead and that players no longer wore shorts that were pushing into 'hot-pants' territory. Professional football in England is a fundamentally different sport to that which existed in this country two decades ago. And one of the main ways that the game has changed, a trend that began in earnest during the 1990s, has concerned ticket prices.

During the first half of the 20th century the cost of going to a match remained remarkably stable, affordable and tended to keep in line with the pace of inflation. In stark contrast to today, it also didn't cost that much more to get into a top-flight game than it did to watch a team playing in the bottom tier.

But nothing that good lasts forever, and the foundations to this golden age of cheap football began to crumble in the 1960s. Cost pressures emanating from the removal of the maximum wage and changes affecting the terms of players' contracts both contributed to the imposition of real increases in admission costs. Although modest, prices continued to creep upwards during the decades that followed, as the days of cheap football began to slowly recede into the distant past. It was a trend that was exacerbated by the decline in attendances; something that clubs sought to accommodate by charging those who still turned up more and more.

'Despite the rises, football was still an event that the average working man could afford to attend. No one likes paying more for something, but a dad could still take his sons to the game without it costing a small fortune. That was about to change though. What supporters have experienced over the past two decades is levels of inflation more characteristic of a banana republic than what you would have expected in the once rather conservative world of English football,' says Mark Longden, chairman of the Independent Manchester United Supporters' Association (IMUSA).

Back in 1990 if you wanted to go and watch a club like Arsenal or Liverpool at home then the cheapest ticket available would set you back £5 and £4 respectively. Fast forward to 2011 and those same two tickets would cost you £51 (Arsenal) and £45 (Liverpool). If football had followed the rate of inflation across the rest of the economy over that same period then those tickets should have cost £8.86 and £7.09. And the picture was just as dramatic when it came to the price of season tickets. During the 1989/90 season the cheapest one available at Anfield cost £60. Again, following the rate of inflation elsewhere, that season ticket should have only set Liverpudlians back just over £100 in 2011. Instead, the average punter was expected to fork out a staggering £725 to get in to watch the reds all season.

Along with these increases in prices, which occurred right across football, by the 2000s, the relative state of homogeneity that had existed between the divisions had also disappeared. In 1960, First Division clubs were charging 25 per cent more than their Fourth Division counterparts for admittance on matchdays. By the 1970 season this difference had jumped to 48 per cent more per spectator. The gap then widened to 64 per cent in 1980, 70 per cent in 1990 and reached a whopping 155 per cent by the year 2000.

The reason most commonly put forward by football clubs for these consistent price rises is the improvement in the matchday experience. The introduction of new and redeveloped stadiums and the development of other facilities, such as in-ground restaurants, better parking and greater levels of security all contribute to a 'football experience' that is incomparable to that 'endured' by fans in the past. For most, the days of standing for hours, crushed against your fellow supporters, with no protection from the elements are now gone. Instead, fans can sit down in a guaranteed seat, while sipping a frappuccino purchased from the club's bar and enjoy the match without being pushed, pulled or having a Kopite urinate in their pocket.

But while accepting some truth in what the clubs claim, Dr Rogan Taylor thinks that you can't really attribute the escalation in price rises to this alone.

He says, 'Of course most grounds have improved out of all recognition. You only have to look around the Premier League at clubs like Sunderland, Arsenal and Swansea to appreciate how different things are today compared to what supporters put up with in the past. There's also probably a case to be made, certainly in the Premier League, that the quality of football on show *is* better and so deserves to command a higher price to be watched. But, let's not kid ourselves that this is the main reason that clubs have put ticket prices up so much. After all, other countries, like Germany for example, have improved their grounds and the quality of their game and yet have not opted to squeeze their fans so much. No, I think that the main reason for the continued escalation in ticket prices is to fund the insane level of wage inflation that has infected our game in the past two decades. Supporters are being squeezed to ensure that clubs can continue to fund this.'

As much as it quickly became a sore point among fans, admission-price inflation was only one of several grievances that infuriated supporters in the 1990s. Others included heavy-handed stewarding at grounds, poor relations with the police and, as the decade wore on, the way in which clubs were being managed financially.

At some clubs the existing supporter organisations took a more activist stance. But most of these were next to useless. The history of such organisations, the way in which they had constantly done whatever the clubs wanted without ever asking for anything in return, made most fans realise that the future of supporter activism lay elsewhere.

Mark Longden, 'Fans needed an independent body to voice the concerns of supporters and to hold their clubs to account, and this is why the game saw a proliferation of Independent Supporters' Associations (ISAs).'

Democratically structured and overtly political, during the 1990s ISAs were at the forefront of club-level supporter activism in English football. One of the earliest examples of an ISA in action concerned efforts by the Hammers Independent Supporters' Association (HISA) to challenge the way that West Ham's owners were choosing to raise the finance to redevelop the Boleyn Ground. Under the board's wheeze, the majority of the £15.5m bill for the ground's redevelopment would be met via the 'Hammers Bond'. Just over 19,000 of these bonds would be made available at three different price levels; £500, £750 and £975. According to the brochure (entitled *We Shall Not Be Moved*) that heralded the launch, in return for purchasing a bond, supporters would then be allowed 'the exclusive right for not less than 50 years to buy a season ticket for your own named seat' and that 'only those supporters who buy a bond will be guaranteed the right to buy a season ticket'.

'What this meant,' says former activist and avid Hammer Steve Barnard, 'was that if fans didn't buy a bond then they couldn't buy a season ticket. So you might think "don't buy a season ticket then". But if you didn't do that it then meant fighting to buy a matchday ticket from the paltry number of seats left available for non-bondholders, which wasn't the most enticing of alternatives.'

Conscious that this exploitation of loyalty might not go down too well among the fans, the club applied extra pressure by adding a healthy dollop of fear into the mix, suggesting that failure to adopt this scheme could mean that other options would have to be considered, including reducing the ground's capacity, ground-sharing with another London club or selling key players.

Despite the backing of West Ham legend Trevor Brooking, the Hammers Bond went down very badly with the fans and over the months that followed its launch, HISA, along with several West Ham fanzines, actively campaigned against it, protesting outside the ground before kick-off and orchestrating pitch invasions.

'It was made very clear to the club that the fans were united in this and that the bond scheme just wasn't happening. In the end I think that of the 19,000 bonds created, less than 1,000 were taken up. The whole thing was a flop and was eventually dropped and quietly forgotten,' says Steve, triumphantly.

In the 1990s, football fans were beginning to discover that if there was something about their club that they weren't happy with then it was in their power, if they acted together, to do something about it. And the most high profile example of an ISA doing just this took place at Old Trafford, where, as the decade drew to a close, the IMUSA took on one of the most powerful figures in English football and won.

In the autumn of 1998, not long after the start of the season, Manchester United fans awoke to the news that the club's board had accepted a £623m takeover offer from BSkyB.

'There were numerous commercial motivations underpinning the bid. There was a feeling that United weren't exploiting their name enough, especially overseas, or charging their fans enough either. But the main reason for Murdoch's interest was the information advantage that ownership of a top-flight club would provide the company in future negotiations with the Premier League, enabling them to be privy to the details of any rival bids. That was the big pull of Murdoch,' says the journalist Michael Crick, one of the key figures behind the fans' campaign against Murdoch.

With the board supportive of the takeover, resistance was left in the hands of the supporters, specifically via the efforts of IMUSA, which had been established a few years earlier in 1995. This supporters' organisation had emerged from a thread of growing discontent among a section of the Manchester United faithful. Along with anger towards rising ticket prices, they were also disgruntled by what was seen as social engineering at Old Trafford following redevelopment of the Stretford End and the United Road stand, during which areas of traditional support had been uprooted and replaced with corporate hospitality. The displaced fans were then scattered around the ground, a process that had a marked impact on the stadium's atmosphere.

In the year of IMUSA's founding, this had been exacerbated when the club had hired Special Projects Security to steward games, with the specific aim it seemed to intimidate those trying to create a better atmosphere at matches into being passive and silent.

Andy Walsh, one of the founders of IMUSA, recalls, 'A few of us kept getting together to talk about these issues and eventually we came to the conclusion that a supporters' organisation that was independent from the club might be a good idea. That way we could use it to start campaigning to address some of the problems that supporters were facing.

Although these issues were a pain in the arse, it was fortunate in a way that they occurred as it gave IMUSA a few years to get up-and-running before the Murdoch bid happened. It meant that we were that bit more organised, which was really useful because the fight against Murdoch was going to be difficult.'

'Difficult' is probably an understatement. This fight wasn't like the one undertaken by West Ham supporters against the Hammers Bond. In challenging the bid not only did IMUSA have to take on the club's board, but they also had to fight Rupert Murdoch, a man who had massive influence in Parliament, the media and in the City. And, as Andy admits, they were doing this without the full backing of the supporters.

'The truth is that some fans didn't really care what went on behind the scenes. For a lot of United supporters all that really mattered was what happened on the pitch. And you can't blame people for only concentrating on the football side of things, because after all, United are first and foremost a football club. Also, although Sky never said how much cash would be available for new players, there was a constant assumption around Old Trafford that the club would be considerably richer. And that's something that appeals to lots of fans because in the modern game, money appears to be everything.'

From inception, figures from the worlds of the media, politics and high finance were targeted as IMUSA attempted to counter the influence of BSkyB wherever possible. In this they were helped enormously by the breadth of the club's fan base. Being the most popular team in the country comes with many advantages, one of which was the fact that there were plenty of politicians, media people and even City directors who were avid fans and, more importantly, sympathetic to the IMUSA cause.

Not long after the bid was proposed for example, the City law firm Lovell, White & Durrant (known simply as Lovells today), approached IMUSA and offered them expertise worth thousands of pounds from a team of five lawyers free of charge.

When their *pro bono* offer eventually expired, the fans struck lucky again when they discovered that a leading expert on competition law was also a keen United fan. Through him they were put in touch with other City lawyers who were again willing to present the arguments for IMUSA on a *pro bono* basis. Corporate lawyers might not be everyone's cup of tea, but without them the anti-Murdoch battle would have been handicapped from the off.

An example of the campaign's sophistication was also evident in the establishment of IMUSA's sister organisation, Shareholders United Against Murdoch (SUAM). Founded by two alumni of Manchester Grammar School, Richard Hytner and Michael Crick, SUAM sought to bring together those shareholders with misgivings about the takeover.

Crick says, 'Along with uniting and utilising the huge amount of talented people that we knew to be shareholders at the club, people working in PR, law and advertising, SUAM also campaigned to build a shareholding block that could oppose Murdoch and stop the club being swallowed whole into his Empire.'

In the autumn of 1998, the campaigning of IMUSA and SUAM, pressure from within the Labour Party against Murdoch (who many Labour people still loathed because of his newspapers' hostility towards the party during the 1980s and 1990s) and opposition towards the bid from other organisations involved in the broadcasting of football, such as the BBC, the Independent Television Commission and the Premier League, helped convince the then Secretary of State for Trade and Industry, Peter Mandelson, to refer the takeover to the Office of Fair Trading, who in turn passed it on to the Monopolies and Mergers Commission (MMC) for consideration.

'The two sides spent the next few months making their case to the MMC and trying to outmanoeuvre each other in the media. I have to say that as effective as our campaign was, we were greatly assisted by the incompetence of BSkyB,' says Michael Crick, gleefully.

For a media company renowned for its business savvy it's widely acknowledged that it ran a bafflingly inept PR campaign during the MMC's deliberation process.

'It's fair to say I think that it might even have been one of the worst examples in British corporate history,' continues Michael. 'It had started badly from the off when their then-chief executive Mark Booth failed to name the United left-back at the initial press conference to launch the bid and things went rapidly downhill from there. During the entire process, BSkyB spent millions on lawyers and lobbyists yet not a single politician switched to the Murdoch camp. For years to come, in business schools around the globe, their campaign will be cited as a text-book example of how not to win over public and political opinion.'

After several months looking into the issue, in March of 1999 the MMC eventually came out against the bid, ruling it anti-competitive and stating that it would have an adverse effect on wider football. In response to the MMC report and judgement, the following month the then-Secretary of State for Trade and Industry, Stephen Byers, halted the bid, effectively rendering it dead in the water.

Andy Walsh, 'To say we were jubilant would probably be an understatement. This wasn't just an example of supporter power in action; this was an example of supporter power succeeding against one of the most powerful figures not just in English football but in English society too. At the start, plenty of people wrote us off, thinking that we didn't stand a chance. And you can understand why. This was Murdoch after all, the man who tended to get whatever he wanted. But we organised, we persevered and ultimately we triumphed.'

The BSkyB affair revealed just how far fan activism had travelled in a very short time. Supporters were now willing and capable of challenging parent clubs and in doing so, altering the way that these clubs were run.

There was even evidence towards the end of the 1990s of fans being willing to get active to support their comrades at other clubs. This was best illustrated during 1997 with the creation of Fans United. The brainchild of a young Plymouth Argyle fan called Richard Vaughan, Fans United was founded in response to a crisis at Brighton & Hove Albion.

Like many clubs at the time, the Seagulls were losing money and taking on debt. Their owners' solution to this was to flog the stadium to developers, a move that raised the ire of the Brighton faithful. A season of campaigning followed, during which Albion fans tried everything they could to thwart the plans of the board.

Incensed by the lack of support from the FA for the fans' cause and touched by the messages of solidarity towards the supporters' plight that had proliferated from across the football community on the nascent forum network, Richard stated on one message board that he intended to go along to an Albion match wearing his own club's colours to show his support for the cause and that others should join in too.

'We received a tremendous response from so many fans of different clubs,' recalls Liz Costa, vice-chairman of the Brighton Supporters' Club. 'The stadium was packed with a variety of different colours. I think there were probably representatives from all of the 92 clubs in the top four divisions as well as a few non-league clubs and some European ones too. It was a heartening example of fans putting partisan loyalties aside and uniting together to show solidarity with our cause.'

As the 1990s came to a close, the momentum was now with greater activism. Although there were still plenty of people, as illustrated during the BSkyB/United takeover bid, who cared little about the politics of football, a growing (and increasingly vocal) section of supporters were beginning to think that the fans had a right to have a say in how their clubs were run.

The natural conclusion to this trend arrived at the beginning of the new millennium with the establishment of Supporters Direct. A few years earlier, Tony Blair's first Labour government had stormed into power, fuelled by a landslide victory and sparkling with an energetic commitment to reform. Although football had undergone something of a renaissance during the 1990s, a change attributable to the launch of the Premier League and the structural reforms that had taken place following the publication of the *Taylor Report*, it was still a sport riddled with problems. Racism, escalating ticket prices and friction between supporters and clubs were just three of the manifold issues affecting the game.

An industry so in need of reform was never going to escape the attentions of Blair and Co. And it didn't. In 1997, with cross party support, the Labour government launched the Football Task Force (FTF), under the chairmanship of David Mellor QC, the former Tory minister and quasi-celebrity Chelsea fan. Drawing on representatives from all sectors of the game, the FTF was charged with the remit of finding solutions to the many problems that still afflicted football.

Although it never turned out to be as radical as most supporters had hoped, the FTF did have a lasting and enduring impact. Many of its recommendations on issues such as racism, disabled access to stadiums and the improvement of links between football clubs and their surrounding communities, were introduced. But arguably its greatest impact was the decision to recommend the creation of Supporters Direct, a body that could take fan activism to the next level through the creation of football trusts, supporter-run organisations whose aim it would be to hold clubs to account and promote the concept of fans ultimately owning and running the teams they followed.

Oddly, considering how much government activity was devoted to football in the 1990s, the idea for trusts didn't originate from some Westminster think-tank or the ideas board of a hired management consultant, but instead from the actions of a group of Northampton Town supporters. Back in 1992, long before a few thousand Mancs had shown the country how impressive fan activism could be, the followers of Northampton Town had formed their own supporters' trust in response to a financial crisis at their club.

Until Northampton's creation of this novel concept, fans had two options if their club faced the prospect of going bust; (1) do nothing or (2) raise money to help it out but receive nothing in return. To this duo, the fans of Northampton conjured up a third option – raise money for the club and this time get *something* in return.

The man behind this simple yet revolutionary concept was Brian Lomax. Given the role he played in the club's history, I was surprised to discover that Brian didn't start out as a Northampton fan. A citizen of Greater Manchester, he had begun life as a supporter of non-league Altrincham. In his youth Brian became an avid follower, cycling around Cheshire to places like Northwich and Macclesfield to support the club. At some of these games, he would be Altrincham's only away fan, a fact that eventually brought him to the attention of the club, who took pity and offered to let him travel with them on the team bus.

Altrincham's form during the early 1960s, when Brian first began to follow them, was pretty poor. At one point in the 1960 season they lost 22 games in a row, a tough run for any fan to suffer. It was around this time that the owners of the club decided to call it a day and pull out, leaving Altrincham on the brink of closing.

In response to this, the young Lomax (just 11 years old at the time), penned a six-page letter to his local paper pleading for someone to come and help out the team that he loved. The editor was so impressed with this impassioned plea that he sent round one of his hacks to interview and photograph Brian and published the letter in full.

Shortly after, two local businessmen, Noel White and Peter Swales (he of Manchester City fame), bought the club, cleared the debts and set about changing Altrincham's fortunes. Their motivation for this, according to the pair, was Lomax's evident passion for the club.

'I think their exact quote was "with fans like that anything is possible",' recalls Brian.

After the arrival of White and Swales, what followed was a mini golden age which saw Altrincham win back-to-back Cheshire League titles and become a founder member of the newly created Northern Premier League in 1968. Key to this success was the signing of ex-Blackburn Rovers forward Jackie Swindells, who in his first season alone for the club scored an amazing 82 goals in just 63 games.

For Brian though, aside from the joy of watching his beloved Altrincham prosper, the experience also gave him his first taste of fan activism. The turnaround might have been achieved in a conventional way, through the arrival of sugar daddies, but without his intervention it might never have happened at all.

Fast forward a few decades to the early 1980s and Brian found himself living and working in Rugby, having moved there after university.

He says, 'When my daughter was old enough I began thinking about taking her to watch one of the local football teams play. We had a couple of choices nearby, but the one that had the "home-town" feel that I really wanted, the feeling which was similar to that which existed at Altrincham, was Northampton Town. So we headed down to the County Ground. To my surprise, my daughter loved it and we just kept on going. At first it was just home games but, as time went on, we started going away too.'

Northampton Town had joined the Football League back in 1920, having been founded years earlier in 1897 by some local schoolteachers. Although most of the club's history has been spent in the lower leagues Northampton did enjoy a spectacular surge up the football pyramid during the 1960s, which saw them rise from the bottom tier of the Football League to the top in just five seasons. But the good times weren't to last and within another four seasons they were back at the bottom again.

By the early 1990s, a cloud had descended upon the County Ground. Under the disastrous financial mismanagement of their chairman, Michael McRitchie, Northampton had a ballooning wage bill, were managing to make a loss every month and had racked up £1.6m of debt; a figure that represented two years' turnover. And all this to fuel a misguided attempt to turn around the club's footballing fortunes. The prospect of folding now loomed.

'It was clear as the financial crisis deepened and time passed that there was no one coming along to save us, no white knight charging to our rescue. In response to this, a few of us arranged a meeting of the supporters to see what could be done,' explains Brian.

The meeting was called in the town in January 1992, attended by 600 fans (tightly packed within a building designed to hold just 250). A representative from the club (which only deigned to send someone at the last minute) informed the assembled crowd about the extent of the problem, including the fact that at that moment the board weren't even able to pay the players' wages and had turned to the PFA for help.

Brian had been asked to chair the meeting because of his political past, which had seen him stand for election four times as the parliamentary candidate for the Liberal Party.

He says, 'The idea of forming a fan-owned trust that would invest in the club was floated during the meeting. A few of us had talked about this beforehand. The option and need was obviously there for some fundraising body to be created. But we felt that this should be one that got something in return for the investment and one that could look after any money the fans raised.'

According to Brian, support for the trust idea was given a boost when during the meeting, those assembled were provided with a stark reminder of how supporters had been treated in the past when they had last raised money for the club.

He continues, 'One of the chaps who attended showed us a blazer badge given to his dad in the 1950s when Northampton fans had bought the first floodlights at the club, which had cost them a lot of money. What the supporters got in return for their considerable investment was six blazer badges and the opportunity for the chair of the supporters' club to have a drink with the club's big-wigs once a year [and who knows if these were free drinks or not!].'

By the time the meeting was closed, the Northampton Town Supporters' Trust (NTST) had been established. Initially it had two basic aims; (1) to raise money to save the club and (2) to seek effective involvement and representation for supporters in the running of the club in order to protect their investment.

The trust was organised as an Industrial and Provident Society (IPS). Legally, these organisations fall into two broad categories, a cooperative (run for the benefit of its members) or a community benefit society (run for the benefit of the wider community). Both categories enjoy limited liability, which means the personal liability of the society's members is limited to the amount of their unpaid share capital.

This share capital is usually not made up of equity shares like those in a joint-stock company, which appreciate or fall in value with the success of the enterprise that issues them. Rather they are par value shares, which can only be redeemed (if at all) at face value. The share typically acts as a 'membership ticket', and voting is on a 'one member one vote' basis.

According to Brian, the inspiration for the development of NTST had come from the Mayday Trust, the housing trust that he ran in Rugby.

He says, 'It struck me that an organisation such as the one I ran seemed the perfect vehicle to provide supporters with the opportunity to come together to buy a part of their club and act as a medium through which fans could democratically influence club policy. I didn't see any reason why what worked elsewhere in society couldn't be translated to football. I also felt, and this was based upon my experience of running the trust, that the more you enfranchised people, the more responsibility you gave them, the more effort they would put in.'

Once formed, the NTST set about raising cash for its aims. Fundraising efforts began across the town, in pubs, clubs and work places, and dozens of individual donations ranging from £1 to £1,000 were sent in to the trust. A bucket collection at the next home match yielded £3,500. Through these efforts, the fans were eventually able to raise £30,000, enough to buy a stake in the club.

This convinced the administrator brought in to run things by the High Court that Northampton could return to solvency (the existence of the trust and its fundraising exercise were given as the main reason why the club could be viewed as a rescue prospect). When the administrator arranged a meeting to organise the future management of Northampton, a new board emerged with four former directors and two representatives of the NTST (each elected by the trust).

'We'd done what other groups of fans had done in the past, provided money to get the club out of a financial hole. But the difference this time was that we were going to be there to make sure our money was being looked after,' says Brian, resolutely.

With the help of the NTST, which had strong links with the local community, the club negotiated with creditors, agreeing to pay back a percentage of the total debts and ultimately emerge from administration.

'Although Northampton has had difficult times since, I still look back on what we did with enormous pride. We established the first supporters' trust and ensured that the club had a future. And that's not bad,' says Brian, a note of pride clearly evident in his voice.

What happened at Northampton was hugely innovative. But because of the club's lowly position in the hierarchy of English football, the trust's efforts only received a fraction of the media attention that other examples of fan activism in the 1990s had commanded. But despite the lack of interest from the media in this revolutionary football concept, some fans *had* been paying attention.

According to Trevor Watkins, one-time chairman of AFC Bournemouth and current head of sports at the international law firm Pinsent Masons, like a lot of clubs in the lower leagues during the 1990s, Bournemouth were struggling financially.

He says, 'Things had been bad for some time, and we'd only really been kept afloat by loans from the bank and sales of players. Put simply, the club didn't generate enough revenue to make ends meet. I think losses at the time were around £50,000 per month. It was in many ways the "classic" football story.'

All this eventually came to a head in January 1997 when it was revealed that the club were around £5m in debt, £2m of which was owed to Lloyds Bank; a creditor itching to get some of this money back.

As a long-time supporter with a legal background, Trevor had approached the board to see if he could use his connections and expertise to assist in the fight for survival.

He says, 'I thought they probably couldn't afford proper legal representation so with my passion for the club and determination to help, I offered my time. It became clear that the club was in serious danger of being wound up. The Inland Revenue and Customs and Excise wanted their money back and were threatening to issue winding-up orders and Lloyds had lost all faith in the current board. Ultimately it was the bank that moved first and on 25 January 1997 accountants from Arthur Anderson were appointed as receivers by Lloyds. That was our very own Black Friday.'

Although the club had wealthy directors and a number of takeover plans had been rumoured including one put together by Roy Pack, a man who had been brought in prior to receivership as a 'company rescuer', nothing came to fruition. Instead, Bournemouth continued to live hand-to-mouth, surviving one week to the next, increasingly dependent upon the fundraising activities of the fans.

'What do supporters do when the club they love is facing extinction? The answer is they do what they have to do to ensure that the club survives,' states Trevor.

With some other long-standing fans, Trevor was instrumental in establishing a fund that was to be used to finance the club's survival. This (along with the trust responsible for it) was officially launched during an evening meeting at the town's Winter Gardens a few days after the arrival of the men and women from Anderson's. The meeting, which was attended by 3,000 people and addressed by fans, local councillors and the club's manager, Mel Machin, succeeded in raising £33,000 in that one night. Although some way short of what was required to ensure the club's survival it was a start and one that gave Trevor hope.

He recalls, 'If the turnout had been poor or the amount we raised quite small then it could have torpedoed the whole enterprise. As it was, we could not have had a better foundation from which to build and from that point on the campaign blossomed. Whitbread the brewers put on quiz nights to raise cash, there were sponsored walks, cake sales, a concert put on by a local businessman. Kids even sent in their pocket money. How encouraging was that? It was wonderful to see how generous people could be with their money and their time.'

Although initially envisaged as merely a body to support the club in its effort to survive, gradually it became apparent to Trevor (and others involved) that the trust charged with organising and running the fund could be something more.

He says, 'While the fans were pumping in money to keep Bournemouth afloat, I talked to many supporters including local businessmen and some of the recently departed directors about the prospect of putting together a rescue package for the club. But the only deal that initially emerged, that of Roy Pack, was dismissed by Lloyds. With no one coming forward we began to think "Why not us?" Just because fans hadn't owned a club before didn't mean that it couldn't be done.'

The odds were certainly against them. From the beginning it was unlikely that the supporters alone could raise the hundreds of thousands of pounds needed to put together a plan convincing enough to persuade the club's creditors that the business could be run in a way that would eventually clear the debts. This meant that wealthy backers would be required to support the bid.

'Considering the club's dire financial position and the fact that majority supporter-control was unheard of in this country this was no easy task,' admits Trevor.

After months of searching, the trust eventually put together a strong group of wealthier supporters, including former director Geoffrey Hayward. With £400,000 in the kitty, the consortium of fans and investors drafted a plan that was presented to existing shareholders, creditors and, most importantly of all, Lloyds Bank.

It was a tense and stressful few days for the trust and any number of things could have gone wrong but on 18 June 1997 the final hurdle was surmounted when Lloyds agreed to back the bid.

'Shortly after four o'clock, I announced to the world that "The assets of AFC Bournemouth, the stand, the stadium, the name, the players, have all been transferred into the hands of the community club. The deal is complete and AFC Bournemouth has survived. We will be seeing you on 16 August at Dean Court against Wigan Athletic." That was a great day and one that I will never forget. The fans of AFC Bournemouth had done something amazing,' says Trevor, proudly.

Along with Trevor's appointment as club chairman, the takeover also gave the AFC Bournemouth Trust Fund majority control of voting shares in the club; making Bournemouth the first club in England to be majority controlled by the supporters.

But despite the innovative nature of what had happened there and at Northampton Town, the idea of fans uniting together to take a shareholding in a club had still not caught on in the game by the close of the 1990s.

'There had been plenty of interest in what we had done at Northampton and I'd been in contact with around 50 different supporters' groups since the NTST had been founded but little concrete had emerged,' admits Brian Lomax.

Although few within the ranks of those responsible for running the game had taken an interest in punk football's emergence, the way that Northampton Town were being run (with the NTST's help) did begin to prick the curiosity of some of those charged with modernising football, most notably Andy Burnham, who was working at the time with the FTF.

He says, 'The task force was charged with looking into lots of different aspects of football, such as better facilities for the disabled, the pricing of tickets and ways to improve the relationship between the clubs and their local communities. I began to hear reports that Northampton were doing good work in many of these areas, putting together schemes that were extremely progressive. The more I delved into this issue the more evident it became that a big reason for this progressive approach was the role being played by the NTST.'

Andy and the FTF started to look into the mechanics of the supporter trust model, talking over its foundation and role at the club with Brian Lomax. They gradually came to the conclusion that what had happened at Northampton, and also at AFC Bournemouth, could represent a panacea to many of the problems that the game was facing.

Andy says, 'Having supporters on the board could change a football club. Not only could fans tell the board what supporters wanted, they also had the power to do something about it. Our view was that if this model could be promoted elsewhere in football then perhaps the sport could start to be reformed from the bottom-up, with supporter power acting as the agent of change.'

At the time the FTF didn't have the power to do anything about it aside from make a recommendation to the Department of Culture, Media and Sport (DCMS). Fortunately, the DCMS was about to be joined by somebody who was very receptive to the FTF's recommendations, as Andy explains: 'In 1998 I was appointed as a special advisor to Chris Smith, minister at the DCMS. So, in effect I became part of the audience to whom the FTF's recommendations were represented. Needless to say, I worked hard to have them accepted.'

With the help of Smith, in 2000 Supporters Direct was launched. Its mission, both then and since, has been to promote sustainable sports clubs based upon community ownership and supporter involvement, to publicise the benefits of the model and also provide support and advice to groups of fans who wish to establish trusts of their own.

According to Dave Boyle, football writer, consultant and someone who worked for Supporters Direct for many years (eventually becoming its chief executive from 2008 until 2011), back in 2000, those involved with the new organisation were heartened and surprised by the response of the fans.

He says, 'Our initial business plan forecasted us helping establish around 50 supporters' trusts in the UK. But it soon became clear that demand massively exceeded expectations. I think the reason for this is that we came at the right time for supporters and with a message that was appealing. Fans were becoming more activist, a reaction to how the game was changing so much.

'The advent of Sky and the Premier League was remodelling football, tearing apart the traditional relationship between fan and club in the process. Ticket prices were rising, clubs were spiralling into debt, the whole notion of "going to the match" was altering. Football supporters as a group were unsettled by this.'

At the same time fans had witnessed what supporter-led action could do, and learned by the examples of what happened at AFC Bournemouth, Manchester United, West Ham and other clubs during the 1990s.

'So when Supporters Direct came along, promoting the idea that if united, fans could not only have a better chance of influencing their club but potentially buy a stake in it, or even one day own it, we obviously struck a chord,' says Andy.

But although the fans were very responsive, initially this wasn't the case with the chairmen and owners.

'The attitude was one of "what do they know about running a football club", they're just supporters,' says Andy, who not only helped found Supporters Direct but remained involved with the organisation during its infancy.

'Although fairly parochial on this issue, the response of owners and chairmen was hardly a surprise,' he continues. 'After all, despite the growing politicisation of supporters few had ever claimed that they had a right to run the club and until Supporters Direct arrived on the scene the concept of fan ownership was confined to the margins of the game.'

But the dismissive nature of some owners gradually began to change as the number of trusts actively involved in running clubs grew. And during the early 2000s opportunities for a trust to grab a stake were plentiful. Administrations were happening at an unprecedented rate and although many clubs were rescued by white knights not all were so lucky. The trust model espoused by Supporters Direct offered these unfortunate clubs a lifeline, one that was eagerly grasped.

Andy continues, 'Quite early on several clubs got into financial trouble and found that the only way they could survive was with the help of the supporters. Because in a number of instances the fans proved able to run things, several owners began to realise that perhaps supporters did know something about the business after all. It wasn't an overnight conversion and it certainly wasn't universal but there was a definite softening of opposition and a gradual acceptance that there could be something to this new idea.'

Since being established in 2000, Supporters Direct has acted as a midwife to the creation of 104 supporters' trusts in English football, 73 of which are in the top four divisions. Some of these own clubs, others simply own a few shares and others have no stake in their club at all. But whatever their role, each is a democratically structured, not-for-profit organisation, whose aim is to hold the 'parent' club to account and advance the cause of supporter ownership (as far away from the original supporters' clubs as it is possible to be).

Many of the stories that have seen supporters get involved in the ownership of football clubs have been amazing; stories that have shown fans in the most positive light possible. But although they are all remarkable in their own way, one of the most amazing concerns the trust that was established by Wimbledon fans back in 2002. Every movement needs a star, that person, group or organisation that pricks the wider consciousness and popularises whatever the movement is peddling. For punk football, that star was initially AFC Wimbledon, a club set up by the fans in the wake of one of the bitterest confrontations to emerge in English football during the past 20 years. Theirs is a story that is almost fairytale-like in its composition; one filled with dastardly villains, noble heroes and that all-important happy ending. It is the story born from a unique misery for the football supporter; the disappearance of the club they love.

5

Punk Football's Poster Boys: The Birth of AFC Wimbledon

THAT owners make decisions which some supporters find unpalatable is one of the few immutable truths of the game. There is a suspicion among some fans, however unfair, that owners aren't true supporters and that the decisions they make are motivated not by a love of the club but instead by a desire to increase the value of their investment.

Barring some financial calamity or hugely unpopular decision, for most supporters the disagreements that intermittently appear rarely mutate into open rebellion. Instead, they become the subject matter of post-match rants in the pub, angry letters to one of the club's fanzines or acerbic posts on supporter forums.

But beneath the angst there is often the tacit acceptance that the 'moneymen' are a necessary evil. So important is cash in the modern game that, despite the disagreements, owners with open cheque books are grudgingly recognised as being the simplest way for a club to compete.

Sometimes this relationship does break down and financial crises at Northampton and Bournemouth created the opportunity for fans to challenge the traditional ownership model evident in English football. But despite any changes, what remained stable in both examples was the focus of the fans' attention; in essence they continued to support the same team.

But what happens when that isn't the case? What happens when the divergent directions desired by both the owners and supporters become irreconcilable? What happens is that one of the fundamental tenets of football, the fact that you can't change the team you love, starts to crumble.

AFC Wimbledon: The Crazy Gang Mark II

On a balmy early autumnal day, the match unfolds before the gathered crowd. The game has something of a bygone age about it; at odds with how football is played in the higher echelons, where the demand for technical perfection and measured passing-play is often placed above the need to entertain. In League 2, creativity and directness still vie for dominance, as they did in the past; making a cultured through-ball as common a sight as a long kick to a big number nine or a crunching tackle inflicted on a tricky winger. It is a joy to behold.

The players themselves feel immediate in this small ground too, less distant and more like the people watching from the terraces. Proximity to the pitch helps, we're not pushed back into the gods here but mere feet away from the action instead. But it's the voices that really do it; the sound of the players' shouts punctuating the air alongside the songs and cries of remonstration and encouragement from the few thousand supporters packed into the ground.

But this tussle between AFC Wimbledon and Accrington Stanley is unexceptional; no vital cup game or title decider. What is happening here differs little from the many other head-to-heads taking place at a similar level on this October afternoon. And yet, it remains remarkable in one way, because one of the teams taking part shouldn't really be here; their existence evidence of a story so remarkable that it sometimes seems difficult to believe.

AFC Wimbledon's chief executive, Erik Samuelson, doesn't seem the revolutionary type. This former partner at accountancy firm PricewaterhouseCoopers looks little different from any other City executive living out their retirement in the leafy suburbs of London. The only incongruous element is the hint of an accent, a hang-up from his Sunderland youth. It gives his measured tones a slight undulation and a suggestion that there might be more to him than meets the eye. And there is. Where most in his position live out their retirement in comfort, Erik has thrown himself behind AFC Wimbledon, a club created by fans, owned by the fans and seen by many supporters as a revolutionary force in English football.

The club arose from one of the bitterest disputes to ever grace the modern game; the decision by Wimbledon FC to dislocate from South London and move 58 miles north to Milton Keynes. According to Erik it was a move that devastated the fans that were left behind.

He says, 'What happened to us a decade ago is probably one of the worst things that can happen to a football fan. All supporters suffer disappointment; the nature of the game ensures this. Obviously some fans endure greater disappointment than others, like those whose clubs face successive relegations. But whatever happens, at least the club remains. They might reside in a lower league but come the next season you can still go and watch them locally. But what happens when that isn't the case? What happens when the club that you love gives up on you and decides to bugger off to pastures new?'

When the proposed move was first announced in 2001, it met with a hostile reaction, but not just among Wimbledon fans. Across the game, supporters of all colours denounced it as an affront to what they believed a football club represented.

'For fans,' argues Erik, 'football clubs are indelibly tied to the community from which they emerge. They're not franchises that can up sticks and move somewhere else. Football clubs are rooted in the community and as such have to be situated nearby that community. This is what the majority of fans that I talk to believe.'

Wimbledon FC's relocation from South London had first been mooted many years before. Back in 1979, the club's then-chairman, Ron Noades, claimed that he looked into moving the club to Milton Keynes when it became apparent that their original home, Plough Lane, was in his opinion insufficiently able to cater for the demands required by entrance into the Football League. Although Noades decided to stay put, the unsuitability of Plough Lane as a home for a league club never really went away.

If you take the time to trawl through the various fan sites looking for answers to the question of the worst ground individuals have ever visited, you'll likely see Wimbledon's old home pop up more than once. Although few English grounds placed much emphasis on comfort or facilities in the pre-Taylor age, Plough Lane stood out among those stadiums belonging to top-flight clubs as being particularly basic.

It had the feel of a ground that belonged to a club that resided in a much lower division. And this was largely because it was. Despite their rapid ascent up the Football League during the late 1970s and early 1980s, the limited financial resources open to Wimbledon ensured that little redevelopment took place and the ground pretty much remained as it had been back when the club were competing in non-league football.

Wimbledon's owner throughout the 1980s and 1990s, as they edged their way towards the First Division and eventually consolidated a place there, was a Lebanese businessman called Sam Hammam. Hammam was an ambitious man and began to think that long-term success had to be built on something firmer than the club's tenacious spirit, the policy of developing and selling players and the paltry gates that Plough Lane could provide.

The first sign of his ambition was a mooted merger with Crystal Palace in 1987. The creation of a South London 'super-club', which would play its games at Selhurst Park, should have given Wimbledon's fans an inkling of Hammam's perspective on football, one that seemed indifferent to notions of heritage and tradition. Although nothing ever came of it, the idea of establishing a relationship with Palace hovered in the ether around the club and sure enough, Hammam's next act of cultural vandalism would once again involve the Eagles. On the final day of the 1990/91 season, Wimbledon supporters were stunned to read in the programme notes that their owner was proposing to abandon Plough Lane and take the club into a ground-share with Palace at Selhurst Park.

His justification for this, a defence that did have a ring of plausibility, was the club's inability to develop Plough Lane to meet the recommendations of the *Taylor Report*, which had been published in 1989. Stadiums are indelibly tied to a club's identity so, understandably, the Wimbledon faithful were dismayed at what Hammam had cooked up. It certainly didn't help his reputation when it was later discovered that he had sold Plough Lane to Safeway for £8m, just over half of which went to his holding company Rudgwick Limited, (who had taken ownership of the ground in 1984 as payment for the loans that Hammam had provided the club).

'The problem with any ground-share is that they very rarely benefit both sides equally. And Wimbledon's deal was no exception,' explains Erik.

Aside from the rental expenses involved, the move also cost Wimbledon significant revenue streams such as matchday sales of pies and pints and the development of commercial relationships with sponsors. Faced with declining revenues and rapidly increasing costs (attributable to the wage spiral that was beginning in the top flight following the creation of the Premier League), the club began to lose money heavily.

With Plough Lane off his hands, Hammam then began searching for a new stadium. But ominously for Wimbledon fans, in the course of this search their owner revealed the same cavalier approach to notions of heritage and history as he had illustrated when proposing the merger with Crystal Palace. Hammam didn't necessarily believe that any new stadium had to be within the borough of Merton (within which boundaries Plough Lane was located). In fact, he seemed unconcerned whether any new stadium had to even be within the borders of London, which was why supporters found their club associated with moves to places as disparate as Gatwick, Dublin and Cardiff. Faced with the prospect of not just the abandonment of any future return to Merton but leaving the capital altogether, the supporters started to make their opposition to such a move felt. And the vehicle for doing this became the Wimbledon Independent Supporters' Association (WISA), which was founded in 1995.

'Things were going wrong at the club and the fans needed a voice. As the 1990s wore on, more and more of us got involved with WISA as a way to try and get the fans' wishes through to the board.'

Ivor Heller, commercial director of AFC Wimbledon, bristles with energy when he talks about those days. His distaste for the 'moneymen' involved with the club remains palpable, and he still recalls with delight the time when around 60 Dons fans got tickets surrounding the directors' box and spent the entire game berating the men inside, causing a response from those within that he gleefully likens to 'rabbits caught in the headlights'.

According to Ivor, despite attempts at establishing a working relationship between the board and the fans, for much of its existence WISA and the owners of the club remained in dispute.

Ivor says, 'The relations weren't good. We got the sense that the people in charge didn't care about the fans. All that interested them was the prospect of getting a new ground, regardless of where it was. Why else would you get stupid ideas like moving a South London club over to Ireland? Within that context you can see why something as dramatic and ill-thought-out as a move to Milton Keynes would make sense to them.'

In 2000, the Milton Keynes Stadium Consortium (MKSC), a group led by the developer Pete Winkelman and supported by the retail giants Asda and IKEA, had put together a proposal for a large commercial and retail development in Milton Keynes, which would include a 30,000-capacity football stadium. The only sticking point in the plans was the absence of any local club that could possibly fill anything more than a 100th of the stadium. The highest ranked local team, Milton Keynes City, were playing in the football pyramid's ninth tier, the Spartan South Midlands League.

But developers are nothing if not resourceful and MKSC ingeniously sought to resolve this problem by simply importing their own team. Several clubs were initially approached, including Luton Town, Barnet and QPR, but each ultimately baulked at the move, sensitive to the hostility that any relocation could create among their fans. Perhaps unsurprisingly, in light of the need for a permanent home, attention then turned to the Wombles.

Although an initial bid was turned down by the Wimbledon board, MKSC came back with an improved offer in 2001, which was accepted. For the men in charge of the club, Kjell Inge Røkke and Bjørn Rune Gjelsten (they had taken full control in 2000 after Hammam severed ties with Wimbledon), the offer was simply too tempting to reject. From their perspective the reason for this was simple; Wimbledon couldn't make enough to cope with the wage spiral that was infecting life in the Premier League. Losses were now a regular occurrence, losses large enough to threaten survival. Like many clubs playing at the time, this left Wimbledon utterly dependent upon the owners and their ability to underwrite the club's finances. For them, the offer was a lifeline they were all too willing to grasp.

In a letter to WISA, which outlined the club's thinking on the move, the then-chairman Charles Koppel wrote, 'The club has neither the assets nor the income with which to finance any development of a new ground. There should be no doubt that our financial plight is extremely serious. The only people funding the club are the owners. Cash flow requirements call for another £7m to be invested in the club this season alone. The club needs the security of knowing that an adequately funded stadium is available to provide a foundation for the future, whether in Merton, its surrounds or in Milton Keynes.'

A move back to Merton had been a desire of the fans since the relocation to Selhurst. In response, the club had made a number of inquiries into its feasibility, looking at two potential sites, the Wimbledon Greyhound Stadium and a return to a redeveloped Plough Lane. Neither of these were deemed suitable; the former because its owner, the Greyhound Racing Association, was not interested in the club's plans and the latter because a feasibility study undertaken by the club revealed that any redevelopment was financially unviable and from a planning perspective extremely remote.

The fans' response to this argument was always one of scepticism. 'The real problem,' argues Ivor Heller, 'was the club's inability to provide a consistent line. They kept putting out different reasons for discounting a move back to Plough Lane that were then proven to be false. For example, along with the feasibility report they also claimed that Merton Council had blocked any prospective move, which was just untrue. They also said the players were frightened of going back to Plough Lane, which again was just a pack of lies. It made it very difficult to believe anything they were saying.'

But even if a move back to Plough Lane, or the borough of Merton, did prove to be unviable, those against the relocation still believed that anywhere in South London would have been better than Milton Keynes. They were also happy to risk the possibility of Wimbledon's relegation and the club's existence on the kind of budget that a continued stay at Selhurst Park would mean.

In response to the proposed move, WISA (backed by an overwhelming majority of the fans) kicked off a protest campaign designed to block Koppel and the board. Picketing, leafleting, black card protests, sit-ins, fans turning their back for the entirety of the game, these were just a handful of the different methods utilised by the supporters.

'One of my favourite memories of back then was when we decided to block in the Sheffield United team coach,' recalls Ivor.

On a cold winter's night, after a home game against the visiting Yorkshiremen, a handful of those who regularly protested after games thought this would be a great idea to grab the campaign some much needed attention.

Ivor says, 'We were always looking for different ways to get into the papers and this seemed perfect. So we lay down on the road, freezing our arses off, surrounded by an army of stewards who could ask us to move but couldn't actually legally move us, which was very satisfying. Then one of our lot got word that the coach was going to back out another way, so a few of us legged it around the stadium, not an easy prospect when your arse is half-frozen, and managed to get there and get down on the road just as the coach was pulling out. I think we managed to prevent them leaving for about an hour.'

At the heart of the fans' campaign was the assertion that although English clubs had relocated in the past, such as Arsenal moving from Woolwich to Highbury in 1913, a move on such a dramatic scale had never taken place. If you wanted to find a precedent then you had to go north of the border where Meadowbank Thistle had relocated to Livingstone in the 1990s, a move that had proven very controversial at the time. The lack of a precedent in the English game gave those opposed to the proposition, and interested neutrals, confidence that the Football League would intervene and stop the relocation taking place.

And initially they did just that; unanimously rejecting Wimbledon's application to move, remarking that 'franchised football' would be 'disastrous' for the industry. The Football League stressed that a club needed to possess some relation to the place from which their name was derived and that it would be wrong to simply up sticks and move the club to another location simply because that offered a better financial return. The consortium and the Wimbledon FC board were informed that any new Milton Keynes club would have to therefore earn Football League membership by progressing through the pyramid, from non-league upwards, as Wimbledon FC had originally done.

And that would have been that but unsurprisingly the club refused to let such a favourable deal slip through their fingers. Charles Koppel took legal advice and appealed. In response, the League agreed to decide the issue via arbitration, which was provided by the FA. A panel to look into the move was established, made up of FA vice-chairman David Dein (also vice-chairman of Arsenal), York City chairman Douglas Craig and Charles Hollander QC (an expert in sports litigation). Craig was an interesting choice by the FA as he was at that time embroiled in a bitter dispute with the fans of York City after he had transferred ownership of the club's stadium to his own holding company and was in the process of expelling the club from the ground.

'Even then we still felt that things would be OK and that they would come to the right decision and uphold the Football League's initial judgement. But that proved to be unfounded optimism,' says Ivor, angrily.

To the dismay of Wimbledon's supporters the panel unanimously decided to pass the buck back to the Football League, asking them to consider the issue more fully. Tellingly, a few comments were included that seemed to suggest that elements within the football establishment were less opposed to the idea of 'franchise football' than had been assumed. In particular, the panel asserted that the move might be a preferable alternative to a club as big as Wimbledon entering administration.

Growing weary of the issue, and with its constituent clubs loath to take on more costs, in response the League asked the FA to establish an Independent Commission to look into the matter. The members chosen for this were Raj Parker, a commercial solicitor, Alan Turvey, chairman of the Isthmian League, and Steve Stride, operations director at Aston Villa. The thinking behind these appointments was never provided by the FA, and prior to the judgement there was little evidence to illustrate which way each member might go.

'We thought that Turvey would probably be sympathetic to our case, Stride perhaps more in tune with the club and Parker, well nobody had any idea what he thought. Despite this, there was still hope that regardless of their leanings, no one would vote for a concept so contrary to what football is about. And that shows how much we knew,' says Ivor Heller, a note of dejection still evident in his voice.

In the end the commission sat for four days in May 2002, delivering a decision on the 28th. Within the 67 pages of the final report, there was plenty for Wimbledon fans to be depressed by, such as the commission being moved by the losses being made (£20,000 per day) and concern for the financial well-being of the Norwegian owners. The report also expressed how impressed the commission was with Pete Winkelman, who they had found to be imbued with 'infectious enthusiasm'. But the most dispiriting aspect of the report for the fans was unquestionably the final judgement. By two votes to one, the commission backed the club's wishes and by doing so ensured that Wimbledon FC would be severing their 113-year association with South London.

'It was a devastating decision. In the context of football unquestionably the worst thing that has ever happened to me,' says Kris Stewart, one-time chairman of WISA. Affable, funny and possessed of an almost zealot-like love of football, along with Ivor Heller, Kris was one of the leading figures of the supporters' opposition to the move.

For him, the way in which the Independent Commission delivered the judgement was indicative of how little the FA thought of the fans.

He says, 'There was no formal announcement. The decision was instead communicated to other parties, the Football League, Winkelman and Koppel and co, but not us. We'd actually found out the night before through someone in the know, so at least we were prepared. A bunch of us decided to head down to the FA to demand an explanation from them, barging our way into the building and basically letting them know that we weren't going anywhere until we'd been told "officially" what was going on.

'Quite some time passed, time that included a few threats to get the police down there to shift us, until eventually the fittingly-named Nic Coward, FA legal head honcho, came down and passed out some printouts of a statement justifying the FA's ruling, which was just a pointless hand-wringing exercise. You hear a lot about money being too important in football but it's not until something like this happens that you realise just how true that is.'

For most Wimbledon fans, the relocation severed their allegiance to the club. Along with a general boycott from visiting supporters of opposition teams, this meant that the last days at Selhurst were poorly attended. At one game against Rotherham United in October 2002, just 849 fans turned up (227 from the opposition), making it the lowest recorded attendance in the First Division's history.

The decline in gate receipts compounded the club's existing financial problems, which had already been exacerbated by relegation from the Premier League to the First Division in 2000. Crippled by losses and with debts reaching £25m, on 5 June 2003 Wimbledon FC went into administration. In September of the same year, following a temporary conversion of the National Hockey Stadium into a football ground, the club moved wholesale to Milton Keynes (being later purchased from the administrators by the consortium and re-branding themselves Milton Keynes Dons). The club currently play their games in the 30,500-seater Stadium:mk, which they finally made their home on its completion in the autumn of 2007.

'It makes me angry to think of how Wimbledon FC ended its days in South London, playing its games to a virtually empty ground. This was a club that had performed miracles, won the FA Cup against one of the biggest teams of the day. It was a horribly sad way for the club to go and I'll never forgive the owners and the FA for that,' says Ivor Heller.

Although the primary focus of the supporters' campaign had been to keep Wimbledon in South London, as the day of the commission's decision loomed nearer and the possibility of a negative outcome became more real, a small number of fans had begun to discuss what would happen if the move was sanctioned.

Ivor says, 'The Dons Trust, a supporters' trust, had already been formed before the move was rubber-stamped, with an aim of possibly uniting fans in a takeover attempt. After the decision there were a few people, such as myself, Kris Stewart, Marc Jones and Trevor Williams who believed that the trust would be the perfect vehicle for setting up a brand new club.'

Conveniently, the WISA annual general meeting had been set for 30 May (a few days after the FA's commission had issued the judgement) giving the fans the perfect opportunity to meet up and discuss options. Ivor continues, 'As you can imagine, with the meeting taking place not that long after the decision, and with all kinds of rumours flying around about what would happen next, there were plenty of people there. Those of us who had thought about setting up a new club decided that this would be the perfect forum to put the idea out there and get a gauge as to the level of support among the fans.'

According to Kris, who was chairing the meeting, although the idea of starting a new club had spread among the supporters over the course of the previous few days, it remained new to a lot of people, and as such there was plenty of concern at the meeting that doing it right away would be seen as giving up the anti-MKSC campaign.

He says, 'There was understandably some concern that starting a new club felt like abandoning the old one and accepting that Koppel and Co had won. I got the sense during the meeting that because of this, momentum might be ebbing away from our proposal. As I was the chair I wasn't really supposed to speak, so I handed the meeting over, went down to the floor and tried to put forward the case for a new club.'

From the floor Kris uttered a phrase that has since entered AFC Wimbledon folklore.

'I said "I just want to watch some football", a quote that has subsequently been seen by some to sum up feeling among fans at the time. The thing is, that was exactly how I felt that night. I was done with campaigning. I wanted to just get back to what I always enjoyed doing on a Saturday afternoon, which was watch Wimbledon.'

Heartened by Kris's simple plea and persuaded by the case put forward by those behind the idea, the meeting voted overwhelmingly to support starting a new club. But what was it to be called?

Ivor Heller, 'We had a meeting with the London FA where it was going to be decided what the club was to be named and establish a founding date. We half-jokingly put forward Real Wimbledon as a name, which was met with a definitive "no". In the end AFC Wimbledon was accepted, even though the AFC part doesn't really mean anything. When it came to our founding date, I cheekily suggested 1889, the same as Wimbledon FC's. To my surprise and immense satisfaction, this was accepted, something I am eternally proud of.'

In several ways this new club could claim an affiliation with Wimbledon FC. There were shared supporters, a similar name and, assuming you don't look at this too logically, a shared founding date. But despite these similarities, there existed one crucial difference. Rather than adopt the financing and organisational model that had proved so ruinous for Wimbledon FC, those behind the new club opted to create a model that placed the fans' interests first. And the vehicle for doing this was the Dons Trust, or to give it its full and less catchy name, the Wimbledon Football Club Supporters' Society Limited.

Erik Samuelson, 'We established the trust, which at the time completely owned the club, as an IPS. This structure enabled fans to buy a single share in the trust (regardless of how much they invested) and become voting members. But these were shareholders whose individual influence could not be increased because everyone is restricted to one share and one vote. We then set things up so that the trust elected the people who run the club on a day-to-day basis. It was important that what was created wouldn't just be another football club; that things were going to be done differently.'

The Dons Trust also provided the club with an immediate means to raise finance without recourse to outside parties, such as banks or local businessmen. Through this they were able to cobble together enough money to pay for a squad of players and cover the initial rent of their new ground, Kingsmeadow, home of non-league Kingstonian, with whom they entered a ground-share.

In June 2002, the new club held player trials over three days on Wimbledon Common, open to any player who felt he was good enough to try out for the team. Fans of football trivia might like to know that one of these hopefuls was Glenn Mulcaire, the private investigator who years later would become embroiled in the *News of the World* phone-hacking scandal. At the time, Mulcaire was a professional footballer and moved to AFC Wimbledon from non-league Croydon Athletic. 'Trigger', as he was affectionately known among fans and players alike, earned himself a special place in AFC history by scoring the team's first ever goal, a beautiful 25-yard volley from outside the box during a pre-season friendly against Bromley.

'In quite a short time we had money, an organisational structure, a manager, somewhere to play and the beginnings of a team. It was a lot of hard work and you need the time and goodwill of others, but we'd done it,' says Ivor, proudly.

In fact, according to Ivor the only real problem that they faced that summer was getting the team enrolled in a league by the beginning of the new season.

He says, 'We wanted to get things started quickly, make the most of the goodwill. A lot of us thought it might have been detrimental to the club's momentum if we had to wait another 12 months before a league would take us. There was still a lot of residual anger over the move to Milton Keynes and still thousands of loyal fans who wanted to follow some local incarnation of Wimbledon FC. Some of us feared that maybe this wouldn't be the case in the future.'

Following a new team, specifically one that would be playing in a much lower division, was going to take commitment from the fans. After a year's reflection, when maybe the issue didn't evoke quite so much anger, would they really be able to attract thousands to a non-league game on a wet and windy Saturday afternoon?

'The answer we feared was no,' admits Ivor. 'There was a race to get us included in a league as soon as possible. The time margin was very slim. The club had been created in June and the new football season started in August. We were really up against it.'

The club's initial choice was entrance into one of the divisions of the Ryman Isthmian League, as they felt this would be low enough to compete effectively but high enough for fans to be satisfied with the quality of opposition. But despite meeting the league's application criteria they failed to get the 95 per cent majority vote needed to allow their inclusion.

'That was a blow but we'd come this far and so we weren't going to fall at the first hurdle,' says Ivor, adamantly. So the club dropped their aspirations slightly and approached the Combined Counties League, one step below the Isthmian.

'And they welcomed us with open arms,' continues Ivor. 'It meant that in the space of a few months we had gone from the utter dejection of losing the club that we loved to having a club that we had built from nothing, that we owned outright, that was going to be run in the supporters' interests and which was all set to debut in a league. It all seemed quite straightforward at the time but when you look back now at what we did and how quickly we did it, it doesn't seem real.'

AFC Wimbledon opened their inaugural campaign away against Sandhurst Town on a blisteringly hot summer's day in August 2002. Keeping in mind that the average gate for games in this league is around 100 people, the travelling army of 2,500 AFC Wimbledon fans presented something of a logistical challenge for the Berkshire club. They surmounted this by the ingenious idea of cobbling together a makeshift stand built from hay bales, which provided the opposition fans with sufficient, if fairly uncomfortable seating to watch their new club earn three points following a 2-1 victory.

Kris Stewart, 'To go from the higher reaches of English football to standing on hay bales while watching your team just about beat someone like Sandhurst Town might to some people seem like a comedown. But not for the AFC Wimbledon fans who attended that game. Our win at Sandhurst was one of the sweetest moments I have ever experienced in football. And I know that others felt the same.'

Despite a slow start, the club finished the debut season very strongly, winning their last 11 league games and only narrowly missing out on promotion.

'That first season was wonderful,' Ivor Heller emotionally recalls. 'After the hell of the previous few years, I think that there was a sense of release among those following the club. We were all just having a laugh again, travelling around London, often visiting places some of us had never heard of. There were some great away days among these. One of my favourites was when we played Bedfont Town FC, which is really, really near Heathrow airport. A few of us were invited back into the club's directors' area and got chatting to members of the board. They were all very friendly but they also had this strange way of talking, where their conversation would stop abruptly mid-sentence, allow a plane to a pass over and then continue as if nothing had happened. It was as if they knew from habit exactly when a plane was going to roar past.'

The solid start the club made to life in the lower leagues laid good foundations for what was to come. In the following season AFC Wimbledon finished top and completed a double by winning the league's Premier Challenge Cup. This form was then carried on into the next season, during which the club ran away with the title and sealed promotion to the Ryman (Isthmian) League Premier Division.

'In the early years we were financially one of the most powerful clubs in leagues we belonged to,' explains Erik Samuelson. 'We had financial muscle because of our large attendances and we were able to build a really strong team. Despite this, we were initially cautious in our first season and were actually outspent by some of the smaller teams. Although we were never extravagant, in the second season we thought "this isn't on" and made sure we spent enough to win. Since then, while always adhering to our principle of financial sustainability (and often being outspent by our rivals) we've worked hard to bring together the right blend of new players and players from the youth system to create sides that can compete and enable us to progress.'

And progress they have. Since their founding, AFC Wimbledon have stormed up the football pyramid and today compete in League 2 of the Football League, an amazing achievement. It means that since the club's foundation just over a decade ago, they have gone from a mere idea dreamed up by a few diehard Wimbledon FC fans to a professional football outfit that now resides just one division lower than MK Dons; the club that deserted them for Milton Keynes.

'In terms of unadulterated joy as a fan, promotion to the Football League in 2011 was probably up there with the FA Cup win by Wimbledon FC over Liverpool in 1988,' laughs Ivor Heller.

Coincidently, their rapid ascent mirrors that enjoyed by Wimbledon FC in the 1970s, when they too crawled up through the non-league system to emerge triumphant in the Football League (ultimately making it to the top flight). But despite this similarity, Erik feels that the two clubs are very different animals.

He says, 'Wimbledon FC was a traditional football club, reliant on the patronage of a few key men. And it was this reliance that caused the crisis from which AFC Wimbledon emerged. The private model of football ownership is great when things are going well. But when matters go awry, such as when form deteriorates or the finances plunge into the red, that's when you see just how ugly this model can be and how little fans matter to the people in charge.

'In our case, the owners couldn't have cared less about the club, the supporters and concepts such as heritage and tradition. By contrast, we are owned by the fans and run things in their interests. We are a proper community club and one that doesn't put money above supporters. Something like the move to Milton Keynes would only happen here if it was the will of the fans. It will never again be in the hands of a few businessmen who get into football for all the wrong reasons.'

The club also aims to run the finances in a sustainable manner, seeking to break even every year. This is in stark contrast to most clubs in the lower reaches of the game, clubs that in many cases are technically bankrupt.

'We won't borrow money to fund transfers or pay exorbitant wages,' says Erik, steadfastly. 'If the club can't afford a player, then that's too bad. And if a player is demanding a salary in excess of what we can manage then we can't afford to keep him; it's as simple as that. Other clubs might be happy to borrow or turn to a benefactor but not us. Sustainability is paramount here.'

Despite this constraint, AFC Wimbledon have still thrived and in doing so challenged the theory that you have to spend in an unsustainable fashion to achieve success. When the club made it into the Football League they did so alongside big-spending Crawley Town, slightly tarnishing that club's achievement in the process. But although this approach has worked to date, according to Erik, the club's ascension up the football pyramid is putting the tenability of their model under stress.

He says, 'The reality is that football remains a game where money matters. Even our success proves that. We thrived very early on because of our financial muscle, which was derived from our relatively large fan base. Money's importance has never changed. And sadly, the higher up you progress in the pyramid the more important money becomes. Right now, we've got enough to compete with our peers. But if we're promoted then things would become more difficult. The time might come when we have to decide whether supporter ownership is something that the fans think is a price worth paying for limited horizons on the football front.'

Members of the Dons Trust have already had a slight taste of this dilemma. Back in 2003 the opportunity arose for the club to purchase Kingsmeadow from the then owners, Anup and Rajesh Khosla. According to Erik, it was the board's feeling that the future of the club would be best served by buying the ground.

He recalls, 'We knew from the problems that Wimbledon FC faced through ground-sharing that it made sense to get our own stadium as soon as possible. It might not seem that important to outsiders, but things like selling food and drink on Saturdays and setting up commercial sponsorships can raise enormous amounts of money over the course of the season.'

Despite being able to conjure up a significant proportion of the cash from the Dons Trust, the club were still short of the total amount. It left them facing the choice of either taking on outside investment (therefore reducing the fans' ownership of the ground) or forsaking the opportunity to purchase Kingsmeadow to maintain the purity of their model.

'In the end, the supporters sanctioned the decision to slightly alter the relationship between the Dons Trust and the club,' says Erik.

AFC Wimbledon chose to establish a new company, AFCW PLC, which owns 100 per cent of its two subsidiaries, AFC Wimbledon Limited and AFCW Stadium Limited (Kingsmeadow). Today, The Dons Trust owns 77 per cent (but 88 per cent of the voting rights) of this new company, ensuring that AFCW PLC could attract the necessary external investment to purchase the stadium, while majority control of both it and the club has remained in the hands of the supporters.

'Although ownership has altered, the supporters' trust remains at the heart of the club, still electing the club's directors and it is to the board of the trust that these people are accountable. AFC Wimbledon remains a club where the supporter is king,' Erik proudly says.

The AFC Wimbledon story is a remarkable one. After all, it is one thing to discuss a concept like fan ownership over a few bevvies but quite another to wake up the next day and turn it into a reality. That the fans did has been to the benefit of football in England. The decision to not give up and instead create a club of their own not only helped expand the plurality of ownership models evident in the game but also provided a clear example that common ownership by the fans and success on the field can go hand in hand.

It was also one that gave the cause of supporter ownership a massive boost. There was nothing like success, particularly when followed closely by the national media, from the outset to raise the profile of punk football. AFC Wimbledon became the poster boys (and girls) for the fledgling movement, the exciting, living example of supporter ownership to accompany the nuts 'n' bolts hard graft that was being undertaken by Supporters Direct. As a tsunami of insolvency events began to wash over English football during the early years of the 2000s, the Dons would soon be joined by a raft of other clubs where the fans, inspired by their example and the thinking behind punk football, began to take ownership themselves.

6

Grecian 4000: The Exeter United Story

DEVON is probably not the first place you think of when football gets talked about. It is a part of the country more synonymous with cream teas, chocolate box cottages and rolling countryside. That said, it's still home to three Football League sides, Exeter City, Torquay United and Plymouth Argyle, which is more than some counties can boast. And while it might not produce as many champions as other parts of the country, such as Manchester, Liverpool or London, or be recognised as a place where stereotypically its denizens eat, live and breathe football, it can still boast something that few other parts can; a fully functioning, supporter-owned professional football club, and unlike AFC Wimbledon, one that hasn't been knocked up from scratch.

Like many followers of clubs that play in the lower reaches of league football, the fans of Exeter City have never had the opportunity to enjoy that much success on the pitch. A couple of decent FA Cup runs, the occasional piece of silverware and a handful of play-off appearances at Wembley is pretty much all they have had to celebrate over the course of a history that stretches back more than 100 years.

'But then, that's what life is like for lots of supporters, isn't it?' says Laurence Overend, current chairman of the Exeter City Supporters' Trust (ECST). 'For a lot of people who follow smaller clubs, things like FA Cup finals, Premier League games and European glory simply aren't factors. Not that this matters. It might seem like something of an anathema to people who follow the big clubs but you can still support a team even if there's little chance of ever winning much. It's more about investing your time and love into a local club for the simple joy of watching football and feeling part of something that matters to your community. Exeter are very, very unlikely to ever win the Champions League but then that doesn't matter. That's not why we support them.'

Just over a decade ago the depth of this passion was put to the test. With the club in dire financial straits and the prospect of liquidation a very real threat, Exeter fans were facing the possibility that the team they loved would no longer be there for them to follow. With no buyers on the horizon and the club several millions of pounds in debt, the supporters emerged as the only group capable of saving Exeter from extinction.

The story of this descent into the abyss begins in the early 1990s. The decade had actually started quite brightly for the Grecians when in 1990 they were promoted out of the old Fourth Division into the Third Division under the guiding hand of manager Terry Cooper. But this promotion would turn out to be the high point in a decade otherwise characterised by abject disappointment. The departure of Cooper (who jumped ship to Birmingham City the following season), along with several key players, such as Shaun Taylor, Richard Dryden and Steve Neville, left the club in a difficult position. After a few unremarkable seasons under the management of Alan Ball, the 1994/95 campaign ended with Exeter finishing rock bottom of the Third Division, an outcome that the returning Cooper was unable to prevent.

During the early-to-mid 1990s financial problems started to become an issue. These were the kind that afflict lots of teams but largely boil down to an inability to raise enough from matchday receipts, sponsorship and merchandising to cover an inflated wage bill. The chairman at the time, Ivor Doble, wasn't a particularly wealthy man, certainly when compared to other league chairmen, and he was finding it difficult to keep the club afloat after the drop.

With losses a regular feature and debts mounting, Doble took Exeter into administration towards the end of 1994. So precarious was the financial situation that the club lost control of St James Park, the stadium which had been their home for nearly 100 years. The ground was sold for the rather modest sum of £650,000 to Beazer Homes and were it not for the interventionist approach of the city council, who stepped in soon after to buy the ground and lease it back to the club, then today St James Park could very well be little more than a modern housing estate.

Although Doble managed to get Exeter out of administration during 1996, they remained mired in financial difficulties and stuck in the bottom tier of league football for the remainder of the decade. These issues, combined with the fact that the chairman wasn't getting any younger (Doble was in his 70s), meant that the hunt for a buyer became paramount. After a search that lasted nearly six years, in 2002 Doble eventually struck a deal that passed control (but not ownership) of the club to a consortium headed by John Russell and Mike Lewis. The idea was that these two would use their commercial nous to turn things around at Exeter, reduce the club's debts and at some point in the near future buy Doble out.

Both men arrived with football form. Russell, who was appointed chairman, had been the owner of Scarborough FC from 1994 to 2000, presiding over a disastrous period for the club which saw them drop out of the Football League and amass debts of £1.25m, two factors that would ultimately contribute to their extinction a few years later. Following a career in the commercial departments of several teams, Lewis (who was appointed vice-chairman at Exeter) had found himself briefly acting as owner of Swansea City during 2001, a tenure described by Lewis himself as 'a complete disaster'. Having been handed the loss-making club by the previous owners, Lewis eventually sold Swansea on for £1 to a consortium fronted by Tony Petty, a man whose mismanagement left Swansea in danger of going under. So incensed were the fans about Lewis's role in the affair that for a time he admitted to being fearful for his safety.

According to Paul Farley, a trustee with the ECST, these factors made many fans wary of the new arrivals. He says, 'Despite the promise of new money from Russell and Lewis and some glitzy PR, such as the appointment of Uri Geller as co-chairman [his son was a fan of the club], a lot of fans that I talked to were canny enough to treat the new owners with caution. Their track record wasn't great and so there was a healthy degree of scepticism around.'

The strangest event to take place during the early days of the new regime was Michael Jackson's visit to the city, a piece of 'glitzy PR' that made national headlines. In an event organised by Geller, Jackson, David Blaine and the soul diva Patti Boulaye made a one-off appearance in Exeter aimed at raising a bit of cash and giving the club's profile a boost (Jackson was even made an honorary director).

In what must rank as one of the least relevant speeches ever delivered on the subject of football, Jackson took to the stage in front of an excited crowd and said, 'Hello to you wonderful people of Exeter. And to you great supporters of the Exeter City football club. Welcome to all the great fans that have come from near and far. And to all you children. I'm very happy, *very happy* to be with you all here today. Today, today we come here to support children, we come here to support children with AIDS. We share our love for the children, to help, to help the youngest of those affected by HIV and AIDS. We will help them to build a good future, all of us working together for them. A future without prejudice for these children and their families. We're here to support and to help the people of Africa to find a solution in the fight against the spread of HIV AIDS. And malaria.'

It is a lovely sentiment, and one that received an enthusiastic response from the crowd, but quite what that had to do with Exeter City no one could really fathom. The razzmatazz of Jackson's visit and stories in the press of Geller using his psychic powers to influence the team's results were making many fans feel a little uneasy. There was a danger of the club becoming something of a laughing stock in English football. A director who bends spoons and strange visits from the King of Pop are not the kind of thing you could imagine happening at Old Trafford or Stamford Bridge.

'Having said that, there are worse things to be than a laughing stock, as we were to find out,' says Laurence Overend, ominously.

During the first season under the new regime it soon became apparent that not all was well on or off the pitch. Behind the scenes, despite claims by Russell and Lewis that the club would be in better financial shape with them at the helm, this wasn't turning out to be the case. The problems that had dogged Exeter for years continued to vex the club, and if anything worsened as the squad expanded under a succession of different managers (four in eight months). A bloated wage bill and continued financial losses led the club to amass more and more debts.

Despite claims to the contrary when taking over, it appeared that the duo's business savvy was non-existent. The worsening financial position meant that bills were going unpaid and creditors becoming restless. The apparent air of financial irregularity was not helped by some of the economies also introduced by the new owners, which included the decision to stop employing NatWest staff to count the gate money on matchdays and to cancel the contract with Securicor to take the cash away. Instead, the owners themselves opted to ferry the money in their own cars after the game, or leave it in the club's safe over the weekend and take it to the bank on a Monday morning. This was behaviour more in keeping with a second-hand car dealership than a professional football club.

Not long after Russell and Lewis had taken control of the club, the FA's financial advisory unit issued a report into the goings-on at Exeter which concluded that the debt was becoming an issue for concern and that the new owners should utilise the services of an insolvency practitioner. The report also recommended that a security firm be employed to bank the club's takings and chastised the owners for neglecting to hold regular board meetings.

As if all of this wasn't bad enough, on the pitch Exeter's fortunes had taken a turn for the worse. The managerial merry-go-round, combined with a squad struggling to gel, resulted in a prolonged period of poor form. The side spent most of the season as relegation candidates and on the last day of the campaign succumbed to what many fans had feared was inevitable, demotion to the Conference.

In truth, their fate had been in the hands of others. The two leading candidates for the drop were Exeter and Swansea City. If the latter won, then their safety was assured. Exeter not only had to beat Southend United at St James Park, they also had to hope that Swansea slipped up against Hull City at home. Exeter did all they could, managing to snatch a 1-0 win with a goal in injury time. But it was to no avail. Swansea thumped Hull 4-2, ensuring that it was the Grecians who would be spending the following season in non-league football. Their relegation made John Russell a unique figure in the game, becoming the first chairman in Football League history to take two clubs into the Conference.

Despite the drop and financial problems dogging the club, both Russell and Lewis said that they were both working '24/7' and would 'battle on' to ensure that Exeter's fortunes would be reversed. The shallow foundations upon which this bombastic defence was built were starkly revealed on the morning of 14

May 2003 when Devon & Cornwall police arrested Russell, his wife Gillian and Mike Lewis and charged them with fraudulent trading.

When the consortium's takeover had occurred both men had claimed that the money was there to support their future investment in Exeter. Russell, who was presented as the bid's moneyman, asserted that he had a significant property portfolio that could be used to underwrite their enterprise. This turned out to be untrue and the reality was that the pair were effectively broke. During their brief tenure in charge of Exeter, debts went unpaid, money was shifted from account to account to obscure the club's parlous finances and the truth was deliberately obscured from other directors.

At the same time, both Russell and Lewis continued to claim generous expenses and award themselves exorbitant 'consultancy' fees. In 2007, following a lengthy investigation by the police, one hampered by a lack of standard financial reporting at the club, the two men appeared at Bristol Crown Court facing several offences of fraudulent trading. Russell and Lewis both pleaded guilty to the charge that they were 'knowingly party to the carrying on of the business of Exeter City with the intent to defraud its creditors', with Russell also adding a guilty plea to the further charge of obtaining a 'pecuniary advantage by deception'.

As the senior figure in the consortium, Russell received a 21-month jail sentence for his role in the affair. Lewis, by contrast, was given 200 hours of community service after the judge accepted that he played a lesser part.

'They got control of our club on the premise that they could use their commercial expertise to turn things around and bring in investment in the future but in the end it was a total fantasy,' recalls Paul Farley, angrily. 'All they did was preside over our drop into the Conference, rack up millions of debt and leave a list of creditors as long as your arm.'

With no white knight to ride to the rescue and the club in a terrible mess, the former chairman Ivor Doble, who had remained the majority shareholder, was approached to take back day-to-day control. But for Doble, who at this point was nearing 80 and lacked the financial capability to accommodate the debt that Russell and Lewis had managed to amass, running the club was too much to cope with and so he felt obliged to decline. This left Exeter in a difficult position.

'I'm not sure many people today appreciate just how close everything came to ending,' says Laurence. 'There were no investors and so there was no money. If it wasn't for the supporters' trust then in simple terms there would be no Exeter City today.'

The ECST had originally been established as an IPS a few years earlier. For an organisation that ended up running a club their initial remit, that of raising enough money for the team to sign forward Gary Alexander, seems quite modest. In the early days the trust's principal focus was assisting Exeter with their manifold financial problems. In this, they differed little from the many supporters' clubs that had been part of English football since the early 1900s. This changed though as the problems facing the club became more dramatic.

During the 2002/03 season, as it became apparent that all was not well behind the scenes, the ECST began to campaign for the fans to have representation on the board. This more activist approach was augmented further in February 2003 when the trust voted to change its constitutional commitment to 'support' the club to that of 'owning' instead. It was this more aggressive approach, combined with a growing sense of unease at St James Park, that led membership to nearly double from 400 in February 2003 to 750 by the end of 2002/03.

With no potential buyers on the horizon and Doble unwilling to take control, the supporters were approached by the club with the idea that they could take on the day-to-day running of Exeter City. It was a move that revealed how bad things had got. No one involved with the trust had any experience of running a football club and yet it seemed to be the only party available to step in and try and save the Grecians from ruin.

In those early days, the job of the ECST was essentially one of fire-fighting. Along with debts to local organisations and businesses which amounted to just over £3m, the club also owed around £230,000 to HMRC and nearly £1m to Exeter players and other football clubs.

'You can only work like this for so long before problems overwhelm you. As a trust, we decided that one of the first things we needed to do was obtain proper control of the club,' says Laurence.

The trust managed to negotiate a deal with Ivor Doble to purchase his shares (along with responsibility for the club's £4.2m of debt) for the price of £20,000, giving it majority control at St James.

Today, the ECST controls 53.6 per cent of the voting shares in Exeter City AFC Ltd. As 12.9 per cent of the club's shares are held in a 'suspense account', this leaves 33.5 per cent of the outstanding amount belonging to other shareholders, meaning the trust is comfortably in control. The trust's stake entitles it to elect two directors on to the club's board, each appointed by the board of the ECST.

'Although a challenge to our members, buying out Doble and securing control of the club was actually the easier part of our attempts to rescue the club. The supporters rallied to our cause and through all kinds of fundraising schemes, we managed to pull it off. But the trust now faced the job of actually running things and that was a daunting prospect,' admits Laurence.

Exeter were still hamstrung by debt. For the trust, escaping these problems had to be a priority.

'We put all our efforts into finding a way out of this, which meant doing everything we could to try and organise a Company Voluntary Arrangement (CVA), through which we could offer a repayment plan to our numerous creditors,' says Laurence.

When a CVA has been proposed, a nominee (who must be an insolvency practitioner) reports to court on whether a meeting of creditors and shareholders should be held to consider the proposal. The meeting, if it takes place, decides whether to approve the CVA or not. If 75 per cent of the creditors agree to the proposal it is then enacted, with all creditors who had notice of the meeting being bound by the terms of the arrangement. Once the CVA has been carried out, the company's liabilities to its creditors are cleared.

CVAs are often complicated for clubs by the role played by the football creditors rule. This Football League stipulation states that debts to players, managers and other clubs, have priority over those owed to other parties. Non-compliance with this can result in the Football League taking action against the club, a procedure that could result in suspension.

What this means for clubs is that there is often less to go round to other creditors once the football debts have been cleared, something that undermines the chances of a proposed CVA being accepted. In Exeter's case, although they were fortunate in being able to broker some favourable deals with players, managers and other clubs, the terrible state of the club's finances still meant that all the club could offer each creditor once the 'football debts' were sorted was a mere 7.2p in the pound.

Laurence Overend explains, 'In October 2003, we nervously put the CVA proposal to our creditors, 88 per cent of whom backed what was offered, which was a very welcome surprise. In one swoop, our debts were massively reduced. We finally had a foundation from which to build.'

But even with debt obligations more manageable, the club still needed to make repayments and at the same time attempt to return Exeter to something approaching financial stability. For once, luck was on their side. In a fortunate turn of fate, the programme of recovery was given a massive shot in the arm during December 2004 when Exeter were drawn away to play Manchester United in the FA Cup third round; a game that would mean Old Trafford gate receipts and a bit of TV money too.

Despite the gulf in league positions between the two clubs, Exeter gave the Premier League team a decent game, and even came close on a few occasions to stealing the win. Although United pushed hard towards the close, a stalwart Exeter defence ensured that the score remained 0-0, meaning a replay back at St James Park; a financial boost that the club could only have dreamed of a few months earlier.

'Although we lost the replay 2-0, the two games had still been enormously beneficial to us. I think in total we managed to reap just under £1m. It's a sum that accelerated Exeter's financial recovery, meaning that we were eventually able to emerge out of our CVA in 2006,' says Laurence.

Alongside their efforts at reducing Exeter's debts, the supporters' trust also began to tackle the long-term financial position of the club. Although the calamitous reign of Russell and Lewis tended to generate the most headlines, prior to their arrival Exeter had hardly been a model of prudence. Aside from the period of administration during the mid-1990s the club had spent most of the previous 15 years in a state of financial disarray, lurching from one crisis to the next. This had to change.

Paul Farley, 'One of the most important things we did was expand the membership of the trust. We got this up from 750 in 2003 to around 3,000 a few years later, a figure that has subsequently increased to 4,000 today. Ironically, without the crisis in 2003 I'm not sure our membership would ever have reached the heady heights it has. The fear of losing our club combined with the sense of camaraderie the supporter takeover created and the feeling that we were all pulling together, acted as a great motivator for people to get involved.'

Just as important as the improvements in Exeter's ability to bring money in have been efforts to stop it leaking out. Like many clubs that have found themselves in financial meltdown, a contributory factor in Exeter's period of crisis was the wage bill.

Laurence Overend, 'We were a Conference club with massive salary expenditure, one almost more commensurate with League 1. Anyone who wanted to come off the wage bill and leave the club was allowed to do so. We were facing a transfer embargo at the time, enforced by the FA because of our financial problems, so we couldn't just bring people in. This meant giving players from the youth system a chance.'

Ironically, the transfer embargo ended up being one of the most beneficial things that could have happened to the club. The players coming through were good enough to suggest that the youth system could supply the foundations for the future. The short-term reliance on youth eventually morphed into a long-term strategy for Exeter, a vital plank in the club's attempts to produce a more financially sustainable business model. Since 2003, Exeter have invested heavily in their youth system and over the past decade, a succession of first-team players, such as Dan Seaborne, Dean Moxey and Martin Rice have populated various Exeter squads.

The board have also chosen well when it comes to managerial appointments, specifically that of Paul Tisdale. Since he took the helm of Exeter in 2006, the club's performance in the league has been remarkable. In his first season alone he managed to turn around years of footballing malaise and lead the Grecians to an appearance in the end-of-season Conference National play-off final.

'We ended up facing Morecambe at Wembley, which was a fantastic day out for the fans. Considering where we had been a few years earlier, relegated to the Conference and facing extinction then you can appreciate how amazing it was for our supporters to be at the home of English football, with the tantalising prospect of promotion back into the Football League,' says Tisdale.

Sadly for the thousands of Grecians who made the trip north to Wembley, despite Exeter going ahead in the eighth minute courtesy of a Lee Phillips goal, Morecambe eventually pulled the deficit back and then, in the dying minutes of the game, went in front courtesy of Danny Carlton's rasping shot. But Exeter's flirtation with promotion was not to be a one-off. During his second season in charge, Tisdale once again steered the club to the play-offs, overcoming Torquay United in the semis to book a place at Wembley against Cambridge United.

'There we were again a year later,' continues Paul, 'just as excited but perhaps this time a little more expectant. After all, the team had proved that the previous season was not an aberration. We were playing really attractive football, the kind that you don't always associate with the Conference and we'd played well enough to deserve our shot at promotion.'

As with the season before, Exeter took the lead, courtesy of defensive stalwart Robert Edwards. But this time there would be no faltering. The team held their nerve and at the final whistle were able to celebrate a return to the Football League.

Paul Farley remembers, 'It's difficult to put into words how I felt as a fan. You see, the whole thing was about more than just promotion, even though that was fantastic. It was like we'd come full circle and were back where we belonged. Only this time, it was better. When we were last in the Football League the club was a mess and everything was out of our control. This time we were back but the fans were in the driving seat.'

Laurence Overend adds, 'I think there was also a sense of vindication when the final whistle went. What the fans had done, giving up their time and money, had shown a great deal of faith in the supporter ownership project. We were taking a path that was different to that trodden by the overwhelming majority of clubs. It was one that was relatively untested and fraught with risks. But we had succeeded. That gave a lot of us a real feeling of satisfaction.'

Prior to his tenure at the club, Tisdale had been coaching with Team Bath, a team founded in 1999 to allow players to combine playing football with a university education. He had taken the helm of the club in 2000 and had quickly turned his young charges into an effective non-league force, earning three promotions in five seasons, guiding the club from Western League Division One to the Southern League Premier.

But as impressive as this was, what really brought him to the attention of the wider football world was Team Bath's FA Cup run in 2002/03. During that season's qualifying rounds, Team Bath managed to defeat Barnstaple Town, Backwell United, Bemerton Heath Harlequins, Newport County and Horsham to book a place in the first round proper of the competition. In doing so they became the first university team to participate in the opening round of the Cup since Gonville & Caius (Cambridge) in 1881.

According to Paul, his happiness at Team Bath was as much to do with the working atmosphere there as it was with the success the team enjoyed.

He says, 'I loved the fact that I was able to work in a steady and patient setting. Because it was a university sports club, there was none of the intense pressure for short-term success that you get with most football clubs. I was given the time to develop my own strategy and construct a side that played the kind of football that I wanted. Although I was ambitious and entertained the prospect of moving on to a bigger club, I was in no rush and was adamant that if I were to move, then my next club would have to share a similar approach.'

In June 2006, Alex Inglethorpe, who had been the first managerial appointment of the supporter-owned incarnation of Exeter City, left the club to take a coaching position with Spurs. With a managerial vacancy needing to be filled the board set about searching for a suitable candidate, with a certain Team Bath coach topping their list.

Paul says, 'When I was approached by Exeter I was really impressed by the club. The environment that existed at Team Bath seemed to exist there too, the sense that football is about more than short-term success and that a manager should be provided with a patient environment to work in. I thought at the time, and it's been confirmed by my experience since, that a huge contributory factor in this is the presence of the trust. Although winning is important and the fans were ecstatic when we won back-to-back promotions and got into League 1 in 2009, it's more important that the club, one, stays in business and, two, adheres to its principles of community ownership. For a young manager like me, there probably could not have been a better environment to work within.'

Proof of the board's patient, long-term approach was revealed in 2011/12 when Exeter were relegated from League 1. The drop back down to League 2 was not accompanied by calls for the manager's head from either the fans or the board. This was surprising when you consider the fact that Exeter had hardly set League 1 alight during their time there and during the final campaign had produced some dismal form, culminating in relegation. Would other clubs show such loyalty to their manager? Compare the experience of Paul Tisdale to that of Nigel Adkins at Southampton. Like Tisdale, Adkins took a struggling club up two divisions with back-to-back promotions. But this didn't stop him being unceremoniously dumped by the board during the 2012/13 season when it looked like the Saints' Premier League survival might be threatened.

Paul said at the time, 'No manager, whatever club he works for, can take his position for granted. But here at Exeter I think that things are slightly different compared to most clubs. The board have goals that aren't necessarily tied up with going on cup runs or earning promotion after promotion. And although we've been relegated, these principles are still being adhered to. They also recognise that I, and any manager that works here, is constrained by the limited budget that the supporter-owned model brings in and by the fact that the accrual of debt to fund lavish transfers and wages is not something that would be tolerated.

'You know, it would have been the easiest thing in the world last season to borrow money to splash out on players in an attempt to stay in League 1. But what would have been the point if in doing so we would have betrayed everything that Exeter and the supporters' trust have worked so hard to build over the past decade?'

The absence of a sugar daddy and an unwillingness to overspend means that supporter-owned clubs need to maximise revenues if they are to survive. For Exeter, entry back into the Football League acted as a huge boost to their finances, improving attendances and providing much needed TV money. Along with these achievements, the club has also seen progress in other areas of revenue generation. The number of hospitality suites at the ground has been increased and the club's bars now open for seven days per week. Exeter have also secured a lucrative, long-term sponsorship deal with Flybe.

'We are by no means a rich club, even by League 2 standards,' explains Paul Farley. 'But our commitment to "live within our means" has meant that everyone at Exeter City has worked hard to increase the money we're able to bring in. And in this we've been largely successful. Yes the club had some luck, such as that massively profitable tie against Manchester United but most of what has been achieved has been done so through careful planning and hard work. Not having a financial benefactor to turn to really sharpens the mind. A club without one operates more like a conventional business and that's exactly what we are.'

But despite the many achievements, there are concerns about the future sustainability of supporter ownership at St James Park. There is a worry among the board, the management and some of the fans that the trust model might have hit something of a glass ceiling.

Paul says, 'I think that as worthy as supporter ownership is at Exeter, and I think it's something that should be celebrated, as long as it's in place this is a club whose fortunes will probably lie within certain parameters. At the top you have League 1, likely the highest point that a club like Exeter can reach. It's not impossible that we could go higher but it is very unlikely. At the bottom, the other end of the parameter, you have the Conference. This is probably the lowest point the club could drop to. Although again it's not impossible, I really don't see us going into a league beneath this.

'So essentially, you'll have Exeter moving between these three divisions, rising during the good times and falling during the difficult ones. Short of the trust suddenly acquiring thousands more fans or abandoning their model and significantly diluting their equity, I don't see these parameters changing in the future.'

There is a concern among some members of the trust, such as Laurence Overend, that for the younger generation of supporters, operating within these parameters could represent something of a problem.

He says, 'If you're a young lad today who has only been supporting the club for a few years, then all you've known is success and us being in the Football League. The problems endured in the past are something only experienced second-hand. The expectations of this group of fans are therefore likely to be quite different from those who went through the ups and downs of the 1990s and early 2000s. For this younger element, maybe the idea of selling the club to an outside investor might not be quite so appalling if it means that we could compete at a higher level. They might also not be so averse to the idea of splashing out on expensive transfers and pushing up wages if it meant having a go at making it to the Championship. This could create some tension within the club and undermine the effectiveness of the supporter ownership model.'

Another worry for the ECST and those running the club is apathy. A lot of what has been achieved since 2003 has been dependent upon goodwill. This is probably most evident in the number of volunteers, both from the ECST and from the wider fan base, who help the club out on matchdays and at other times during the week. By the club's estimation, these volunteers currently contribute in the region of £200,000 of work annually. Allied to this, membership numbers, which stand at around 4,000, are also dependent upon the goodwill of fans to put their hands in their pockets and provide support to the club year in year out.

'What happens if this starts to trickle away?' asks Laurence. 'In the early days, when we were still recovering from the awful crisis of nearly folding, getting fans to join the trust or volunteer was relatively easy. The sense of fear and desperation that almost going out of business created was, ironically, a great motivator. My concern is that the further away we move from that time, combined with the fact that Exeter are now in sound financial shape, might make people less inclined to get involved because the sense of drama has dissipated. Trying to ensure that the fans remain motivated is going to be a big challenge over the coming years.'

Despite the many challenges, those involved in the trust feel that the future remains bright nonetheless. One reason for this is Exeter's geographic position. Paul Farley thinks that because of its relative isolation in football terms, there exists the potential to grow.

He says, 'There are no big clubs down here for us to compete against. The nearest Premier League outfit, or certainly the easiest to get to are Southampton, and they're nearly 100 miles away. If we can tap into our surroundings then there is no reason why the club can't expand. No one thinks we're going to turn into Barcelona overnight but the potential to grow is there. And if we can do that then I think that it will only strengthen our community model because the more members that we can get involved, the greater our ability to compete at a higher level will be.

'The one thing that is clear to everyone involved in this project is that we can't afford to stand still. As long as we look for new opportunities, ensure that the club grows all the time and remain true to our philosophy then there is no reason why this club can't become the Barcelona of the West Country, albeit on a slightly smaller level.'

7

Life at the Top: Supporter Trusts at the Big Clubs

THERE is a suspicion in the game that as worthy as supporter ownership is, it might be best suited to non-league football and the lower reaches of the Football League. It is a suspicion born from the fear that the levels of cash involved the higher up you go in the game act as a barrier for ordinary fans to obtain a stake in the club. Although the fan bases might be bigger in the top flight and the Championship, raising multi-million pound sums is always going to be logistically trickier than raising tens of thousands.

At many big clubs too, the need or the opportunity for fans to gain a stake hasn't arisen that often. Wealthy investors, usually promising deeper and therefore more alluring pockets than any supporters' organisation can rival, have tended to outmanoeuvre trusts whenever shares have become available or takeovers undertaken. And they have done so with the tacit support of the fans too. Despite the manifold instances of private investors coming in and failing at clubs, in most supporters' minds the tantalising riches on offer as a team inches towards the top are still most easily accessible if the business is backed by a few quid, something that tends to not be the case if fans become the partial or total owners of a club.

In the early days of punk football, when trusts took control or founded clubs, such as AFC Wimbledon and Exeter City (along with others like Brentford, York City and Notts County), it certainly appeared to be the case that this new phenomenon was a lower-league thing. And in reality little has changed that perception since. Most of the instances of supporter ownership that have popped up in English football during the past decade have continued to be in the lower reaches of the game, at clubs such as AFC Rushden & Diamonds, Wycombe Wanderers and Chester FC.

But just because ownership, whether total or partial, is more common in League 1 and below doesn't mean that it necessarily has to stay there. And if you want proof of this then look no further than Swansea City.

When Swansea took to the pitch to face Valencia away in their first group game of the 2013/14 Europa League, it marked the culmination of a remarkable journey for the Welsh club. In 2002 they had been mired in the bottom tier of the Football League and caught in a financial quagmire. Yet here they were, just over a decade on enjoying a third season in the Premier League, earnestly defending their Capital One Cup triumph of the previous campaign and, alongside Spurs, representing the Premier League in Europe. For the fans, the journey from adversity to success must have been hard to believe.

'It might be something of a cliche, but it's been a roller-coaster ride. There aren't many fans that have experienced what we have over the past decade. We've had some great times but equally there have been some real lows too, times when we thought this football club could go under,' says James White, long-time fan and current vice-chairman of the Swans Trust.

Prior to their recent incarnation as the Premier League's sexiest football team, Swansea City spent an age in the doldrums. Although they had tasted top-flight success in the past (under the guiding hand of John Toshack) the club's time as First Division starlets in the early 1980s had been brief. The latter part of that decade and the entirety of the one that followed had been fairly bleak in football terms.

If Swansea became famous for anything during these years it was the regularity with which managers were dispensed with. The high point (or low point depending upon your perspective) of this managerial merry-go-round was 1996, when four bosses came and went in one season. Among these, the most dispiriting appointment must be that of Kevin Cullis, whose previous experience was as youth coach with non-league Cradley Town, looking after their young side in the West Midlands Junior League. Although Cullis only managed to last a grand total of six days before being sacked, in that time he was able to suffer the ignominy of being ejected from the club's dressing room at half-time during a home game against Blackpool.

As mediocre as much of the late 1980s and 1990s were, fans could console themselves with the fact that although what they were watching might no longer have the glamour and excitement of the Toshack era, at least the club still played League football and, while never that flush with cash, held their own financially. But this wasn't to last. With the arrival of the new millennium, Swansea City were beset with problems on and off the field.

Like with many clubs at the time, the way that Swansea had been run for decades was proving incapable of adapting to modern football. Rising wages, escalating transfer costs, commercial naivety, an antiquated ground and falling attendances had resulted in a loss-making club and one that was racking up debts season by season.

For the owners, Ninth Floor plc., this was bad news. A business like the Swans was hardly the most welcome addition to their balance sheet, one that was already heading in the wrong direction. Keen to concentrate on their security and IT projects (the perfect bedfellows for any football club), Ninth

Floor began looking for a way to extricate the company from the football world, finding the answer to this problem in the shape of Swansea's then commercial manager Mike Lewis (the same man who would later go on to run Exeter City into the ground). In July of 2001, 99 per cent of the club was passed to Lewis for the princely sum of £1 (and the promise to repay Ninth Floor's loans to the business, which totalled just over £800,000).

Although not a wealthy man himself, Lewis took on the club believing that he would enjoy the financial support of several local businessmen. In his autobiography, *The Trains Don't Stop There Anymore*, he explains what happened to this promised support once he had become Swansea's head honcho, 'Anyone with substantial funds in a position to help hid for cover when the moment of need arrived. I should have known better than to expect a queue of investors to be banging on the gates of the club eager to help. Excuses given to me by local businessmen when asked to help the Swans were wide ranging:

'"My company is going through a rough patch at the moment…"

'"We're poised for a takeover and I dare not make any investment at this time."

'"My wife hates football and she will kill me if she sees me investing in the Swans."'

Lewis managed to keep Swansea going but within three months of taking control he was already looking to follow Ninth Floor's lead and palm responsibility off to someone else. That someone else turned out to be Tony Petty, a London-based businessman and a self-confessed West Ham fan, who bought the club and the debts for a quid towards the end of 2001. With unusual honesty, Petty arrived claiming to be no 'white knight', promising fans that they shouldn't expect any injections of cash into the club.

'And he was true to his word,' states Leigh Dineen, one-time chairman of the Swans Trust and current vice-chairman of Swansea City. According to Leigh, what the club got instead was a thoroughly businesslike approach. 'Petty acted like this was an ordinary company. And the first thing you do if you take-over an ailing company is try to remove as many high-paid staff as you can from the payroll. So one day the fans woke up to the announcement that he was planning to sell seven of our best players. The problem is that although this technically makes business sense, in football it's a stupid thing to do. Among the fans the hostility directed towards Petty was palpable.'

At the time, Petty claimed that he had acted like this to show potential investors the Brisbane Lions that he had the club's finances under control and that the £800,000 of debt that he had inherited from Mike Lewis was manageable. According to Petty, representatives from the Lions were put off buying the club by the hostile reaction of the Swansea faithful in response to the new regime's age of austerity.

Back in the summer of 2001, concerned about the way that Swansea were being run, a small group of supporters had already set up the Swans Trust (established as an IPS). Adversity seems to be the key for the popularity of trusts and in this Tony Petty was a gift. His decision to try and sell the club's key players galvanised the fans against him and support for the trust blossomed. Subsequently, life became fairly unpleasant for Petty whenever he attended a home game at the Vetch Field, Swansea's dilapidated ground. At one match against Rushden & Diamonds, the club's owner was verbally assaulted for the full 90 minutes and had to leave the stadium surrounded by stewards.

'On the terraces and behind the scenes, the Swans Trust became the voice of the fans. We organised marches, campaigned inside and outside of the ground and put a lot of effort into getting rid of Petty and looking at ways that the trust, along with other local businessmen, could take control of the club,' says Leigh.

The size of the Swans Trust, the limited finances it was able to accrue through fundraising and the extent of the debt that Swansea carried meant that it had little hope of success in the fight if acting alone. Fortunately it didn't have to. From the beginning, the trust and the campaign to oust Petty received vital support from former directors and local business people, among them Mel Nurse.

In the autumn of 2001, Nurse (a former player and something of a hero at the Vetch) made another invaluable contribution to the club by purchasing the £800,000 owed to Ninth Floor. By becoming the club's principal creditor, it gave Nurse, who was in constant conversation with the supporters' movement and broadly supportive of their desire to gain a stake in the club, the ability to pressurise Petty to sell to alternative owners or force the issue by placing Swansea into administration.

'There was a lot of pressure on Petty now,' explains Leigh. 'There were legal moves to try and get him to sell, there was hostility on the terraces and there were demonstrations in the town and outside the Vetch. It felt inevitable that he would finally get the message and sell up. When he did, vitally for us at the trust, any new regime at the club had to be one that included an element of supporter ownership.'

Working with local fans from the business community, the Swans Trust was able to become part of a consortium that approached Petty with an offer to take over the club, an approach that was ultimately accepted at the beginning of 2002. Building upon its initial £50,000 investment, today the trust currently owns 100,000 shares, representing a 20.4 per cent stake in the club. This significant concern allows the trust to have one executive director and one associate director at the club, each elected by the Swans Trust's board.

Leigh says, 'It's a testament to the generosity of the fans and everyone involved with the trust that through all kinds of fundraising schemes and the ubiquitous bucket being passed around at games, the Swans Trust came up with that initial investment. It was a lot to ask of our supporters but they came through when it mattered most.'

Although the power struggle at the club might have been resolved this didn't mean that Swansea's problems were suddenly over.

James White recalls, 'The early years of the consortium's time in charge, a period when we were all still trying to recover from the hangover of the Lewis and Petty era, were difficult to say the least, specifically the 2002/03 season. I remember that Brian Flynn had built a new team pretty much from scratch and results hadn't been that great. It came down to the last game of the season and a home fixture against Hull that we had to win or risk going down. It's hard to explain the feelings that games like that evoke. There's so much at stake that you're all over the place really.'

The game started well for the home side when local boy James Thomas put them ahead through a penalty. But things quickly turned sour and a couple of defensive mistakes gave Hull the opportunity to bag two quick goals and grab a 2-1 lead.

James continues, 'It didn't seem possible that we could have gone through everything we had with Petty and then go down. It was one of my worst moments as a Swansea fan when that second goal went in.'

Anyone who has every read *Roy of the Rovers* might find parallels with that comic's storylines in what happened next. Just before half-time Swansea managed to get another penalty, which Thomas put away with aplomb. The second half opened in sensational fashion as Lenny Johnrose fired home through a crowded goalmouth to restore the hosts' lead. Then, on the 57th minute, Thomas latched on to a through-ball and chipped the Hull goalkeeper from 30 yards, a finish to match any that took place that afternoon. With that goal, the local hero got his hat-trick and Swansea killed the game off, ensuring their survival in the process. The win gave them 49 points, just enough to avoid the drop.

James White says, 'You probably couldn't have written a more dramatic end to the season. We'd survived. Just. I think everyone who followed the Swans was emotionally drained by what had happened. The trick now was to never get in that position again. We had to rebuild the club financially and on the pitch, start making us candidates for promotion rather than relegation.'

And that's exactly what's happened. From that point on, in financial terms there has been no return to the grim days of the past. Losses might have been incurred here and there but the club has remained averse to unnecessary borrowing and in the Premier League today, Swansea are one of the few clubs to have no debt, which is an amazing accomplishment.

'It would have been pointless to have run the club any other way,' explains Leigh Dineen. 'Everyone who got involved in the consortium that took over, from the big shareholders to the thousands of fans who are part of the Swans Trust did so to ensure that this club was saved and it was never run in such an unsustainable fashion again.'

Despite the absence of a backer to bankroll them and the presence of a budget that has often been dwarfed by league rivals, Swansea have managed to combine financial stability over the past decade with a miraculous climb up the football pyramid. First under the management of Roberto Martinez, and then Paulo Sousa and Brendan Rodgers, the club edged their way up the league system, eventually gaining promotion to the Premier League in 2011. How has this happened?

Leigh says, 'The board recognised early on that we were financially limited. Our investors were not overly wealthy and there are only so many times that you can keep going back to the supporters asking for hand-outs. We came to the conclusion that we would have to do something different to other clubs if we were to thrive. The team had begun playing attractive football under Kenny Jackett and had some success. This is a style that you don't often see in the lower leagues and it struck us that there might be something in it.

'But the real catalyst for our development of this playing style was the appointment of Roberto. He came with a football vision, centred on his sides playing attractive, attacking football and not the long-ball, kick-and-rush approach so common in the lower divisions. This style of playing became the "Swansea Way" and it worked. It accommodated our deficiencies elsewhere, turning a club with limited resources into one that could compete with much wealthier rivals because of the way we played.'

Another aspect of the Swans' success has been the ability to manage such a large and disparate consortium. When a club is run by a consortium, there is always the possibility of a clash between different personalities and different perspectives on how to run the club. And that's just when it's a handful of people in charge. When you're talking about a consortium in which there are thousands of fans too, then the potential for conflict must increase exponentially.

And yet at Swansea this hasn't been the case. Leigh Dineen is well placed to comment on why their model has worked. Although he was instrumental in the establishment of the Swans Trust and served as its supporter director for two years, Leigh has subsequently become a major shareholder himself and now works with the trust rather than for it.

He says, 'Along with all interested parties sharing the football vision for the club, which has been hugely important, it also helped that we formed the consortium during a period of adversity. It forged a sense of unity among the interested parties that might not have existed had it been a conventional takeover. The fact that we took over a club that had been so disastrously managed in financial terms helped too because it created a shared desire to make sustainability paramount. If this hadn't been the case then over the past decade there might have been more disagreements between the different parties on the issue of spending and transfer budgets, which could have led to a collapse of the consortium.'

Despite the level of agreement that has existed, Leigh admits that all parties involved have had to make slight compromises over the past decade, because none have a majority shareholding. Not that he thinks that this is necessarily a bad thing.

He adds, 'What's great about Swansea is the fact that this is not one man's vision but that of thousands of fans, including shareholders like me, who are working together. How many clubs in the higher divisions can claim to have that?'

Along with delighting anyone who enjoys a story of success against the odds, Swansea's arrival in the Premier League also gave a significant boost to the cause of supporter ownership. Although the Swans Trust is only a minority partner in the consortium, Swansea's success in getting into the Premier League and impressive performance once there, suggests that perhaps punk football need not solely be confined to the lower leagues.

James White says, 'You hear a lot in football about this model being unsuitable in the Premier League. And it is probably difficult to imagine a club like Manchester United suddenly being entirely owned by its fans.

But what we've illustrated is that an element of supporter ownership is compatible with success in the higher divisions. It doesn't have to hold a team back. In fact, I can't see any reason why every club in the top flight couldn't have some percentage of this. It works in Germany and look how well their clubs are doing in Europe. I think at the moment English football is stuck with a perspective that still sees private owners as the best option available, despite the overwhelming evidence to the contrary.'

Although Swansea are technically a Premier League club with an element of supporter ownership, the top flight is not where their experiment with punk football began. Anyone sceptical about the ability of fans of teams in the Premier League or even the Championship to gain a share of the clubs they follow could rightfully point to the fact that when the Swans Trust entered the consortium, it did so at a time when buying a share in the club came at a relatively modest price. It would be much more difficult for that to happen today, a time when Swansea are awash with European and Premier League television money, enjoying life in a brand new stadium and have become a club with a turnover that those in League 2 could only dream of.

Gaining a stake in a top-flight club is always going to be difficult for a supporters' trust because of the costs involved.

But it's not impossible. Arsenal are one of the biggest clubs in England. According to Deloitte, during the 2012/13 season the Gunners generated €284m of revenue, a figure only bettered in England by Manchester United, Manchester City and Chelsea. On an international level, the club was eighth in Deloitte's Money League, gradually pulling away from traditional domestic rivals such as Liverpool and Spurs.

In short, this is not the kind of club where you would expect to find an active supporters' trust complete with its own portfolio of shares. But since being formed back in 2003, the Arsenal Supporters' Trust (AST) has proven that even at the very highest levels of English football, supporters can gain a foothold at the clubs they follow.

'There's little chance that the AST will ever own the club. But that doesn't mean that supporters have to just sit back and have no say in how their club is run. A share, however small, gives you a voice. And that's what we're all about, giving our members a voice,' says Emma Shepherd, who has been following Arsenal for as long as she can remember.

Emma talks happily about the club's past triumphs, the players she has met over the years and about her admiration for Arsenal's long-serving manager Arsene Wenger. And this enthusiasm is equally apparent when she talks about the AST, within which Emma serves as a board member.

She says, 'To me, and to the 850 members that we have in the trust, supporting Arsenal doesn't end at 5pm on a Saturday afternoon. I want to have a say in how my club is run and the AST provides the medium for this. It's cheap to join and involvement makes you feel like you're doing more than simply following the club like a customer.'

Today the AST owns three shares in Arsenal plc. Although this might not sound much, and actually isn't when you take into account that the company is divided into just over 62,000 ordinary shares, the fact that the AST holding has a market value of around £48,000 illustrates how costly it is to gain any stake at a big Premier League team. Although the finance for these shares has principally come from trust members, the AST has also had some assistance from the club.

Back in 2005, just as Arsenal were issuing more equity to fund the Emirates Stadium project, it was noted that the club had one authorised but unissued share. Dubbed the 'orphan share' by the AST, its members campaigned to have it transferred to their ownership to provide a 'safe home', something that the club eventually agreed to in 2007.

Although the AST only owns a very modest shareholding, according to Emma, possessing it does provide certain rights.

She says, 'At the very simplest level, it gives us a seat at the AGM. It means we get to question the board, officially register our opinions on certain matters and vote on club issues. And I think that because of this, the club takes us seriously as a supporters' group, more so than if we had no stake. It's the reason why we have such a good relationship with the board and why the levels of communication between both parties have always been very strong.'

Key to the AST's relationship with Arsenal is the concept of 'custodianship'. Like other trusts that have taken a share in football clubs, the AST sees supporters as a group within the Arsenal community best placed to guard the club's values. From their perspective, owners come and go but the fans endure. Because of this, the AST has been keen to extend the plurality of ownership and include more supporters as shareholders. The problem, and this is one common to all big clubs, is that a share in Arsenal costs around £16,000, a figure well beyond the means of the average fan. The AST's solution to this problem is a novel idea called Fanshare.

'Fanshare is designed to make investment affordable because it significantly reduces the cost of a share,' explains Emma.

The scheme works like this: you become a member of Fanshare by paying a one-off fee of £20. After that, punters decide how much they would like to invest each month in buying Arsenal Fanshares, the minimum being £10 and the maximum £1,000.

'Say then for example,' continues Emma, 'we have 1,000 fans each saving £10 per month and the cost of one ordinary Arsenal share is £15,000. After two months those savers would have reached £20,000 in total, giving them cumulatively enough to purchase one share (with £5,000 left in the kitty).'

Once this share is purchased, it is divided into 1,000 Fanshares with each member being given one share and a cash balance of £5. In return for their investment, along with obtaining a stake in the club, members of Fanshare also get a place in a ballot for a seat at the club's AGM. So far, the uptake of Fanshare has been pretty good and to date around 2,000 people have invested.

'The only problem,' admits Emma, 'has been acquiring shares to buy. As you can imagine with a club like Arsenal, one in which two people, Stan Kroenke and Alisher Usmanov, own around 95 per cent of the stock, not a great deal of shares are available. Despite this, Fanshare's still managed to acquire 104 shares, making it the third largest stakeholder at the club.'

Through Fanshare and the stake acquired by the AST, the Arsenal faithful are doing their bit to expand the role that ordinary fans can play at the club, ensuring that supporters can have a voice even at one of the Premier League's big boys.

According to Dave Boyle, obtaining a share and building upwards from there will always represent the best way for fans to influence policy at their club and hold that club to account.

Dave says, 'Ownership is king. That's what my experience of working with trusts and clubs has taught me. Total ownership is obviously best but any degree of shareholding is beneficial. Even one share can provide fans with a voice, one that the board can't dismiss out of hand. Of course, that's not to say that fans are powerless without ownership. There are many examples of fan groups at big clubs, such as Spurs, Newcastle and Fulham, campaigning on certain issues and achieving a positive result. It's just that, from my experience, the cause of the fans is a lot stronger if they also possess a stake in the club at the same time. And the bigger that stake the better their position will be.'

But sometimes this is easier said than done. As the examples of Exeter and Swansea revealed, although horrible to endure, financial catastrophes at clubs often present an opportunity for fans to gain a stake. But in the higher reaches of the game, even when a club is in a financial mess, organising fans to mount a takeover is not always that easy.

In 2007, Tom Hicks and George Gillett, two American businessmen with a background in sports ownership, seized control of Liverpool. Although they arrived claiming to respect the traditions of the club and also promising to invest in the squad and provide the funds for a new stadium, it was soon revealed to the fans that the plans of the new regime were built on shallow foundations. Liverpool's new owners had borrowed £185m to fund the takeover of the club and a further £113m to accommodate player signings and running costs. They later refinanced the entire package and took out a new loan which came to a total of £350m.

Through the way that Hicks and Gillett had organised the ownership structure at Liverpool, the supporters discovered that the club would be paying the interest on this loan from cash flow. As long as the duo stayed at the helm this figure would be around £40m per year. It became clear to the fans that this was not the deal that the supporters had been sold and there was also no way on earth that Hicks and Gillett had enough cash to fund a new stadium – a development that was estimated to cost a minimum of £300m.

As supporters of a club which until that point has always enjoyed financial stability, the takeover unsurprisingly caused disquiet among the fans. Angered by the debt the club had taken on and concerned that the team's performance on the pitch was beginning to suffer, the supporters were spurred into action. Led by the club's supporters' union, the Spirit of Shankly (SOS), marches and protests against the new regime became a common sight at Anfield.

'There were rallies in Liverpool city centre, sit-ins at Anfield, flag days, leafleting campaigns, and marches on the ground.

Probably the most high-profile example of our campaign was a rally outside Anfield before a home game against Blackpool in 2010 which saw between 5,000 and 7,000 supporters in attendance. We tried anything we could think of really to highlight our cause and make sure that the media's attention was fixed on what these two cowboys were doing to our club,' says current SOS secretary Paul Gardner.

But as useful as these methods were in galvanising opinion against Gillett and Hicks and keeping the issue alive in the media, for another group of fans it appeared to make more sense to try to tackle the issue head-on by engaging directly with the new owners. Share Liverpool FC (SLFC) was established in 2008 with one aim; to unite fans in an attempt to buy out the club. Lifelong Red Barrie Baxter was one of the leading figures behind the scheme:

'Liverpool's owners at the time only ever had one concern and that was money. They didn't care about the club, its history or its culture. They saw Liverpool FC as an investment, pure and simple. It made sense then to the people involved with SLFC that what you had to offer Hicks and Gillett was a financial way out that would ensure that they weren't needlessly out of pocket and that they could leave honourably. Liverpool possess one of the biggest supporter bases in the world and we thought that if we could tap into this then the financial power to put together a buy-out could be unlocked.'

Their aim was to turn Liverpool into a scouse version of Barcelona, with around 100,000 members buying a single share at around £5,000 a pop (giving SLFC enough cash to mount a £500m takeover).

Although it was envisioned that any supporter organisation that arose from these plans would be run as an ISP, initially SLFC faced something of a credibility gap with the fans, as Graham Smith, one-time secretary of SOS, explains: 'We were a democratic organisation. SLFC weren't. No one doubted that everyone involved with SLFC was a committed Red but they'd been brought together by Rogan Taylor, the man behind the plans, and not elected. They were also talking about £5,000 like it was nothing. Most Reds, specifically those from the city, would not regard £5,000 as a drop in the ocean.'

To address this credibility gap, during 2010 SLFC went into partnership with SOS, providing several members of the fans' union, such as Graham, with seats on the SLFC board. Together these two groups then set about furthering the cause of supporter ownership at Anfield, which as the year rumbled on was becoming a more realistic proposition by the day.

'By 2010 it was clear that Royal Bank of Scotland (RBS), the club's principal creditor, had run out of patience with Hicks and Gillett,' says Barrie Baxter. 'The bank was desperately looking for a solution to the crisis that had engulfed the club, even if that meant forcing the owners to sell Liverpool for less than they valued it.'

Around this time, the club appointed Barclays Capital with a mandate to find new owners and hopefully restore something approaching financial sanity at Anfield.

Graham Smith says, 'As part of this process SLFC were invited down to London to talk with Barclays Capital about the possibility of the supporters taking over the club. At this point the scheme had received about 30,000 people registering an interest. And you could add to that probably another 20,000 further supporters from SOS that were open to the idea of investing if the price could be brought down. So there was considerable support out there.'

Despite this, according to Graham, any attempt to take over Liverpool was hampered by the approach of Barclays.

He says, 'For a start we weren't given access to the books, so we had no idea what size of bid to put in. We were also in something of a catch-22 position. You can't sit down and negotiate with people without the money, or at least a significant part of it, being on the table. But people were loath to hand over money, and equally we were wary of taking it, until it was proven that we were the kind of organisation that people would negotiate with. Barclays wouldn't let us tell anyone about the meeting. I don't think they fundamentally saw us as a credible option, largely because our access to money was so uncertain. In truth, I think they were just going through the motions, talking to us just to ensure that they couldn't be criticised later on for failing to explore all options.'

In October 2010, any notion of a supporter takeover was rendered moot when Gillett and Hicks sold Liverpool to Fenway Sports Group (FSG) for a fee of around £300m, far below the pair's valuation of between £600m and £1bn. The arrival of Fenway effectively ended the SLFC's attempts to buy the club and recently the scheme has been placed into cold storage; several years of cordial relations and the sense that the club is back on track robbing the group of its impetus. Despite this, there are still some fans, like Graham, that harbour dreams that one day a scouse version of Barcelona could become a reality.

He says, 'The truth is that FSG are a sports investment company (or a hedge fund if you're being less kind) and they're probably not in this for the long haul. Their primary focus is not the club's heritage and traditions. They got Liverpool cheap and their medium- and long-term aim is to increase the club's value and sell it on. Because of this, the fans should be setting themselves up as FSG's exit route. What's to stop the owners selling parts of the club bit by bit to the supporters with a long-term aim for us to have 100 per cent ownership or majority control at Anfield? The numbers are certainly out there. Liverpool FC have told SOS that there are about six million people worldwide with a connection to the club. We've also got commercial relationships with several big companies, who could be part of the solution, in the same way that Adidas and Audi are at Bayern Munich. If FSG, the club and the supporters worked together on this incrementally, there's no reason why it couldn't become a reality.'

A lot of what's happened with trusts to date has been reactive, supporters responding to a crisis. But it doesn't have to be this way. As Graham argues, with the right organisation and a positive relationship with the owners, there's nothing stopping fans at big clubs from believing that partial or total ownership is one day possible.

'But the key to this I think is the ability to build a mass membership,' suggests Duncan Drasdo, chief executive of the Manchester United Supporters' Trust (MUST).

With Manchester United being worth more than a billion pounds, those fans who desire to one day own a stake in the club arguably have one of the most difficult jobs in English football. Despite this, Duncan feels that expanding the trust is the best way to secure the long-term aim of having a degree of supporter ownership at Old Trafford.

He says, 'Fans that follow big teams obviously have a harder time obtaining a stake because the sums involved can be astronomical. But, on the plus side clubs like United and Liverpool also have huge, international fan bases. Our aim is to access this and build MUST into a huge organisation. The bigger we are, and the more members we have committed to the concept of supporter ownership, the easier it's going to be to react to any opportunity to gain a stake at United in the future. Asking hundreds of thousands of members to contribute a small amount is going to be a lot easier than asking a handful to contribute millions.'

In the absence of such opportunities, if in the meantime trusts at big clubs want to be more than just a pressure group, there are other things that they can do. And one area where there has been particular development has been that regarding a club's assets.

Under the 2011 Localism Act, introduced by the Coalition Government, communities, and by extension local organisations, have the right to bid for 'assets of community value'. The idea behind this piece of legislation is to ensure that land and buildings of value to communities, such as village shops, pubs and even football stadiums, are not taken away from local people without them first having an opportunity to purchase them.

For an asset to become officially of 'community value', an application must be made to the local authority which will then judge whether it can be added to its list. If the application is successful then should the asset come up for sale, the community organisation that made the request is given a six-week period to decide if it wants to make a bid for it. If it does, then it has a further six months to raise the necessary finance, effectively delaying any sale.

Several supporter trusts at big clubs, including those at Manchester United, Liverpool and Birmingham City, have already had their club's stadiums added to the local authority's list of community assets.

'Safeguarding the future of the stadium is vital to us,' says Steven McCarthy, chairman of the Blues Trust at Birmingham City. 'Over the years there have been several clubs where the fans have had to endure the horror of their stadium being sold off. Not only is a stadium often something that is intrinsic to the identity of both a club and the fans, it is also the most important asset any club has. This is certainly the case with St Andrew's. Our successful application now means that the fans and not just the board will have a say in any future sale of our stadium.'

Of course, grounds cost a fair few quid, and although purchasing one would be cheaper than buying out a top-flight club, it still represents a big ask for most supporters' trusts. But then the assets of a football club don't end at the stadium. Many big clubs have varied property portfolios and it is here that some fan organisations in the higher reaches of the game have sought alternative ways to become stakeholders.

In 2012, a group of Evertonians got together to form Trust Everton, the driving force behind which was Tony L'Anson.

He says, 'The initial rationale for the founding of Trust Everton was to explore thoroughly the feasibility of a supporters' vehicle providing sustainable long-term funding for the real estate assets of the football club, such as the training ground and the stadium'.

Of key concern to the trust was the future of Finch Farm, Everton's 55-acre training facility, which lies just outside the city. This had been acquired by the club in 2006 and then sold not long after to the development firm ROM Capital for £2.1m. ROM developed the site to the club's specification, valued it at £17m and then leased it back to Everton.

'In 2011 it was announced that the owners were selling the training facility, offering it at a price of around £15m, a sum which Everton couldn't afford,' says Tony.

For Trust Everton this represented an opportunity to acquire the asset, placing it in the hands of an organisation that would work with the club rather than solely seeking to maximise what it could earn from them. The idea was to use a subscription-based membership system and other forms of finance commonly employed by supporter trusts to raise the necessary finance to purchase the training facility.

Despite considerable interest among Blues in what Trust Everton was doing, its plans to buy Finch Farm never came to fruition. The scheme was rendered moot when Liverpool City Council stepped in and bought the asset for £12.9m. Despite this, what was attempted by a small group of Evertonians does reveal that in the absence of shareholding, a trust can still try to be more than just a pressure group, that there are other options available.

It might be drastic but for those fans who have found that influencing a club via a trust is simply impossible in the higher levels of the game there is another path to follow. Manchester United are the biggest club in Britain and certainly, alongside Barcelona and Real Madrid one of the biggest three in the world. Privately-owned and with a market valuation way beyond the reach of any ordinary supporter organisation, opportunities for fans to gain a stake are limited to say the least. For a small section of the Old Trafford faithful, a group that was growing disillusioned with the way that United had changed over the years the answer was simple: do an AFC Wimbledon and start a new club of your own.

8

Manchester's Other United: The FC United of Manchester Story

BELYING its reputation for endless drizzle, for once Manchester is basking under the heat of a clear blue sky, deciding for a change to join with the Indian summer the rest of the country is enjoying. For the few thousand supporters scattered around Gigg Lane, traditional home to Bury FC, it represents a chance to cast off their coats and reveal the sacred red shirts of the home team.

And it is red, rather than the white of Bury, that's on show here because the assembled horde has come to watch the club that shares Gigg Lane with Bury; FC United of Manchester.

This is a team that might play in the same colours as the city's other, more famous United and share fans that have an affinity with both clubs but which is the antithesis of what Manchester United have become. It is a club that embodies the idea of fan power, functions democratically and which hopes to be living proof that Old Trafford could one day be run differently.

But to discover the club's origins we have to leave Gigg Lane and travel back to 2005 and the storm that was brewing over Manchester.

Prior to his arrival at Old Trafford, few people had ever heard of Malcolm Glazer, unless you were one of those rare few in this country with an interest in American football. Glazer, who made his fortune from an eclectic array of businesses including real estate, nursing homes and oil, became the owner of the Tampa Bay Buccaneers in 1995. Under his stewardship these perennial underachievers have enjoyed periods of unparalleled success, the high point being their clinching of the Super Bowl in 2002.

First and foremost a businessman (Glazer has presided over a tripling of the Buccaneers' franchise value since taking control), according to his advisers he became attracted to the idea of taking over United because of the belief that the current owners were failing to fully exploit the brand. Although this might sound incredible considering just how much tatty rubbish United are willing to have their crest emblazoned upon, when you bear in mind that rival clubs such as Arsenal and Manchester City have sold their stadium naming rights in multi-million-pound deals then it's possible that Glazer might have had a point.

Starting small, initially buying a three per cent stake in the club during 2003, by the autumn of the following year Glazer had increased his share in United to nearly 30 per cent. His incremental build-up created a fervour of speculation regarding a possible takeover, rumours that were finally confirmed in the autumn of 2004 when the American approached the club's board with outline plans of a buy-out package.

With Glazer's offer supported by an enormous amount of borrowing, United's board were aware that acceptance of the bid would place hundreds of millions of pounds of debt on the club, a large enough amount to make them reject his advances.

Undeterred, Glazer returned with a more detailed bid a few months later, this time backed with a reduced degree of leverage. But for a club like United, one that had been relatively debt-free for some time, even this diminished level of borrowing proved more than they were willing to risk and once again Glazer found his amorous advances rebuffed.

Despite this rejection, speculation persisted, now concentrating on the belief that Glazer was going to bypass the opinions of the board and launch a hostile takeover. The critical move came in May 2005 when it was announced that he had bought the 29 per cent stake previously held by the Irish racehorse owners John Magnier and J.P. McManus. This gave him a controlling stake in the company, a move he then followed up by launching an offer to buy the remaining shares in United. Glazer eventually reached the point where he passed the magic 90 per cent mark, giving him the right to initiate a compulsory purchase of the company's remaining shares.

Considering the furore that had been created when Murdoch had tried something similar a few years earlier, unsurprisingly none of this had gone down too well among the fans. Despite the gap between the two takeover attempts, United's supporters, or at least the more activist element among them, had not spent the intervening time twiddling their collective thumbs. Aware that a debt-free, publicly listed football club of United's stature would always be a potential target for takeovers, IMUSA, Shareholders United (who had dropped the 'Against Murdoch' part of their name after that particular foe had been vanquished) and the club's various fanzines had eventually collectivised under the umbrella of the Not for Sale Coalition, a group determined to oppose any corporate predator with an eye on the club.

When the Glazer takeover started to gather momentum, these various fan groups inevitably began to mobilise. With no conflict of interest arising from the bid, it meant that the political route utilised by IMUSA and Shareholders United during the Murdoch affair was unavailable to the coalition, necessitating a change in tactics. This time around, it was Shareholders United that took the lead. After the scare of the attempted BSkyB takeover, Shareholders United had already been encouraging fans to buy shares in the club to provide them with the power necessary to block any future takeover attempts (the ultimate ambition being a controlling stake in the club). Once the prospect of a Glazer takeover became a reality, efforts to increase the stake in the club held by ordinary fans gathered momentum.

This approach was then complemented by IMUSA concentrating on attacking United's revenue-earning potential, a tactic that threatened the club's potential future income, thereby theoretically undermining Glazer's ability to secure loan finance. There were protests against leading sponsors, Nike and Vodafone, including instances where their stores were 'flash-mobbed' by IMUSA members. Life was also made difficult for anyone who collaborated with Glazer. Taking inspiration from the average 15-year-old prankster, the Brunswick Group (hired by Glazer to undertake PR during the bidding process), was inundated with phone calls, black faxes, emails and unwanted pizza deliveries.

The campaign against Glazer was organised, well supported and one of the most sophisticated put together by any supporter organisation in football. But by the terms of its own aims, it was also an abject failure. Shareholders United never came close to achieving its targets and the IMUSA campaigns were a nuisance but nothing more.

'On reflection,' says Michael Crick, who had remained one of the leading figures behind Shareholders United, 'you wonder sometimes whether we would have been better letting Murdoch take control of the club. We fought hard against someone who at least has an understanding of English football and who had the money to fund a takeover. We won that fight but in doing so left the door open for Glazer, a man who has subsequently saddled the club with enormous debts and whose long-term impact on United is yet to be understood.'

Despite being unable to stop the sale of their club, resistance has continued. One campaign, known as Love United Hate Glazer, (already in existence prior to the takeover), has involved the spreading of the slogan and the acronym LUHG around various locations in the city via stickers and graffiti. The campaign also encourages fans to wear green and gold at home games (the colours of Manchester United's precursor club, Newton Heath). To complement this, the Manchester United Supporters' Trust (which grew out of Shareholders United) has tried, unsuccessfully, to bring together a number of wealthy United fans, known affectionately as the Red Knights, in an attempt to organise a buy-out of the club from Glazer.

But the most high profile response to the takeover, the one that has created the greatest number of column inches and the most interest among fans of Manchester United and other clubs alike, was that undertaken by a small group of supporters for whom the buy-out was the final straw in their growing disillusionment with the club.

Andy Walsh is a United fan to the core. Talk to this genial Mancunian for any length of time and his love of the team he has supported for decades is clear. But he has still been one of the leading figures in the creation of FC United of Manchester, the non-league club that has become a refuge for those fans tired of the way Manchester United has been run.

According to Andy, for those behind the founding of the new club, the Glazer affair was merely the catalyst rather than the cause of their decision to break away from the Old Trafford faithful.

He says, 'For a long time I (and others who would go on to help create FC United of Manchester) had been involved in efforts to try and increase the role of fans in football by setting up different networks where supporters could get together and try to achieve change in the game. The problem, from our perspective, was that clubs, especially in the top flight, were treating fans in a way that I would describe as dismissive. At Old Trafford you could see this in the growing heavy-handedness of stewards during the game, the moving of match times to suit Sky and by the way the club ignored our protests and changed the name of the Stretford End to the West Stand.'

But most galling of all for Andy has been the escalation of ticket prices. Back in 1990, the cheapest ticket available for Old Trafford cost just £3.50. If the club's pricing structure had kept in touch with the rest of the economy, then that same ticket should have cost around £6 in 2011. Instead, the cheapest ticket available to watch Manchester United play set punters back £28. And that's a figure that has only increased over the past few seasons.

'Like any system run along such nakedly free market lines as the Premier League, the last few decades have rewarded the wealthy and punished the poor. This has been most acutely felt among working-class supporters,' argues Andy, angrily.

Many fans from working-class communities are now priced out of the game and for a lot of low-earners the days of taking your kids to the match on a Saturday afternoon are a thing of the past.

Andy says, 'It's meant that increasingly the only way to support the club is down the pub watching Sky, which is not how most fans want to view a game week in week out.'

According to Andy, for a section of the supporter base, this groundswell of discontent morphed into open rebellion once the Glazer takeover became a reality.

He continues, 'A group of us had just had enough and started to look at ways we could register our opposition to the club. We felt that one way was our custom. People like Glazer always assume that fans will take any treatment meted out to them. They look on us like a herd of sheep that will meekly turn up season in season out, regardless of the despicable way that the club treats us. It was one of the hardest decisions of my life but we felt that the only way that we could make our feelings known was to challenge this assumption and to say "enough is enough", we won't come through your turnstiles and you're no longer getting our money.'

But among many of those who decided to withhold their money, there was also the sense that the Glazer affair represented an opportunity. The idea of starting a new club had first been mooted during the proposed BSkyB bid. It was regarded at the time as a 'nuclear option', the fans' last resort should Murdoch become the new owner. Over the years that followed, the idea never really went away. By the time Glazer took over, a significant cadre of United supporters, the majority of whom were actively involved in the influential fanzines, *Red Issue*, *Red News* and *United We Stand*, were ready to go 'nuclear'.

Andy says, 'In 2005 a group of us began talking about the feasibility of starting a new club. At first it was probably just talk but it kept coming up again and again. Over time we began to realise that there were enough of us seriously committed to the idea to give it a go. And in June of 2005, that's exactly what happened. We knew that we needed to be robustly organised, so in an eight-week period a steering committee of 15 people was established, which started to actively recruit members, developed a business plan, looked into finding somewhere to play, drew up a constitution and made an application to the FA and the Football League to participate as a new club.'

Like other supporter-owned clubs, FC United are constituted as an IPS. Currently, membership is obtained by paying a minimum annual fee of £12 to the club, with each member receiving one share and one vote, regardless of the amount paid. Shareholders get to attend the AGM, the parliament of members that holds the club to account and debates overall policy. At the AGM, ideas and suggestions from members and the club board are voted on and members also get the opportunity to stand for and be elected to the trust board, the body that appoints those who oversee the day-to-day running of the club.

If one word could be said to define the steering committee's business plan in those early days it would be unrealistic; but unrealistic only in the sense that they hopelessly under-estimated just how popular an endeavour FC United would be. The initial business proposal was based upon the assumption that they might be able to get a few hundred people through the gate on matchdays and that membership would be around 1,000; an estimate that turned out to be exceptionally cautious.

Within a few months FC United had raised £180,000 from around 3,000 people and although they did get some large investments of around £5,000, most of what was raised came in small amounts. There was even one donation of 50p from a young girl from Bradford which touched everyone involved in the club.

Almost all of those who applied for membership understood the vision behind the club, the idea that regardless of the financial contribution you made you would only ever receive one share and one vote.

'There was one exception though,' laughs Andy. 'Some bloke from down south wanted to invest quite a lot of money in the club but seemed to think that this would give him a greater say, as is the case with clubs run along traditionally capitalist lines. Needless to say, we didn't take his money.'

Despite high levels of local interest, approval was not universal. For a while the Love United, Hate Glazer sticker campaign was hijacked by stickers featuring a new slogan, Love United, Hate FC. And then during a derby against Salford City in the club's early days, a bunch of Manchester United loyalists in the crowd unfurled a banner calling FC United supporters 'Judas Scum'.

'On a personal level there are some lads that I went with to the match for years who I haven't spoken to since the club was set up, which was something I never expected to happen. I can understand where some of this feeling is coming from, the feeling that what we were doing was splitting the anti-Glazer campaign. But I stand by what we did and ultimately, despite Manchester United's success on the pitch, Glazer is still there and the club remains laden with debt,' explains Andy, sadly.

The club's first game, a friendly at Leigh, took place in mid-July, just a few weeks after the idea of starting a club had first been seriously suggested. Under the guiding hand of manager

Karl Marginson, FC United took to the pitch in front of just over 2,500 fans and earned a respectable draw. The game ended with an exuberant pitch invasion (long forbidden at Old Trafford) and players being carried off shoulder high, a rare sight in English football following a goalless friendly.

In the following weeks the club secured a ground-share with Bury at Gigg Lane and successfully applied for membership of the Second Division of the North West Counties Football League. The team then made their league debut against Leek County School Old Boys, at Harrison Park in Staffordshire.

'What a journey that first season was, from that debut in August right through to promotion at the end of the campaign. There were amazing home games, fantastic away days and even an end-of-season European away game in Germany against FC Lokomotive Leipzig. But promotion was unquestionably the highlight. It was like a dream come true. We'd turned an idea into a reality, building a club for the fans and one that was becoming a success,' says Simon Howles, editor of the FC United fanzine, *Under the Boardwalk*.

And after that initial promotion the success continued. During the following two seasons FC United climbed up the pyramid, reaching the Northern Premier League Premier Division by 2008, just one step below Conference North.

'We had a few tough seasons as we adjusted to the higher level but recently things seem to have picked up. We managed to reach the play-offs last season, the third successive time we've done this, and we came very close to gaining promotion to Conference North, which would have been an amazing achievement,' says Adam Brown, one of the founders of the club and a current director.

During that first season FC United enjoyed average home gates of around 3,000, much higher than the norm for the league they were playing in. Although over time numbers have declined, they still regularly have a home presence of around 1,700 supporters at Gigg Lane, which by some margin remains the highest for the division.

Freed from the repressive atmosphere of all-seater stadiums where groups of mates can rarely watch the match together (assuming they can afford to get in), the fans have also rediscovered the joy of collective singing, something that has inspired a succession of YouTube hits.

Their songs mix the proud, the weird and the simply funny. Some are Manchester United classics given an FC United twist, while others are new, forged by fans enjoying the creative release of being freed from the stifling constraints of Old Trafford.

For this book there's this fitting chant, sung to the tune of Herman's Hermits 1964 release, 'I'm Into Something Good':

'Woke up this morning feeling fine/ Got punk football on my mind/ We play football the way, the way that we should/Oh yeah/Something tells me I'm into something good.'

Or if you want something with a slightly (very slightly) more modern feel then there's the reinterpreted version of 'This is How it Feels', from Oldham's greatest musical exports, the Inspiral Carpets:

'This is how it feels to be FC/This is how it feels to be home/ This is how it feels when you don't sell your arse to a gnome/ Arse to a gnome...Arse to a gnome...'

And then there's my personal favourite, sung to the tune of 'Lord of the Dance':

'Glazer wherever you may be You bought Old Trafford but you can't buy me/I signed not for sale and I meant just that You can't buy me, you greedy twat.'

'The thing is, going to watch FC United feels like it used to do when I'd go and watch Manchester United when I was younger,' thinks Simon Howles. 'Going down with your mates on a Saturday, paying to get in at the gate, and then being with them in the ground. It's so different to what was on offer at Old Trafford, where you'd be lucky to get a ticket at all and if you did get in then you'd probably be sitting on your own, policed at every moment by ever-present stewards.'

One of the biggest differences for those heading down to Gigg Lane on Saturday afternoon is the price to get in. Although it's hard to compare a game in the Northern Premier League to one taking place in the Premier League, for many years a lot of Manchester United fans have been priced out of attending the match.

'Football, specifically in the Premier League, has mutated from a working-class game to one where it's middle-class, middle-aged men who dominate the average crowd,' says Andy Walsh.

And the research backs this up. According to a recent Premier League Fan Survey, just nine per cent of those regularly attending games were under the age of 24. By contrast, the average age of a Premier League season ticket holder was 44. They were also largely middle-class, comfortably-off men and women who have replaced the massed ranks of the working classes that once populated the terraces (who now only make up around nine per cent of attending fans). And the reason for this is simple: cost.

Andy Walsh says, 'If you're a mum or dad and you want to take a couple of your kids to the match, then just to get into Old Trafford today, even with the concessions that you get for kids, you're looking at paying a minimum of around £60. And that's before you include getting to the game and buying food and drinks when you're there, which will also set you back a few quid. It means that the days of working-class families going to the game, something that used to be the backbone of football in England, are a thing of the past.

'Here at FC United to get in on matchday, adults pay just £8 and under-18s £2. It means that for £12 an adult and couple of kids can enjoy a day at the game together. It is all part of what this club is all about, making sure that there are people in the city who are not completely disenfranchised from watching live football.'

Whenever possible, the people behind FC United are keen to point out that this is more than just an ordinary football club too. Although success on the field and progress up the pyramid matter to those behind the project, it's felt that FC

United's success needs to be measured in other areas too. And paramount among these, according to Adam Brown, are their efforts to serve the local community.

He says, 'Many clubs have become divorced from the communities from which they emerged, ignoring the people that live near or around the ground in favour of fans from elsewhere in the country, simply because this is often an easy way to make money. We don't want our club to be like that, we want it to be rooted in the local community and for us, this means doing things to help that community.'

One area that illustrates this is the club's partnership with Street Soccer Academy (SSA), a professional service provider that specialises in the rehabilitation and reintegration of vulnerable and 'at-risk' individuals, such as the homeless, ex-offenders and those who are not in employment, education or training. FC United have recently opened a Regional Centre for SSA operated by the club's community coaches and volunteers, which offers a professional football environment for these people to access high-level coaching and wrap-around support.

Although this interaction with the people of Manchester is motivated by a genuine desire to address social ills, there is also an element of reciprocity about it too. FC United want the community they serve to increase their financial stake in the club and so feel that the greater their involvement in that community, the more willing that community will be to provide the necessary support. And it's an approach that is already paying dividends, as illustrated by the amazing response that the club's received following their decision to build a new stadium.

As AFC Wimbledon discovered before them, the disadvantages of ground-sharing are manifold. Aside from the rent to Bury, FC United also lose the income that they would have gained from matchday services and from non-football revenue-generating activities, such as the provision of conference facilities. With this in mind, the club have been raising the finance to build their own stadium in Moston, in the north of the city. The planned 5,000-capacity ground is being built in conjunction with Manchester City Council, which is providing some of the funding and offering the land at a peppercorn rent.

The cost of this new stadium is estimated to be around £5.5m. In order to access the funding that is being provided by organisations such as the city council, Sport England and the Football Foundation, FC United have had to raise around a third of the money themselves, something they have chosen to do via a community share scheme.

Raising money in this way is increasingly popular in the third sector, helping to finance everything from wind farms to health shops to football stadiums. Unlike 'normal shares' community shares carry no voting rights and cannot be traded. Along with specific rules governing when and how you can withdraw your money, there is also an individual investment limit of £100,000 and the IPS running the scheme can only pay limited interest on shares, which according to Co-operatives UK should only be 'sufficient to attract and retain the investment'.

Under the FC United scheme (which has already exceeded its target yet remains open), people purchase shares in the ground's development. Although only open to club members, anyone willing to invest in the project can do so by becoming one. Regardless of the level of investment, each share is only valued at £1 and can only be sold to another FC United member. But although investors can't benefit from a rise in share values, from the third year anniversary of the issuing, the holder could potentially receive an interest payment of up to two per cent above base rate (dependent upon the club's financial position). In spring of 2012 the target of £1.6m for the share issue was reached and having recently overcome a few legal hurdles regarding the ground's location, building has recently started on the new stadium.

'Reaching our target from the share issue is a fantastic achievement, especially in the current economic climate,' Adam Brown proudly says. 'We at the club believe that community shares provide a great way for supporter-owned clubs to raise a lot of money whilst preserving the notion of community ownership. Here at FC United we believe community shares are a better way of raising finance to borrowing from banks and are more sustainable than relying on wealthy individuals who may not always have the best interests of the club at heart and who can always disappear at a moment's notice.'

Regardless of any future financial return, Adam believes that the amazing response to the community share issue by local people is largely attributable to the fact that the planned stadium will transcend narrow football interests and embrace a wider social remit.

He says, 'Yes it's going to be a football ground but equally it is going to serve the people of Moston and the wider community of the city. Beyond sport, the building can provide a space for meetings for local community groups, pre-school provision and possibly a venue for delivering education, training and employment services for local people. In both its financing and its remit this is at heart a community endeavour which is something that we have always wanted FC United to be. And I think that's an aim which has resonated with local people.'

Obtaining the stadium will also enable FC United of Manchester to compete effectively in the future too. Although they have enjoyed crowds several times in excess of the league average every season they have been in existence, future progression will be dependent upon increasing financial revenues.

At the moment they are a big fish in a small pond, a position that will diminish if the planned upward progression continues without the necessary improvements in the club's commercial reach. The new stadium, combined with greater investment in their youth system, will be FC United's response to the financial limitations of their supporter ownership model. But even with these improvements, Andy Walsh is unsure that his club could repeat the levels of success enjoyed by AFC Wimbledon, not that this is something that particularly worries him.

He adds, 'We're a different club to AFC Wimbledon, a smaller one. That might change in the future but there's a possibility that it won't. But for us, progression isn't necessarily as important as it was for them. From the off, they wanted to get back into the Football League, back to where they thought they should rightly be. Luckily for them they had the financial muscle to do this. Of course we need success on the field, otherwise our supporters and members aren't going to be willing to make the necessary sacrifices of time that following a football club requires.

'But for us it's just as important to be of benefit to the local community and to show other clubs that if we can do it, start a club, build a new ground, with our relatively small number of supporters, imagine what a club with a fan base of hundreds of thousands could do? It's our hope that supporters of Manchester United can see that what we have done is possible and that there are real alternatives to the current model; that people like Glazer don't have a monopoly on the ownership of football clubs in England.'

9

Does it Always Work?

YOU might get the impression from reading the previous few chapters that everything in the world of punk football is pretty straightforward and that supporter ownership is the panacea to the manifold problems facing the game. But when is anything connected to football ever that straightforward?

In reality, for all the successes like AFC Wimbledon, FC United of Manchester and Swansea City, there are also the times when things haven't turned out quite so rosy. One of the most combustible examples of this took place at Notts County a few years ago, an episode that reveals everything that is good and bad about fan ownership.

It is fair to say that Notts County are something of a footballing institution. They are the oldest club in the world to currently play at a professional level, the team that has played the most matches in the English professional game and they even had their black and white home colours adopted by Juventus, no less. So, there's plenty to be proud of there. Less impressively though, they also hold the record for enduring the single longest period of administration in English football; an unprecedented (and subsequently unbeaten) 534 days.

The club's problems began towards the end of the 1990s, following a takeover by American businessman Albert Scardino, who had acquired County from local plumbing and heating merchant Derek Pavis. Scardino was an unusual figure to become so deeply immersed in the world of Nottingham football. Back in the 1970s, the Savannah-born Scardino had co-founded a weekly local newspaper, the *Georgia Gazette*, with his wife Marjorie. Although tiny, the paper developed a reputation for campaign journalism and following a crusade against local corruption, Albert eventually won a Pulitzer Prize for his work. After they had sold the paper, Scardino later went on to have stints working for the *New York Times* and the Mayor of New York before he and his wife washed up on these shores in the early 1990s.

While his wife would go on to become a major figure in the media, first as chief executive of the Economist group and later CEO of Pearson PLC, Albert set his sights on the world of English football, motivated by a strong belief in its investment potential. Unencumbered by local tribal loyalties, Scardino first had a stab at Nottingham Forest, becoming part of a £20m consortium takeover supported by venture capital firm Mercury Asset Management. When Mercury cooled on the idea and a rival consortium took control of the club, Scardino simply shifted his focus to the local rivals, approaching Pavis about a possible deal.

Under their eventual agreement, Pavis decided to sell Albert his 90 per cent shareholding for around £300,000, with Scardino further liable for £2m of loans owed to the former owner. These would be repaid in three instalments over the coming years. Part of the problem with this deal was that Scardino wasn't a wealthy man and certainly didn't have the finance in place at the time to pay back the loans. Theoretically, there was every possibility that he would be unable to raise sufficient cash to pay Pavis what was owed to him. Conscious of this, Scardino had approached the city council (which had always had a close relationship with both local clubs) in the hope of receiving some financial support. Although no formal contract was ever established, the American emerged from his meetings under the impression that the local authority would provide loan guarantees worth £3.4m to Notts County, thereby enabling him to raise the finance to pay Pavis back.

Confident that the money would come, with the help of Peter Storrie – who had arrived from West Ham as the club's chief executive – Scardino next sought to put in place the second aspect of his strategy, namely County's push for promotion out of the Second Division. Players were brought in on big contracts, such as Darren Caskey, Ian Baraclough and Tony Hackworth (all rumoured to be earning in excess of £100,000 per year) as the club assembled a squad supposedly fit for the First Division. Sadly, as seems all too common in football, despite the splurge the club could only manage a disappointing eighth in the league, four points off the play-off running.

At the same time that the first team were failing on the pitch, Scardino was also failing behind the scenes. High wages, disappointing attendances and no sign of the loan guarantees he had hoped for from the city council, all conspired to undo the American's grand plans. Although he managed to raise a loan of £560,000 to enable County to repay the first instalment to Pavis, further finance proved difficult to acquire. The club defaulted on the second instalment, which led to a gradual breakdown in the relationship between Scardino and Pavis. Other creditors, including HMRC and NatWest Bank, were also becoming anxious as County's debts rose steadily to £6m. With an untenable wage bill, inability to borrow money without guarantees and creditors clamouring for their money back, by the middle of 2002 Scardino had little option than to place the club into administration.

'What followed were 534 days of hell, and for a time it looked as though the club might face extinction. There were no realistic signs that anyone wanted to buy, which is a frightening prospect for any fan,' says Mike Scott, most recent chairman of the Notts County Supporters' Trust (NCST).

The NCST was formed in 2003 to provide supporters with a voice during the crisis, to raise money for County and to explore the possibility of the fans becoming part of any bid for the club. Like other trusts, it was constituted as an IPS and established on the democratic principle of one member one vote.

To raise the necessary amount to secure ownership of the club was beyond the means of the trust so its plans were always dependent on finding investment partners sympathetic to the concepts of punk football. Fortunately for the fans, such sympathy did eventually arrive. A group calling themselves the Blenheim Consortium, which included former club directors Peter Joyce and John Mountney, along with former Leicester City director Roy Parker and dotcom entrepreneur Haydn Green, came forward with a plan to take over County in conjunction with the NCST towards the end of 2003.

As part of its commitment to the consortium, the trust was set a target of raising £250,000. Through a mix of celebrity dinners, quizzes, raffles, and collection buckets being passed around both at Meadow Lane and at other grounds, the supporters eventually reached their target.

The trust's cash gave it a share in County and provided it with the right to elect a supporter director on to the board. This position was then improved a few years later when the consortium's leading shareholder Haydn Green provided the trust with enough shares to give it majority control and three seats on the board.

Mike Scott says, 'Haydn was a great Notts County man. He never sought the limelight and without his money Blenheim would never have succeeded. He was already respected by the fans. But to then put us in a position where we effectively controlled the club was amazing. I think Haydn envisaged the fans as the perfect long-term custodians of the club's future. It's a real shame that we weren't able to repay his generosity by embracing this.'

What followed the Blenheim takeover, certainly compared to the years that preceded it, was a period of relative calm for County. The influx of new money had to a large extent cleared a sizeable chunk of the club's debt, the wage bill was trimmed and an era of financial solidity seemed to beckon, with the trust committed to the principle of sustainability. The only downside was the team's relegation to the bottom tier of English football in 2004 and their inability to mount an effective campaign for promotion thereafter.

But the calm was not to last. Personal agendas, diverse political opinions and differing perspectives on the role that supporters should be playing at the club, gradually coalesced to produce considerable friction within the trust.

For Mike Scott, one of those who often found himself in opposition to the supporter directors, the core disagreement centred on the issue of democracy.

He says, 'Essentially, are supporter directors elected like MPs, to do as they see fit between elections, or are they there solely as representatives of the supporters, who must refer back to those fans (or at least the trust board) before taking any decision of major significance? I believed in the latter definition, whereas others believed in the former. And I think it was this difference of interpretations that ultimately led to so many disagreements.'

The future of the NCST then reached a dramatic crossroads in the spring of 2009 when John Armstrong-Holmes, the supporter-elected chairman of the club, revealed to members he had been in talks to sell County to Munto Finance Ltd, a Middle Eastern consortium backed by Qadbak Investments.

Although the supporter ownership model could have kept the club going, several members of the board had been on the look out for new investment because they felt that this was the only way that Notts County could progress up the leagues. Over the years they'd had discussions with several parties but nothing ever came to fruition. Then out of nowhere the club had received an approach from Peter Trembling on behalf of the Middle Eastern consortium.

In response, the chair and the vice-chairman of the club went to Bahrain (at their own expense) to meet with Trembling and his colleagues. There followed several days of intensive discussions, which culminated in them returning with a proposal, one that appeared to promise a future in which the club would be provided with the kind of investment that could fuel long-held dreams of a return to the higher reaches of the football pyramid.

But despite the promises of riches to come there was one stipulation to the takeover that appeared controversial. Munto claimed to be wary of becoming involved with the club should they have to undertake an expensive buy-out of the existing majority shareholder. What this in effect meant was that prospective owners would only countenance taking the club on and providing future investment if the NCST was to hand over its shares to Munto. It was a proposal that was met in some quarters by fierce opposition.

Mike says, 'There were some members of the trust, such as myself, who had concerns about what was happening. Personally, I wasn't convinced by the evidence supplied to us that the money claimed to be available was actually there. And I also felt that Haydn Green had given us his shares in good faith, with an aim for us to be custodians of the club. To me, handing these over to Munto could be seen as a betrayal of that trust.'

Munto's proposal was shared with all supporters at a fans' forum, with both those for and against presenting their arguments in public. Following this, a postal vote was undertaken by the trust, the final result of which revealed a whopping 93 per cent of members in favour of the takeover.

The new owners took control of Notts County in July of 2009, after their bid had been given the green light by the football authorities, and immediately set about wowing the fans with a whirlwind of activity. Headline-grabbing moves such as the appointment of Sven-Göran Eriksson as director of football and the signing of high-profile players on big contracts like Sol Campbell and Kasper Schmeichel seemed to reassure fans that the arrival of Munto really did herald a new era for the club. But despite the initial flurry of action, events at County soon began to take a turn for the worse.

Far from being backed by Middle Eastern billionaires, it seemed that the Munto takeover was a bit of a con.

'There simply was no money. The club had been taken for a ride. We'd signed over the supporters' stake and got absolutely nothing in return,' says Mike, angrily.

While rumoured to be simultaneously taking money out of the club, once in charge at County, Munto initiated a plan for success that will be familiar to most football fans: borrow and spend. The new owners seemed to hope that the club could recoup what was borrowed through footballing success and the increased commercial revenues that this would bring.

Six months of shelling out on players that were unaffordable and racking up unsustainable debts eventually caught up with County. In their short spell in charge Munto had turned a sustainable business into one that owed £7.5m and which was threatened with administration for a second time.

In an interview with *The Guardian* around this time, Armstrong-Holmes said, 'I was told that Munto's backers, Qadbak Investments, were owned by hugely wealthy investors who would take Notts County to another level financially. Instead, just a few months later, we have a club that has left several debts unpaid, with county court judgments and a winding-up petition having been issued against it, and major questions still unanswered about Qadbak's ownership. Far from believing that the club is now on its way to climbing up the leagues and the bright future Qadbak promised, I am now dreadfully worried about what the future holds.' (Reproduced with the consent of *The Guardian*.)

With creditors clamouring for repayment and threats of administration coming from several quarters, in December 2009 Munto decided to get out and put the indebted club up for sale. The extent of the financial calamity at County ensured that few people were interested in taking the business on. Despite this, help did ultimately appear in the form of former Lincoln City director Ray Trew, who stepped in to clean things up. Under his ownership the past few years have been spent slowly recovering from the disaster of the Munto era.

Ray says, 'It was a pretty perilous time. We knew it would be bad, but the extent of the debt that we uncovered as the weeks and months passed following our takeover was truly staggering. There were unpaid bills for all sorts of things and a lot of ill feeling among sponsors and suppliers, which is completely understandable. We had to take each debt on its own merit really and speak to the company or individual to find a way forward, whether that be through structured payments or return on investment through sponsorship, etc. There was a lot of hard work just to get the club back from the brink and then a lot of time and effort has had to go in continuously since then to try and restore faith in the Notts County brand and to get us moving towards a more prosperous future.'

The example of Notts County doesn't show supporter ownership in the most flattering of lights. So much so that when stories appear in the media extolling the virtues of fan power, it's rare for County to get much of a mention. But their inclusion matters. Running a football club is no easy business and a lot of the time the human relationships involved are important. Supporter ownership can be a wonderful success, as the examples of AFC Wimbledon and Exeter City reveal. But equally, these experiments can fall foul to the same forces that have been picking apart the dreams of club owners since the dawn of the professional game.

And this needn't always be because people fall out or get their heads turned by Middle Eastern sheiks waving wads of alluring (yet non-existent) cash. As the examples of Stockport County, Brentford and York City reveal, sometimes majority ownership by the fans can struggle because the task of running the club is simply beyond the power of those involved.

Stockport County

Life can be difficult for the smaller clubs that surround Manchester. Struggling for attention against the city's football behemoths must make survival a daily grind. Edgeley Park is just seven miles away from City and United, so Stockport County probably have it worse than most. Even their novel decision in the past to play games on a Friday evening only partially solved this problem. The depth of their dilemma was perfectly illustrated during the 1998/99 season when despite residing in a higher league than Manchester City, they were still drawing much smaller average crowds.

Although Stockport have enjoyed periods of success, such as under Danny Bergara and then Dave Jones during the 1990s (with the latter even getting them into the pre-Championship First Division), for most of County's history, life has been spent in the Football League's lower reaches. And occasionally beyond! Since they gained entry into the Football League back in 1900, they have applied for re-election on four separate occasions.

And their supporters will surely hope that a fifth application will come one day soon because the past few years haven't been much fun. At the end of the 2010/11 season, following a dismal campaign, the club were relegated to Conference National. As if this wasn't tough enough, the run of poor form continued and just two seasons later, Stockport were cast down into Conference North, in doing so gaining a new record, becoming the only team in Football League history to drop from the second tier of the pyramid to the sixth.

Along with this footballing demise, there has been an equally torrid time behind the scenes over the past few years, a period which has seen owners come and go, a managerial merry-go-round and a rare example of a supporters' trust taking the club to the brink of financial oblivion.

The seeds of Stockport's malaise were sown back in 2003. The owner at the time, Brendan Elwood, under whom the club enjoyed their greatest period of success, chose to sell. Although

County had been doing well in football terms, becoming a regular fixture in the second tier, financially the club was less successful. Championship-level wages and the collapse of ITV Digital were just two of the many factors that were gradually causing Stockport to become one of the growing legion of clubs suffering regular losses and over-reliance on borrowing to cover these. The apparent answer to those problems was a white knight by the name of Brian Kennedy.

Kennedy, described generously in the media as a local entrepreneur and less generously as a double glazing salesman, was the owner of the local rugby union club, Sale Sharks. His vision, as outlined to Elwood, was to unite the Sharks with County under the umbrella of his company, Cheshire Sport, with both clubs playing their home fixtures at Edgeley Park.

Although he had no experience of running a football club, as proof of his pedigree, Kennedy could point to his time with the Sharks, time which had seen him turn a loss-making club that had never won a trophy into one making a profit and which finished second in rugby union's Premiership. Swayed by the promise of a future secured, Elwood sold up and Cheshire Sports took control of County in 2003. Ominously for the club, as part of the deal Kennedy became the sole owner of Edgeley Park.

Over the years, Kennedy has come in for considerable criticism from the fans, some of it justified, some of it a little unfair. The most commonly levelled criticism is that he favoured his first love of rugby, and in doing so placed more emphasis on the Sharks rather than County. Although there is certainly evidence to back this up, during the early part of his association with the club Kennedy appeared committed to both teams. Not only did County welcome a raft of new signings after the new owner took control but the club also enjoyed a hefty playing budget, the second largest in the division.

This all changed in 2005 when Kennedy announced that he no longer wanted to run the football side of things and was planning to sell the club to the local supporters' trust. Prior to this, Kennedy had already made it clear that the days of simply handing over money to either club were in the past, telling the local press at the time that he wanted both Stockport County and the Sale Sharks to stand on their own two feet.

'I think Kennedy genuinely believed that the fans were the best custodians for the club from that point on, the people who could really run things in a sustainable manner. Supporter trusts elsewhere had already earned a decent reputation in running lower league clubs, so there was a good reason to believe that we could do the same,' says Norman Beverley, one-time chairman of the Stockport County Supporters' Trust (SCST).

The SCST took control in July of 2005 for a nominal fee of £1. It was an agreement that, initially at least, received broad support from the fans. Elected as vice-chairman of the club by members of the trust, Norman still looks back on that moment fondly.

He recalls, 'Regardless of what happened subsequently, that was a great day for County. I am a passionate believer that supporters, and the wider community, should have a stake in their local clubs. Elsewhere in football at the time, trusts were appearing all over the place and it felt like we were really part, and in some ways at the forefront of a revolution in the game.'

Despite the optimism of the SCST and goodwill that existed among the fans there were difficulties from the start, in part because of the agreement struck with Kennedy when taking over. Although the deal contained several positive aspects, such as a six-year sponsorship agreement with Cheshire Sport (that amounted to around £750,000) and a ten-year option to buy Edgeley Park for a sum of £4.5m, there were some other elements that were less beneficial to the club's future. Key among these were stipulations that Cheshire Sport would take a share of matchday revenue and a 30 per cent cut of all transfer fees.

But the main problem facing the SCST, and one that would have vexed any group that had taken over the club, was the loss of Edgeley Park. Any club that loses a stadium can attest to the fact that surviving without it is a difficult prospect. The fact that so many football clubs are able to function at all, specifically in the lower leagues, is dependent upon what they can generate at their ground from corporate hospitality and the selling of pies and pints on matchday. In a few short years, Stockport County had gone from being kings of their own castle to become in the eyes of many fans the junior partner in the relationship between themselves and the Sale Sharks. Norman Beverley admits that this is something that constantly held the club back.

He says, 'Despite the romance that surrounds football, the bottom line is that you need to make money. What had happened in the past had certainly undermined the football club's ability to do this. We tried our best to remedy the situation but in reality it was always going to be a very difficult task in light of the situation that surrounded the stadium.'

According to Norman, the trust actually came close to solving the problem long before the ten-year option to buy Edgeley Park expired.

He says, 'It's a real case of "what if". We had an investor lined up who was willing to provide us with a way to regain ownership. This venture was going to be financed by building new houses on a vacant site next to the football ground.'

Under the strategy put forward, once the development had been completed the person funding the project (a very well-off local businessman) would be given the actual cost of the build and the profit from selling the houses would be given to the trust. The figures involved were considerable; enough to have enabled the club to buy back their stadium.

'We, along with the person financing the project, held a number of meetings with the council chief executive, where we presented the plan. All we needed was the OK from the local authority, which sadly wasn't forthcoming. The trust's future and that of the club could have been very different had the council shown a little more understanding and a bit more vision,' says Norman, dejectedly.

As it was, County remained tied to their old home and tied to a deal that was becoming more unsustainable by the day. During the 2008/09 season it was revealed that along with many smaller debts to other creditors, County owed £450,000 to HMRC and £300,000 to David Farms Ltd, a sum that was originally borrowed to assist in the search for a new stadium but which ended up being used to sustain the business and provide cashflow.

'The club was ultimately forced into administration in April 2009 owing over £7m,' says Norman, a palpable sense of regret still evident in his voice. According to him, by this point the atmosphere at the trust had begun to sour.

He continues, 'New people had come in, often people who didn't completely "buy in" to what punk football is all about, and other people, such as myself, were being forced out. There were competing philosophies about which direction the club should take with some elements wishing to revert to private ownership and others wanting to stay true to our original vision. Meetings went on with developers which I knew nothing about, and at one point I was informed that I was not clever enough to be involved with these negotiations. That was the final straw for me and so I left. This air of conflict, combined with the fact that the club was clearly in financial trouble, all added up to a difficult time towards the end. It was hardly the most dignified way to run things.'

With the accountancy firm Leonard Curtis appointed as administrators the all-too-common search for a saviour began. 'What was certain,' concludes Norman, 'was the supporters were not going to be part of the solution. What had happened at Stockport County had effectively, in the eyes of many people involved with the club, sullied the idea of the fans being in charge.'

The legacy of debt created during that era also cast a long shadow. Although County performed well during the time when the supporters were at the helm, managing to earn themselves a promotion to League 1 in 2008, successive owners have struggled to rebuild the club since and, inevitably perhaps, performance on the pitch has suffered, leading to Stockport's drop into Conference North.

In the aftermath of the supporters' time in charge there were many accusations thrown about as to whose fault the whole debacle had been. Some blame the SCST, others Kennedy and those with longer memories, Brendan Elwood, criticising him for abandoning the club in the first place.

'In truth, there were so many things wrong at County it would be difficult to pinpoint any one factor or person as being chiefly responsible,' thinks Norman. 'On a personal note, I just think of it as an opportunity wasted. With a bit of help from the council, and there are plenty of local authorities that have helped football clubs, things could have been so different. But that didn't happen and Stockport suffered and continue to suffer to this day. It's going to be a long road back to the Football League.'

Brentford FC

Brentford have never been one of London's big beasts. Despite a history that stretches back to 1889, the club have rarely lingered amidst the loftier heights of English football. Their best period was in the 1930s, when they spent a few seasons in the top flight, even managing a couple of top-six finishes before the Second World War interrupted this particular golden age. Since then, they have lingered in the lower tiers of the Football League.

Despite their lack of on-field success, for much of the club's history those in charge faced little in the way of organised opposition from the fans. The club might have struggled financially and possessed limited football horizons, but in the most part the fans left the board to run matters as they saw fit. But this didn't last forever and, in keeping with the rest of the game, this benign environment started to disappear during the 1990s.

The first signs of fan activism came with the establishment of the Brentford Independent Association of Supporters (BIAS) in 1998, formed in response to the behaviour of David Webb, who had recently acquired the club. Not long after taking control, Webb initiated the sale of any player he could get rid of, including leading goalscorer Carl Asaba. Although the whole spine of the team was eventually ripped out, the combined deals only recouped £1.2m. To the fans' ire, despite claims to the contrary by Webb and his chairman Tony Swaisland, the money wasn't reinvested in 'quality replacements' (that is, unless you call a few non-league hopefuls and some Spurs reserve players 'quality replacements').

BIAS began life as a single issue pressure group, an organisation whose sole purpose was to rally around its 'Webb Out' campaign and agitate for the removal of their owner. And it got what it wanted. Webb eventually tired of the aggravation and sold his majority share in 1998 to Ron Noades.

Like many new owners, Noades arrived with big talk and big promises, claiming that he would push Brentford up to the First Division. As many fans have experienced, 'big talk' costs nothing and is pretty pointless if not backed with investment, good players and the appointment of a manager who knows what he's doing.

At first it looked as though Noades was covering at least two of these factors. Money and players arrived, banishing memories of the Webb years and doing much to placate the fans. The only issue that appeared was the owner's very unusual decision to manage the club himself. But to the surprise of the supporters (and many interested neutrals) this decision turned out to be a shrewd one (in the short term at least). During his first season at the helm, Noades guided Brentford to promotion, ending the campaign as Third Division champions. He even managed to bag himself the Manager of the Year award for good measure.

But the good times were not to last. Unlike his predecessor, Noades was not averse to a gamble. Regardless of the unusual step of managing the club himself, his model for progression up the pyramid differed little from that adopted by many owners in football: spend more than you have and hope for the best.

Brentford's promotion, and the club's attempts to progress further, had been fuelled by borrowing. By the time Noades eventually parted company with the club, they would owe millions.

'I think his plan was always to borrow some money, chase success, get us into Division Two and then sell our ground to cover the debt, hoping that progression on the pitch would convince the fans that he knew what he was doing,' says Donald Kerr, vice-chairman of the club and supporter-elected director.

It might be a bit knackered, but Griffin Park is a piece of valuable real estate in south-west London, worth millions to whoever owns it. To a businessman like Ron Noades it probably made perfect sense to sell it, realise its value, and then move to a new ground somewhere cheaper.

'But the problem for the fans,' continues Donald, 'was the owner's desire to sell before an alternative stadium was built. We were facing the prospect of our owner selling our ground and then tying us into a ground-share with Woking. And who knew how long that would have lasted?'

The campaign against the Woking ground-share was led by BIAS, for whom the move acted as the perfect recruiting tool. Along with conventional tactics, such as leafleting, picketing and raising the issue in the local media, BIAS also attempted to rally support from around the world of football and started to lobby Football League officials, as it would be that organisation that would rule on the move.

At the same time, occurring to David Merritt, long-time fan and current supporter-elected non-executive director, the idea of forming a supporters' trust started to be talked about among those more activist members of the Brentford faithful.

He says, 'I think one of our members, Brian Burgess, was the first to mention the idea but a lot of people who'd been either involved with BIAS or who were simply concerned about what was happening at the club were intrigued by this new form of organising. The idea began to germinate in a lot of people's minds that if we had a stake in our club then maybe in the future, fights such as these could either be avoided or at least if they occurred then the fans would be in a stronger position to negotiate.'

After an initial public meeting in the spring of 2001, during which the response to the concept was favourable, the fans behind the original idea started to work with Supporters Direct to put together a constitution and prospectus for what would become Bees United, Brentford's very own supporters' trust. Although they didn't know it at the time, the foundation of the trust in 2001 would prove to be timely.

Despite Noades's best efforts, the Football League ruled against the Woking move in June of that year. Not long after that, another proposed ground-share, this time with Kingstonian, also floundered. With his plans scuppered and the club's debts mounting, in 2003 Noades announced he was cutting his ties with Brentford and selling up. But with a crumbling ground, massive debts and a wage bill that was exceeding annual turnover, it wasn't as though people were queuing up to bite his hand off. The club faced something of an impasse. On one side, their owner wanted to sell and was unwilling to invest into the club. On the other, no one appeared to be riding to the rescue.

'It began to dawn on many of us that the obvious answer to this problem was the trust,' says Donald.

Although Ron Noades is held in low regard by many Brentford fans, for Donald, his approach during the negotiations to sell the club to Bees United should be appreciated. Donald says, 'He was very helpful, something that's not always highlighted. I always got the impression that he really wanted the fans to be the next owners.'

To acquire Noades's 60 per cent controlling stake (owned by his holding company Altonwood) the trust had to arrange a financial restructuring of the club's debts and release Altonwood from £4.5m of bank guarantees.

'Achieving this outright alone would have been impossible, simply beyond the means of the fans,' admits Donald.

To accommodate this problem, the trust managed to secure help from several outside sources, such as Barclays Bank and Hounslow Council. Interestingly, according to Donald, they also received help from Noades too.

Donald says, 'Altonwood offered to provide a £1m interest-free loan for three years and to maintain a £1m bank guarantee against a reduced level of bank borrowing of £2.5m. Proof I think of Ron's desire for the supporters to be part of the solution.'

The trust was then faced with the prospect of raising £1m towards the buy-out, which was a large amount but one that was still achievable.

Donald proudly explains, 'Along with membership subs, loans from supporters and all kinds of fundraising events, like sponsored bike rides, raffles and jumble sales, we eventually got there. Combined with the help we were getting, this enabled us to buyout Altonwood's shareholding in the club and effectively become the majority owners of Brentford FC at the beginning of 2006.'

But although the acquisition by the supporters solved the impasse created by Noades's desire to sell, it didn't necessarily solve the other problems that Brentford faced under the previous owner. The club remained heavily in debt, saddled with an over-generous wage bill and the owner of an aging ground through which it was difficult to raise much commercial revenue.

Griffin Park might have character by the bucketload but it's also the only stadium in the Football League which has a pub on every corner. While this might be the traditionalists' idea of heaven, it hampered attempts to raise money from selling food and drink on matchdays.

'Brentford only had average gates of around 4,000 and our members could only provide the trust with so much to keep the club going. There simply wasn't enough coming in to cover what was going out,' admits Donald.

During that period when the fans were majority shareholders of the club, Brentford lost around £300,000–£400,000 per year. Although these financial issues face many lower league clubs, the problem for the Bees was the absence of a sugar daddy to take up the slack.

'The financial situation at the club,' continues Donald, 'effectively meant that the fan-owned version of Brentford was better suited to a lower league, one where our incomings more accurately matched our outgoings.'

Given the problems encountered with the previous two owners, selling Brentford to an outsider was not something that many fans considered a tenable option, even if the alternative was watching the club slide inevitably towards non-league football. But this is exactly what would go on to happen. In 2010, Bees United handed control of the club over to local businessman Matthew Benham, a long-time supporter and someone who had provided financial assistance during the era of fan ownership.

David Merritt says, 'It took us a long time to get to the stage where we were happy giving Matthew the majority ownership of Brentford. We went through years where he just had some loans to the club [he helped get rid of the debts to Ron Noades], then years of a partnership deal where we retained ownership while Matthew put more money in, and got more influence.

'Eventually though the trust reached a point where we were comfortable enough with Matthew to move to a situation where control was transferred. I guess the conclusion is that Matthew is a pretty exceptional guy and we went through a long period of getting used to each other. It also helped that there are Brentford fans who remembered him attending games as a kid, so he had good pedigree!'

Under the deal offered by Benham, in return for an initial stake of 35 per cent representing the non-trust shareholdings of former chairman Martin Lange (25 per cent) and the Wheatley brothers (ten per cent), he would invest a minimum of £1m per year for the following five years. This investment gave him operational control.

At the end of those five years (2014), Bees United would be given the option to repay the loans that they already owed Matthew (amounting to £4.5m) and buy out his stake in the club. If they chose not to do this, Benham would then be provided with the opportunity to take over control of Brentford FC by buying most of Bees United's 60 per cent shareholding.

Donald Kerr says that is was an agreement that most people involved with the trust were happy to approve: 'We put the deal to a vote and 99 per cent of those who turned up backed it. No agreement to sell our stake was ever going to be risk-free but we thought that this deal was a good one and that there are enough safeguards in place, such as having board representation to ensure that the fans will be part of the decision-making process at the club.

'In all honesty, we never really imagined we would be able to pay back the money Matthew had loaned us and so, sure enough, last year we agreed, with the consent of our members, to grant him an early takeover of our share.'

The members of Bees United were faced with a problem common to any group of supporters that ends up running a club; is their model of ownership strong enough to accommodate the expectations of the fans? In their first full season involved with the club, Brentford suffered relegation to League 2, at one point going sixteen games without a win.

'It might not be kind to say this, but the quality of football in the bottom tier leaves plenty to be desired,' thinks Donald. 'As a fan, you want to watch good football and feel that your team has a chance of doing well. When the trust was in charge this simply wasn't the case. If anything, the club seemed more likely than ever to drop down into the Conference. How long would it have been before our supporters became disillusioned with Bees United? If we'd found ourselves in non-league football, something that without Matthew Benham's input I think could easily have happened, would the trust still be seen as the saviours of the club? I doubt it.

'I'm a huge supporter of the "trust model". Without it, we couldn't have got out of the impasse that Ron Noades faced us with. But after that, it was clear that supporter ownership would only work at Brentford if the fans were willing to accept us playing at a much lower level. I for one wasn't and I'm eternally grateful that Matthew Benham came along and, so far at least, has proven to be a man of his word.'

Brentford are not the only example of supporter owners struggling and ultimately accepting that outside money is the only way to survive. Travel a few hundred miles north from London and you arrive at York, home to the Minstermen.

York City

Compared to most of those teams that currently compete in the top four flights of English football, York City are relative newcomers to the game. The current incarnation of the club only formed back in 1922 and didn't play their first Football League match until 1929. Since then it's fair to say that the club have remained one of the game's perennial minnows, spending most of their time in the lower echelons of the Football League (aside from a brief dalliance with the Second Division in the mid-1970s).

At the dawn of the new millennium things on and off the pitch weren't going too well for the Minstermen. On the playing side, they were plying their trade in the old Third Division, having been relegated during the 1998/99 season. During their inaugural campaign in the Football League's then bottom tier, rather than challenge for promotion, as the fans had hoped, York flirted with the possibility of relegation and were it not for the arrival halfway through the season of new manager Terry Dolan, who ultimately guided the club to 20th position, York may well have ended up dropping into the Conference.

But as disappointing as events were on the pitch, they were overshadowed by what was happening behind the scenes. Since 1992, York had been under the chairmanship of Douglas Craig, the club's majority shareholder. He had acquired his position following the abdication of York's previous chairman Michael Sinclair, who had quit the club, his business and dispensed with all his worldly assets in 1990 to become a priest.

There had long been a tradition at York City that involvement represented a form of public service, a privilege and one that it would be unseemly to benefit from financially. In this the club's board shared something of that Edwardian sense of civic virtue which motivated so many people to get involved in football when the professional game was in its infancy. With this in mind, Sinclair had allowed Craig to purchase his equity, some 123,000 shares, for £1 each, a figure well below market value. It was a civic-minded approach to business that Craig would later shun.

John Lacy has been a York City supporter for over 60 years and more recently become a co-opted member of the York City Supporters' Trust (YCST) board. Long before the financial meltdown that Douglas Craig presided over, he feels that few supporters were endeared towards their chairman.

He says, 'There are not many supporters to gain first-hand knowledge of a club chairman or board members. My opinions of Douglas Craig prior to the club's financial problems were, as for most fans, influenced by local media, comments from other fans and, of course, gossip. However, I was present at a couple of open forum meetings at which he answered questions put to him by fans about the club. His attitudes and responses to supporters at those meetings tended to confirm my impressions, and those of others, of a determined but stubborn and opinionated man.

'For instance, he steadfastly and in the face of much criticism at the time, refused to sign the club up to the Kick Racism out of Football campaign. Because of his intransigence, I think we were just about the only Football League club not to endorse their message.'

Although never popular among the fans, Craig was at least tolerated and regarded as a solid if fairly unlikeable steward whose cautious approach to club finances ensured a degree of stability. But according to Ian Hey, current chairman of the YCST, this opinion of Craig was about to undergo a radical transformation.

Ian says, 'We obviously weren't happy with what had been happening on the pitch. Relegation, flirting with life in the Conference and games that were often difficult to watch are not things that any fan enjoys. But that's all part of football. There might have been a hardening of opinion towards Craig but I think most fans still thought of him as part of the tradition at York, which saw chairmen as having the best interests of the club at heart. This began to change in the summer of 1999, when he announced that ownership of our ground was shifting from the club to an outside holding company, Bootham Crescent Holdings (BCH), which was owned by Craig and other directors.'

The chairman argued that this transition of the club's main asset to another company was being undertaken to escape the FA's Rule 34. This ancient statute stated that when a club folded, once shareholders had received what they had originally paid for their shares, all remaining profits from the sale of assets, such as stadiums, had to be paid to the FA's Benevolent Fund or to other charitable organisations.

The rule was originally put in place to protect clubs from asset-strippers by removing the possibility of shareholders making a profit from the deliberate closure of a club and dispersal of assets. But Craig claimed that should York suffer liquidation in the future, these provisions threatened the possibility of any successor club being able to play at Bootham Crescent. By transferring ownership to BCH, he asserted that the ground would always remain in the hands of York City supporters and therefore available to whatever incarnation of the club existed in the future.

'Craig wrote to all of York City's shareholders asking them to approve the move. But really this was something of a fait accompli because, as the chairman outlined in his letter, he and the club's directors, John Quickfall, Colin Webb and former playing hero Barry Swallow, owned 94 per cent of York's shares and had already approved the plan anyway,' recalls Ian Hey.

Although it was possible, if you really, really tried, to interpret Craig's move in a positive light, it was equally possible and much more realistic to view what was happening as a deliberate attempt to circumvent the FA's ruling and strip the club of Bootham Crescent.

To those who have never ventured to this part of the world, York's stadium lies just outside the city centre in a largely residential area. York has always been a pricey place to live by northern standards (there's no chance of picking up a dilapidated terraced house for £1 here), lying as it does in the 'Golden Triangle', a term commonly used by estate agents to describe the affluent area of west and north Yorkshire between Harrogate, York and North Leeds.

Back in 1999, the land upon which Bootham Crescent stood was worth a few bob, an amount estimated at the time at around £4.5m. Considering that BCH paid the club just under £166,000 for the ground then it is understandable why what happened later would raise more than a few eyebrows among the supporters.

The veracity of Craig's assertions, that he was in essence protecting the ground in perpetuity, would soon be put to the test. York's rapid descent to potential contenders for Football League relegation precipitated a financial crisis at the club. By 2001 the wage bill had topped £2.2m, a figure that represented 151 per cent of the club's total income, the worst wages/turnover ratio in either the Football League or the Premier League at the time.

Their problem was one that was endemic to football and one that has continued to be a problem since. In short, they were a Third Division club, with the attendance figures and commercial revenue that this implies, that had a wage structure more in keeping which a team much higher up in the football pyramid. York were running at a loss (£1.2m that season alone) and racking up debt along the way.

In response to this, in December of 2001, Douglas Craig surprised fans by announcing that the club and the ground were up for sale.

'It came as something of a shock,' recalls Ian Hey. 'The club were losing money but the situation wasn't terminal. There were plenty of other clubs that were in a bad way. The fans thought that Craig was using the financial issues to cash in on his investment. His asking price was £4.5m, a price that represented a staggering return for his and the other directors' initial investment.'

Tellingly, considering everything that he had promised when transferring the stadium over to BCH, an alternative was also offered to potential investors whereby they could buy the club for £1 and leave Bootham Crescent in the hands of the holding company. Should they go for this option they would have to vacate the ground, with BCH providing £1m for the redevelopment of the nearby Huntington Stadium.

'In light of this, it's hard to see what happened as anything other than Craig trying to make a fast buck, attempting to get as much as he could from the small amount that he'd invested in the club. Whatever occurred he was set to make a fortune, all at the expense of York City,' says Ian, angrily.

This perspective was then given further credence by Craig taking the unusual step in January of 2002 of stating that should no buyer be forthcoming by the end of March, the club would resign from the Football League, an unprecedented move by a football chairman. In his defence, Craig claimed that, as York were losing thousands per week, possessed no assets to borrow against and were reaching the limit of their overdraft facility, it was simply untenable for the club to continue to trade beyond that date.

Unsurprisingly, the fans were having none of this. A protest movement sprang up quickly, accompanied by the establishment of a supporters' trust. Marches outside the ground were well attended and a campaign was started to have what Craig had done investigated by the FA.

'But that turned out to be something of a waste of time,' explains Ian. 'Even though it was clear to everyone who followed the club that Craig was effectively asset-stripping York, the FA simply stated that he and the board had "broken no rules". They were of no help whatsoever.'

Although the supporters' trust considered bidding to buy the club (but not the stadium, as this was beyond its fundraising capacity) its plans were quickly undermined by the arrival of John Batchelor, who bought City for the nominal fee of £1 in March 2002.

The late Mr Batchelor, scion of the Cup-a-Soup dynasty, who rebuilt his family's lost fortune from scratch and who realised a lifetime's ambition by establishing his own rally-driving team, ended up becoming a figure of loathing among the supporters. He arrived, as many new owners do, with big ideas and big promises and managed to turn a crisis into a complete disaster.

John Lacy says, 'Few people knew who John Batchelor was or where he came from, other than he may have had something to do with tinned peas! But he seemed to offer a last lifeline for survival and we all grabbed at it. He appeared genuinely delighted to take on the role of saviour and had exciting (if somewhat bizarre) ideas to attract investment and develop the club. On occasion, he would join the fans on the terraces, incognito. I stood next to him once. He seemed like a committed and enthusiastic supporter. How wrong we were.'

Were it not for the fact that his actions impacted upon the hopes and dreams of thousands of innocent York City fans, you could almost regard his time at the club as a piece of comic genius. First, York were rebranded as a 'soccer club' and, in an exercise of 'marketing-synergy' linked up with his racing car team (the extent of this seemed to be the inclusion of a chequered flag on York's redesigned badge). Luther Blissett then turned up for a time as coach only to leave shortly after.

Everyone loves Brazilian football, so Batchelor's next 'wheeze' was to bring in Brazilian striker Rogerio Carvalho. So good was Carvalho that he played a grand total of four games for the club, scoring an amazing no goals. Batchelor also promised to establish a club radio station, a sports bar and to provide the supporters with two seats on the board only for none of this to come to fruition.

You could probably, just about, write all of this off as the behaviour of someone who had got into something he didn't fully understand were it not for the fact that at the same time that Batchelor was revealing how ill-equipped he was to run a football club, he was also rumoured to be systematically taking money out of it. Not long after he had taken control, the house builders Persimmon gave £400,000 of sponsorship money to York. But only £100,000 ever made it into the club bank account. The remaining £300,000 is thought to have been lavished by Batchelor on his racing team.

Despite promising to pump money into the club, all York's new owner had really done was allow the financial problems that had built under Craig to mount. Unwilling to support the business from his own pockets, and now reliant upon the PFA to pay the players' wages, in December of 2002, just eight months after he had taken control, Batchelor placed City into administration.

'That was a devastating time for fans. There was a very real prospect that no one would come in to save us and I think a lot of supporters feared that York were in real danger of being wound up. It certainly didn't help matters that we had lost control of our ground. In fact, over the course of 2002 it had become clearer and clearer to us that a future in which York City played at Bootham Crescent was becoming more unlikely by the day,' says Steve Beck, former chairman of the club and current treasurer of the YCST.

During that torrid year for York City fans, BCH had given further proof that perhaps the best interests of York City weren't at the forefront of the company's mind. Not only did the supporters learn that BCH had sold ten per cent of the company's shares to Persimmon, it was also revealed in the summer of 2002 that developers had put in a planning application for 93 homes to be built on the site of the stadium.

After this news was announced York was buzzing with rumours. There was the mooted move to the Huntington Stadium, a possible ground-share with Scarborough, and an ambitious plan announced by Batchelor proposing the building of a brand new 17,500-seater stadium within York.

'The latter was obviously off once the club had gone into administration,' recalls Ian Hey. 'If you can't even pay your players I doubt you're going to be able to build a new ground. With regard to the other two, as time passed and the situation became bleaker and bleaker by the day the question was, with no one interested in taking the club on, would there even be a "York City" playing football come the following season to use these grounds?'

In response to the growing crisis, the YCST kicked into action. Steve Beck explains, 'The trust and the fans undertook a tremendous effort to try and rescue our club. There were the usual fundraising activities, like raffles, quizzes and the ubiquitous collection bucket, all done in the hope of raising the £500,000 it was thought needed to convince the administrator that the trust had the financial resources necessary to run things and start tackling our debt.'

According to Steve, along with huge support from the local paper, the wider community and the fans, YCST also received help from elsewhere in football.

He says, 'When we were trying to get money together our very good friends at AFC Wimbledon held a collection at one of their games. One night, not long after, I received a call from a "Wakefield Womble" wishing to meet, so we arranged to get together at a pub in York one Sunday evening. I was slightly... but pleasantly surprised when he arrived with over £3,000 in change in the boot of the car! Here I was transferring cash from one car to another in a dimly-lit car park...desperately hoping it wasn't being recorded on CCTV! That £3,000 bought us enough time to raise the required price for the purchase of the club and we will always be indebted to the people of AFC Wimbledon for that.'

Ultimately, the trust managed to just about cobble together enough cash to reach an agreement with the administrator in March 2003. But it was a close-run thing and would have been impossible without the help of Jason McGill, a local fan and owner of a packaging business in York who stepped in to help financially. McGill's assistance meant that he became a minority shareholder, with an agreement that it would be the YCST that had majority control.

But the takeover only represented the first step in reversing York's fortunes. The club now had to be run. The problem for the trust was the fact that York City regularly lost money, and had been doing so for some time. For most clubs, the obvious answer would be to turn to a benefactor, someone who could accommodate their debt with some generous soft loans. York only had the trust which had spent everything it had in gaining control of the club.

Steve Beck says, 'The upshot was some really difficult times and we had to cut costs. I remember at one point early on I somehow ended up in front of the players to inform them that there was no money to pay their wages at the end of the month. I was conscious that within a room full of concern and anger, one player (the Brazilian Rogerio) was looking at me with a big smile on his face. It suddenly dawned on me that he hadn't got a clue what I was saying and as the meeting finished I had to ask our captain to explain the situation to him in broken Portuguese...the smile soon disappeared from his face!'

During the first full season that the trust was in control of the club, their new manager Chris Brass (chosen because he was the highest paid player on the books) put together a side that cost three-quarters less than the average for the division. Despite winning their first four games and rising high in the league, form then deteriorated markedly. In the end the team managed to take just four points from their last 22 matches and were relegated to the Conference.

'It was hardly the most impressive of starts to our experiment in supporter ownership,' admits Steve, dryly.

Although they might have been competing in a lower league, in 2004 the club did manage to successfully ensure that Bootham Crescent was once more in their hands. Since the summer of 2003, the board of York City had been negotiating and arguing the case for provision of funding from the Football Stadia Improvement Fund (FSIF) to secure Bootham Crescent as the home of the club.

Ian admits, 'This money, which was available to all Football League clubs, could have been claimed by Douglas Craig, but he didn't bother; another example of his neglect. Fortunately Jason McGill was on board and he managed to convince the FSIF that a non-league club should still be given access to this funding as the money had been unclaimed by Craig when York had been a League club. Without him and the money, there's no way we could have secured Bootham Crescent.'

The FSIF provided York City with a £2.2m loan, which was used to a buy a 75 per cent share in BCH, giving the club majority control over Bootham Crescent. The only catch with the deal was the obligation that York would have to sell Bootham Crescent and move to a new, all-seater stadium within the boundaries of the city by the beginning of the 2014/15 season. But at least once this happened the club would be eligible to turn part of the loan into a £2m grant for the development of this new ground.

Ian says, 'It's been a lengthy process but we've worked closely with the council and in 2012 it was announced that we would soon be moving into a new community stadium, built by the local authority and housing both York City FC and the York City Knights Rugby League Club. I suppose the only downside from the whole deal from the fans' perspective was the fact that Douglas Craig and the other shareholders of BCH managed to do quite well from the FSIF money.'

Although the club, under the stewardship of the trust, managed to establish some degree of financial stability and resolve the stadium issue that for so long had been a cloud hanging over York, by 2006, Steve Beck admits that after just a few seasons in charge it was becoming clear that promotion back to the Football League was not going to be as easy as initially envisioned.

He says, 'It's a problem faced by lots of trusts. By and large, supporters are not rich people. And while appealing to them to dig into their pockets during a crisis is one thing, to keep going back to them again and again naturally leads to diminishing returns. We did have our membership cash, but this wasn't enough to bankroll things. As a trust, we simply didn't have the financial might to push the club onwards.'

Had Bootham Crescent been in better condition the situation could have been different. But repairs were a constant drain on resources and the stadium's revenue-generating potential wasn't the best.

'We also weren't helped by the fact that the financial crisis had affected the team's performance and naturally less people were willing to pay to watch Conference football. But even taking those factors into account, I still think that the trust model at York was probably holding the club back,' acknowledges Steve.

Although there had been an initial belief – common to most teams that get relegated – that York would bounce back into the Football League right away, after a few seasons in the Conference it was apparent that this wouldn't be the case. This realisation, combined with the fact that the trust was struggling to make a profit, led Jason McGill to make an offer. In return for a 75 per cent stake in the club, he would wipe the debt for the small amount of money he had already provided and promised to give additional finance over the coming years.

Ian Hey says, 'We were faced with the choice of, do we maintain majority control and possibly stagnate in non-league football, or do we risk it and take on an outside investor and hopefully advance up the football pyramid? I have to say that the feeling at the time was that if this was anyone but Jason, then the answer would probably have been no. But Jason was trusted.

'Without his investment there would have been no supporter buy-out, without his help we wouldn't have secured the loan from the FSIF and without his financial assistance, the club might well have got into difficulty again. It's for these reasons, and the fact that so many of us naturally wanted York to be playing in the Football League again, that we were receptive to his offer.'

In June of 2006, the YCST held an Extraordinary General Meeting at York's Barbican Centre, attended by some 700 members. McGill's offer was put to them and a substantial majority opted to accept it, bringing to an end the period of majority supporter ownership at the club.

Steve Beck says, 'You can arguably look back and say that what we did made sense. For a start, the trust retained a 25 per cent stake in the club, meaning that we've always had an input in the decision-making process. There's been no return to the bad old days of Douglas Craig. By taking on an external investor, we've made sure that York City have had the necessary finance to compete in the Conference and eventually get out of it, something achieved in 2012.

'We also picked someone in Jason McGill, who has worked hard on the new stadium project; and that is a development that we believe is essential for the future financial security of the club. But it's not perfect and there are times when being a junior partner is difficult. I would prefer it if the fans still had majority control, and maybe one day they will again, but until then we'll just have to make the best of it and be thankful that the club is doing OK.'

Although supporters at York and Brentford found ownership of the club a greater burden than they were able to carry, at least both trusts maintained some influence; giving the fans more say on the club's future than many other supporters in football have. From this perspective, it's difficult to compare what happened at these two clubs with what happened at

Stockport and Notts County. Even so, the examples in this chapter certainly illustrate that failure is just as possible under supporter majority ownership as it is when a private individual or a consortium take control of a club.

But if this doom and gloom has thrown into doubt the effectiveness of punk football in your collective minds, then take heart from how clubs are organised in mainland Europe, where supporter ownership has been knocking around for decades. From Greece in the east to Sweden in the west, the continent is dotted with examples of clubs where it's the fans that call the shots. There are even whole leagues that adhere to the principle of supporter ownership, going so far as to enshrine the concept in law.

England might have greedily embraced punk football over the past decade but if you want proof of how well it can work and how popular it can be then your best bet is to take a gander at what our continental comrades have been up to.

10

They Do Things Differently Over There: Supporter Ownership in Europe

ALTHOUGH the English have certainly been the most active in the realm of supporter ownership over the past decade, it's fair to say that as a country we have come a bit late to the party. If we take the time to cast our collective eyes across the English Channel and have a look at how clubs are organised in Europe, then it's evident that punk football has a much longer history among some of our continental neighbours.

And you could see some of these clubs in action during the latter stages of the 2012/13 Champions League, when Bayern Munich, Barcelona, Real Madrid and Borussia Dortmund comprised the teams that made up the tournament's semi-finals.

In an age when Russian oligarchs and Middle Eastern sheikhs pour millions into the game in the hope of success here was an example of four clubs either completely or partially owned by their fans reaching the pinnacle of European football. Although still a minority on the continent, supporter-owned clubs have been competing there for decades; and one of the best known and most successful of these are Barça.

Based in the Catalonian region of Spain, Barcelona are the 22-time champions of La Liga, four-time victors in the European Cup/Champions League and 26-time winners of the Copa del Rey. They are also the second biggest football club in the world in terms of revenue, with an annual turnover in 2012/13 of €482m. But what's really amazing about Barcelona is that this has been achieved not through the largesse of some deep-pocketed billionaire but through a model where it is ordinary fans who own the club.

When football was first establishing itself in Spain in the late 1800s, rather than take the path that England took, Spanish football maintained the membership model that had also characterised the game's early years in this country. In Spain, members became known as *socios*, a role that gave them a say in how their clubs were run.

As of 2013, Barcelona had around 176,000 registered *socios*, with each adult member paying €177 for the right to own a share in the Catalan giant. Membership entitles the *socios* to vote for the club president and exercise their opinions on an array of other matters. In 2003 for instance, members voted to allow shirt sponsors for the first time in the club's history.

Becoming a *socio* also provides the opportunity to join the assembly of delegates, the highest governing body at Barça. This 3,000-member parliament is comprised of *socios* drawn at random by computer and has the power to censure the president and the board should they not comply with the club's statutes.

Just try and imagine something similar happening at a big Premier League club and it's possible to appreciate how radical a structure Barcelona's is. It seems almost impossible to picture

Roman Abramovich compelled to stand for re-election every four years and being held to account by an assembly of ordinary Chelsea fans.

Although once common in Spain, clubs run like Barcelona are actually in the minority today. During the 1980s, the *socio* model unravelled spectacularly, providing proof that poor governance is still possible even when it's the fans that own the club. Spiralling wage and transfer costs created a period of unparalleled profligacy in Spanish football, during which many clubs managed to get into a terrible mess. So great was the problem that the government had to step in and bail out those with untenable levels of debt. In return, it forced the majority of Spanish clubs to convert to publicly limited sports companies, via the introduction of the 1990 Spanish Sports Act.

It was hoped that by running the clubs as conventional businesses with stakeholders and a board of directors, both financial management and accountability would improve. It hasn't. Spanish football remains troubled, beset with all kinds of financial problems, specifically debt. Over the past five years many clubs, including some big names like Real Betis and Deportivo La Coruna, have gone into administration and collectively members of the top two divisions now owe around €4bn.

But back in the 1980s not every club got itself into a mess. A handful – Athletic Bilbao, FC Barcelona, Real Madrid and CA Osasuna – had actually kept their finances in pretty good shape. Under the Seventh Additional Provision of the Spanish Sports Act, any club that had managed to stay in the black for five years, starting from the 1985/86 season, was permitted to maintain their existing organisational structure. This meant that the *socio* system was allowed to continue, albeit only at a minority of clubs.

When talking about the *socios* of Barcelona and their role in owning and influencing the running of the club, it has to be appreciated that for a big chunk of the last century, their power was heavily curtailed. Between 1939 and 1975, Spanish football, along with every other aspect of life in the country, was dominated by the personality and politics of General Francisco Franco. The 'Generalissimo', as he liked to be called, had come to power during the Spanish Civil War (1936–1939). Like Fascists all over Europe at the time, Franco was big on nationalism, regarding the creation of a unitary national identity as vital for the country's social and economic prosperity.

In football this meant the suppression or eradication of elements that contradicted Franco's nationalist vision. For a club like Barça, which had a strong affiliation with the cause of Catalan nationalism, this was always going to spell trouble. The Catalans of the north, the area in which Barcelona is located, have long sought greater independence from the rest of Spain, regarding their region as a separate country in its own right. Aware of the potency of this political force, FC Barcelona's founder, Hans Kamper, began cultivating a distinctly Catalanist identity at the club, by for example adopting Catalan rather than Castilian (Spain's national lingo) as their official language. It was all part of an attempt to conflate supporting Barcelona with supporting regional nationalism.

Kamper hoped this would make the club more appealing to a wider section of society, specifically the local professional middle-classes who were mobilising behind a Catalanist, nationalist ideology. And it was and approach that worked. From a low of just 34 in 1908, the number of *socios* rose at the club to reach 20,000 by 1922.

The only downside to this brilliant strategy was that it worked too well, leaving Barcelona indelibly linked with the cause of Catalanist nationalism and 'political' in a way that is almost unimaginable in England. This was all fine when the political climate was benign but unfortunately for Barcelona it became less favourable when Spain was taken over by a military dictatorship hell-bent on suppressing any examples of regional independence.

'Under Franco the ability of *socios* to influence decisions at the club was significantly undermined. Overseen by a newly created sports ministry staffed by right-wing sympathisers, *socio* control was circumvented by the regime, primarily by the installation of "Fascist friendly" members on to the club's board. It was through them that a process of de-Catalanisation was attempted, with efforts made to make the club more Castilian in appearance. The most totemic example of this was a change in the club's name from the Catalan-sounding FC Barcelona to the more Castilian-sounding Barcelona Club de Futbol,' says Dr Jim O'Brien, author and expert on Spanish football at Southampton Solent University's Lawrie McMenemy Centre for Football Research.

During the Franco era, Barcelona were not the only club to undergo such changes. In the Basque Country, another region of Spain that considers itself a separate nation, Athletic Bilbao suffered the humiliation of having their name changed to the Castilian-sounding Atlético Bilbao and their *socio* model of ownership undermined by government interference.

But nothing and no man lasts forever and on 20 November 1975 a tearful Carlos Arias Navarro, Spain's Prime Minister, announced to the nation that the Generalissimo had passed away. Although Franco had made efforts for the continuation of his regime, they would prove to be flawed. Within two days of his death, his anointed successor, King Juan Carlos, had begun the process of dismantling what Franco had created and started the transition to democracy.

Football, which had already begun to shrug off the controls that had been imposed upon it, greedily embraced its own return of people power. At Barcelona this was signified, at the instigation of the *socios*, by the re-adoption of the club's original name, FC Barcelona. This was a move that was echoed elsewhere in the country wherever Franco had intervened to force the adoption of Castilian-sounding names, such as at Real Gijón (reverted to Real Sporting de Gijón) and Atlético Bilbao (reverted to Athletic Bilbao).

The crowning glory of the *socios'* regaining of power though was the election of club president Josep Lluís Núñez in 1978.

Núñez became the first president to be elected by the entire membership of FC Barcelona since the outbreak of the Civil War in 1936. A local businessman who had made millions from more than two decades of involvement in the development of the city, Núñez arrived in his position promising to find the money to make Barcelona as big, if not bigger, than their arch-rival, Real Madrid. And over the past 35 years that's just what's happened.

Although, just like their arch-rival, Barcelona have become a dominant force in European football while retaining their democratic structure, at times it has to be acknowledged that it's been a struggle for the members to maintain the model's purity. Despite being a beneficiary of the re-establishment of democracy, Núñez didn't always appear to operate within the constraints imposed by members.

One of the main criticisms levelled at the president was the lack of transparency at the club. Under Núñez, for the first time in Barcelona's history (something that didn't even occur under Franco's acolytes) the names of assembly members were not made available to *socios*, meaning that club members were unable to find out who represented their interests and who to approach with concerns. There was also a lack of transparency concerning the process by which individuals were chosen for the assembly.

As worrying as this was, of greater concern to many *socios* was Núñez's desire to introduce far-reaching commercial reforms. The president thought that Barça should improve their commercial strategy to bring revenues more in line with the club's European rivals. As proof of the club's poor commercial model he could point to facts such as the 30 per cent gap in merchandising revenue that was said to exist between Barcelona and Manchester United during the 1990s.

It was this motivation that lay behind the construction of the FC Barcelona museum (later renamed the President Núñez museum), which ended up being a big money-spinner for the club and which today attracts 1.2 million visitors a year, ranking it second to the Museu Picasso as the most visited museum in the city of Barcelona. This desire to improve the commercial reach of the club was also the driving force behind the president's next big idea, Barça 2000; a hugely ambitious and expensive project that aimed to convert the area surrounding Camp Nou into a massive theme park and leisure centre which Núñez believed could attract millions of visitors per year. He probably had in mind something akin to Disneyland but with Johan Cruyff in the role of Mickey Mouse.

For a section of the *socios*, Núñez's marginalisation of members combined with fears that greater commercialisation could lead to privatisation began to create a general sense of unease about the direction the club was heading. It was a sense not helped by the president making no attempt to hide his admiration of the way in which privately-owned rival clubs such as Manchester United, AC Milan and Arsenal were run and organised. What emerged from this discontent was L'Elefant Blau, an opposition group formed in 1997 to campaign against the presidency of Núñez and to re-assert the notion of *socio* power.

The first concerted campaign against Núñez from the *socios* emerged in the spring of 1997, when L'Elefant Blau initiated a vote of censure against the president and the board. Although ultimately unsuccessful, with only 15,000 *socios* backing the motion from a total of 40,000 votes cast, the fact that a significant minority had opposed the president at all made it clear to Núñez that he could not take the membership's support for granted.

It was also the first time that the president had been seriously challenged by ordinary fans during his long reign, an event that revealed his vulnerability to supporter power. Although Núñez managed to maintain his position for a further five years, continued campaigning by L'Elefant Blau, combined with violent crowd protests against his tenure led to his eventual resignation in 2000, and with it an end to the Barça 2000 project.

The establishment of L'Elefant Blau re-energised the *socio* system, reminding ordinary members that Barcelona are not Manchester United or Chelsea and that authority at the club really did lie in their hands. The culmination of this surge in supporter power was the election of the L'Elefant Blau candidate, Joan Laporta, as president in 2003, with roughly a 20 per cent margin over his nearest rival. In keeping with someone who during this election campaign had stressed the important role played by *socios*, under his presidency member democracy was enhanced at the club. Along with a recruitment drive that saw numbers rise from 105,000 in 2002 to 163,000 in 2008, Laporta also improved transparency by developing the club's communication strategy.

But as worthy as all this was, it's doubtful that fans, specifically fans as accustomed to winning as those of Barcelona, would have been happy had this surge in *socio* power also coincided with a period of poor form on the pitch. After all, despite his many faults in the eyes of some supporters, Núñez had delivered on his promise to make Barcelona as big as Real Madrid. His final decade in control of the club, one that had seen the increased marginalisation of the *socios*, was a particularly impressive one on the pitch, with Barcelona securing six La Liga titles, two Copa del Reys and one European Cup.

Fortunately for the L'Elefant Blau movement, Barcelona were just about to embark on another period of mesmerising success. By the time the president stepped down in 2010, the club had bagged four La Liga titles, one Copa del Rey and secured two Champions League victories. Barcelona also became the most feared and respected team on the planet. This was a side that included the likes of Lionel Messi, Xavi and Andres Iniesta, and which many commentators regarded as one of the finest to ever grace European football.

Along with that all-important success on the pitch, Laporta and his successor Sandro Rosell have also illustrated that it's possible for Barcelona to pursue a more aggressive commercial strategy without compromising the social and cultural heritage of the club. Over the past decade, turnover at Camp Nou has risen from €123m in 2002/03 to €482m in 2012/13. In the Deloitte Money League, this is an increase that has enabled Barcelona to go from being outside the top ten to second position behind Real Madrid.

Several factors lie behind this improvement. Along with the increase in *socio* numbers and the appointment of successful professionals to key positions, Barcelona have also sought to apply financial discipline to activities and improve the way in which the club has been marketed. The success of this more austere financial environment is perfectly illustrated in the way that the club has altered the wage structure, which has been reduced from 83 per cent of turnover in 2003 to just 48 per cent in 2012.

On the revenue side, the club has become extremely adept at selling the 'Barça brand'. Despite the English Premier League's international profile, according to the 2010 European Football Merchandising Report, it's actually La Liga that comes top of the European merchandising league, generating €190m of revenue. From this figure, the big two, Real and Barça, gobble up around 80 per cent of the total, which is around €152m to share between them.

Through these changes, which have been accompanied by improvements in commercial relationships, Barcelona have become considerably better at generating revenue than privately owned rivals in Spain. According to leading football blog theswissramble, in 2010/11, Spain's two leading member-owned clubs, Barcelona and Real Madrid, had turnovers of €451m and €479m respectively, which dwarfs the figures of their nearest challengers Valencia (€120m), Atlético Madrid (€100m) and Sevilla (€83m). And this is a trend that is only widening. Between 2008 and 2011, Barcelona and Real increased their revenue growth by €142m and €113m respectively. Of their rivals, only Atlético Madrid (€21m) and Valencia (€16m) managed to do the same. Other challengers, such as Sevilla and Villarreal, actually saw their revenues fall.

The two Spanish giants are also more profitable than their rivals. During 2011/12 Barcelona made a pre-tax profit of €48m, a figure that even outdid their traditionally more successful rivals Real, who only managed €32m. In La Liga, few clubs ever turn a profit and even those that do rarely manage anything higher than €5m. Real and Barça are in many ways in a league of their own.

And this has all been achieved without a sustained hike in ticket prices. The influence of the *socios* has ensured that the pockets of fans have been protected over the past decade. According to *The Guardian*'s Datablog, during 2011/12 the cheapest season ticket available at Camp Nou would set you back £172. This compares pretty favourably to rival clubs, such as Atlético Madrid (£257), Malaga (£239) and Sevilla (£340). Cast your eyes beyond Spain and compare it to a leading English club like Arsenal, where the cheapest season ticket at the Emirates cost £985 around the same time, and you can really appreciate how effective the *socio* system has been at protecting the interests of ordinary supporters.

But (and there always is a but), in enjoying their balancing of success on the pitch, greater commercial expansion and supporter protection, Barcelona have had a few advantages over other clubs that have helped their position. For a start, unlike teams in the top flight in England or elsewhere in Europe, Spain's big two, Real Madrid and Barcelona, command considerable support among football followers in the country. Barça enjoy the following of 25 per cent of Spanish fans, with a further 11 per cent regarding them as their second team. Combined, both Real and Barça are believed to account for 60 per cent of all fans (once second preferences are taken into account). When it comes to generating revenue, specifically related to merchandising, this gives both clubs a potential market incomparable to any other club in the country.

Barcelona also do pretty well out of domestic television money. Unlike the Premier League, in recent years Spanish clubs have been able to negotiate individually with broadcasters. This has meant that the bigger teams, the ones that have the largest constituencies of potential viewers, have been able to obtain a more favourable slice of the pie. Real and Barcelona each receive €140m a year from domestic rights, a figure that amounts to just over half of that made available. The remainder is split unequally between La Liga's 18 other clubs, with some such as Levante, Malaga and Sporting Gijon receiving as little as €14m each.

With these natural advantages, perhaps it's easier for clubs like Barcelona or Real to balance a supporter-friendly ownership system with success on the pitch as they are inured from some of the harsher financial realities faced by many other clubs in Spain and Europe.

'Clubs like Barcelona and Real Madrid are special in many ways. They possess massive support, both domestically and internationally, and enjoy television deals that rivals can only dream of. This is possibly why the other examples of *socio*-owned clubs in Spain, Athletic Bilbao and CA Osasuna, haven't had comparable levels of commercial or footballing success,' suggests Jim O'Brien.

Spain is of course not the only game in town. If we cast our collective eyes a little further north then we light upon somewhere that evangelists of supporter ownership often herald as the Promised Land. It is a place where fans of almost every team can have a say in how their clubs are run, a land where ticket prices cost a fraction of what they do elsewhere, and one in which the curse of spiralling wages and excessive debts seems to be well controlled. The place is called Germany and their league, the Bundesliga.

By English standards the Bundesliga is a mere infant. They might be one of world's leading football nations but the Germans were slow to come round to the attractions of the professional game. Although football arrived in Germany not long after it had begun to establish itself in England, it wouldn't be until the 1960s that the country finally embraced professionalism and at the same time established its first centralised, national league.

'The main reason for this delay was the long dominance of the middle-classes in the game,' argues Dr Kay Schiller, a German sports historian at Durham University. 'Unlike in England, where the sport was quickly embraced by the working-class, in Germany at both club level and within the principal football authority, the Deutscher Fußball Bund (DFB), the middle-classes remained dominant for many years.'

For this class, professionalism was seen as an affront to the values of amateurism, specifically as it introduced the unsavoury element of monetary reward. In this, they shared much in common with the old boys of the English public school system, who had attempted to stem the tide of professionalism that had swept over football during the 1880s. But where they had eventually lost control of the game, in Germany the middle-classes managed to maintain a position of strength for a lot longer, meaning that it would be some time before the Germans aped their Anglo Saxon cousins and adopted professionalism.

In English football the need to pay regular wages encouraged the adoption of the joint-stock system, marginalising the membership model of ownership that had originally been dominant. In Germany, football remained less developed than the game which existed in England so the pressure to adopt professionalism, and by extension the joint-stock system, was less pronounced, meaning that the membership model of ownership was given the space to thrive.

In Germany this type of organisation is known as an *eingetragener Verein* (e.V) and tends to be the model adopted across many different sports. An e.V is characterised by the following rights and responsibilities; the members democratically elect representatives who manage the Verein, liability is limited to the assets of the Verein, the club must not distribute any of these assets to its members or representatives and all cash flows have to be directed to the club's non-profit objective (the promotion of sport).

The thing about e.Vs is that they are often not just football clubs. There are usually many other sports, both professional and amateur, housed under the umbrella of the club. And this is often revealed in the name. At VfB Stuttgart for example, the VfB stands for Verein für Bewegungsspiele, which in English roughly translates as a club for movement/exercise games. And at Stuttgart, these movement/exercise games include hockey, fistball and table tennis clubs that compete on an amateur basis.

'This embracing of more than one sport means that the club as a whole provides a "community benefit", something which allows them certain tax advantages. It's also the case that most clubs, because of this "community benefit" function, have received financial support from local and city authorities over the years, the most beneficial of which has often been the provision of the stadiums they play in,' says Dr Schiller.

The relatively undeveloped nature of football in Germany, certainly compared to somewhere like England, and the numerous financial benefits awarded to the e.V model, meant that supporters developed a very distinctive relationship with their clubs as the sport grew.

'German football fans never acquired the perception of themselves as customers, like the English did. In fact, most fans would be horrified today if you ever labelled them as a customer,' argues Uli Hesse, author of *Tor!: The Story of German Football.*

According to Uli, because the Verein model became the accepted way for clubs to be organised, Germans developed an alternative idea of what it means to be a 'fan'.

He says, 'Supporters saw themselves as part of the club and this was because they could become members of the Verein, people who had a say in how things are run. It meant that the concept of involvement being limited to simply paying to watch your team and little else became alien.'

Although amateurism dominated thinking within the German game long after it had disappeared in England, it would be wrong to think that demands for professionalism were non-existent. The issue continually raised its head during the inter-war years, usually if Germany's amateur national side got battered, such as the 6-0 mauling it received at the hands of Austria in 1931. Like England during the 1880s, there were also plenty of examples of players being given 'under the table' payments in return for joining certain clubs.

But it wouldn't be until after the Second World War that an element of professionalism overtly appeared. In 1945, the Oberliga Süd (Southern League) allowed the paying of players, albeit no more than the modest sum of 30 Reichsmarks per game. A few years later in 1948 they also introduced the *Vertragsspieler* (player-under-contract) system, which although not technically professional did make players something akin to employees rather than simply members of a sports club. Under this system a salary cap, which would stay in place for the next 15 years, was set at 320 Deutschmarks (DM) per month. Players were also expected to have a regular job and to prove that they were actually doing it. Today it would be like Bastian Schweinsteiger having to split his time between playing for Bayern Munich and putting in a shift at the local car factory.

Although this half-hearted approach to professionalism became the standard in Germany during the 1950s, it came under pressure as the decade wore on. One of the reasons for this was the slow drain of German talent to countries where footballers were rewarded handsomely for their efforts. Players such as Horst Buhtz (Torino), Reinhold Jackstell (Lens) and Kurt Clemens (FC Nancy) were part of a small but growing trend which saw Germans choose to move to leagues which had already embraced professionalism, such as Serie A or Ligue 1, rather than wait for the football authorities to introduce it (and a better wage) at home.

Allied to this was a growing concern towards the end of the decade that German football might be falling behind that played by its professional European neighbours, a fear not helped by the national side's early exit at the quarter-final stage of the 1962 World Cup. So disappointing was this exit, that when the team arrived back at Frankfurt airport a few days later, there were just 300 fans there to greet them.

This national humiliation proved to be the catalyst for the creation of a professional league. Following pressure from several regional football associations, on 28 July 1962, the DFB voted to introduce a new, single-tiered nationwide league. The Bundesliga, as it was called, would kick-start its inaugural season that August and was comprised of 16 clubs drawn from West Germany's five Oberligen.

But although professionalism arrived with a bang, it came with some caveats. For a start the Bundesliga maintained a system of wage control for several years. The new maximum basic salary was set as 500 Deutschmarks per month, with the potential addition of a 700 Deutschmark bonus. There was also a transfer cap introduced. This limited fees to a maximum of 50,000 Deutschmarks (with 20 per cent of that going to the player).

Along with continued control over pay, one other area that the new professional league continued to differ from those in countries such as England, France or Italy was in the ownership structure of its participant clubs. In the Bundesliga the Verein model persisted, a move attributable to the continued tax and financial benefits that the model enjoyed and its popularity among fans, many of whom had grown accustomed to having a stake in the clubs that they followed.

'As professional football became popular and more money started to flow into the game across Europe, specifically during the 1990s, it was this different perspective of fans that I think was key in helping the Verein model survive. Even though many German football fans looked to England and admired what was happening in the Premier League, there were very few calls from supporters for the Bundesliga to abolish the Verein model. For us, it went hand in hand with our identity as supporters and became something absolutely fundamental to German football culture,' argues Uli Hesse.

Although the e.V model survived, it's not been immune from a little bit of tinkering here and there and back in 1999 some changes to the way that clubs were organised were introduced. Along with the creation of a new league association to run the top two divisions, the Deutsche Fußball Liga (DFL), a new regulatory framework, was also introduced to provide the option for e.Vs to spin-off elements of the club, such as the football side, into separate companies.

The idea behind the spin-off was for clubs to sell equity in these companies and by doing so attract outside private investment. Crucially for fans of supporter power, any spin-off comes with one major restriction. According to the 50+1 ownership rule, the e.V members must retain a minimum 51 per cent stake in the voting rights of the company.

This rule was designed to provide investment opportunities yet at the same time prevent outside investors from having overall control of the direction of the company, ensuring that the culture of the Verein remained endemic within the Bundesliga.

Bayern Munich, that Bavarian footballing powerhouse, is one such club to have taken advantage of the freedom provided by the change. Over the past decade they have sold two nine per cent stakes in their football company to Audi and Adidas. The €165m raised through this contributed to the €346m cost of constructing the club's new stadium, the Allianz Arena. Although this has diluted the e.V's ownership, Bayern's members still control 82 per cent of the club's football company (a figure that cannot fall below 70 per cent following a recent ruling passed by the e.V).

'In the purest sense, the only exceptions to the 50+1 rule are two clubs, who because of their peculiar history were granted exemption from the regulations. Vfl Wolfsburg and Bayer Leverkusen are works teams, established and wholly owned by German corporations [Volkswagen and Bayer respectively] and so their structure adheres more towards the "Anglo Saxon" model common in England,' says Uli Hesse.

There are also two other clubs, TSG 1899 Hoffenheim and RB Leipzig, that while strictly speaking still adhere to the 50+1 rule, have because of the nature of their ownership, ventured into something of a grey area.

Just a few seasons ago, Hoffenheim were playing in the fifth tier of German football. Around 2000, Dietmar Hopp, a software entrepreneur and one-time 698th richest man in the world, arrived at the club he had played for and supported as a boy to become their financial backer. Hopp's millions transformed Hoffenheim's fortunes, and over the following seasons the club scaled the greasy pole of German football and arrived in the top tier in 2008.

Although Hopp only owns 49 per cent of Hoffenheim's voting rights, critics believe that his €240m investment has given him excessive influence at the club and produced an over-reliance on his generosity. It was an opinion given credence when he sanctioned the sale of Luiz Gustavo to Bayern Munich in 2011 without the knowledge of the manager Ralf Rangnick (who later resigned in protest). This was behaviour more reminiscent of an English Premier League owner than that commonly seen in Germany.

Just over 200 miles away from Hoffenheim, in the state of Saxony, RB Leipzig have been causing headlines since their establishment a few years ago, largely because of the way in which they are funded. The 'RB' in the name ostensibly stands for Rasenballsport (lawn ball games) but it is understood across the game to really refer to Red Bull, the Austrian energy drink giant that stands behind the club.

The company first tried to get involved in German football during 2006 when they approached Sachsen Leipzig, then playing in the fourth tier, about the possibility of investing millions into the team in return for the club changing their name to Red Bull Leipzig. But this plan ultimately floundered following a vehemently hostile response from the fans, who were wary of having their club absorbed into a private company, and a ruling from the German FA that prevented e.Vs competing in the country's top four divisions from being named after a commercial product.

Undeterred, Red Bull withdrew for a bit and had a little re-think about their strategy. They returned a few years later in 2009 and this time with a new approach. Rather than take over an existing club, Red Bull founded a new one, RB Leipzig.

Uli Hesse says, 'In Germany you need a minimum of seven members to officially register a club. RB Leipzig has eight, each one of them an employee of Red Bull.'

To acquire players, the new club approached SSV Markranstädt, a small e.V just eight miles east of Leipzig, suggesting an incorporation (and financing) of some of Markranstädt's teams.

'In reality though,' continues Uli, 'what they really wanted was Markranstädt's top senior side, which at that time had the right to compete in Oberliga Nordost, German football's fifth tier.'

After Markranstädt agreed, the regional FA of Saxony then approved the deal and also sanctioned the new club's logo, which amazingly bears a striking resemblance to the image found on cans of Red Bull.

'There's no doubt in most fans' minds that despite the existence of 50+1, here is a club that is just as dependent upon its private backers as Hoffenheim,' Uli concludes.

Although it's taken longer than at first predicted to climb from the fifth tier to the third (the club were only promoted during the 2012/13 season) the aim remains entry into the Bundesliga and ultimately promotion to the top league. Should this happen then, assuming Hoffenheim are still knocking around the top division, it would mean that Germany's top flight would have two clubs adhering to the law but not the spirit of 50+1.

Surprisingly, considering how much German supporters defined themselves as members rather than customers, when the changes affecting the Verein model were introduced, few fans raised objections towards what was happening even though these changes represented the first concerted attack on the model since the game took root in the country.

'Most supporters had confidence in the DFL. The maintenance of member control through 50+1, plus the fact it was at the clubs' discretion whether they wanted to "spin" elements off, meant that fans were sure that the Bundesliga wasn't heading down a path that would make it one day a carbon copy of the Premier League,' argues Uli.

Although the DFL has purposefully prevented the league from becoming a *laissez-faire* 'free-for-all', this has not harmed it in any way financially. According to Deloitte's 2013 Annual Review of Football Finance, although the English Premier League might be Europe's highest revenue-creating division with its teams generating a combined total of €2.9bn, the Bundesliga is the nearest challenger with its €1.9bn equivalent. This puts the Germans ahead of rival leagues on the continent, such as La Liga (€1.8bn), Serie A (€1.6bn) and Ligue 1 (€1.1bn).

Unlike these other leagues, where media rights tend to dominate the way in which clubs make their money, often accounting for between 40 and 60 per cent of revenue generated, the Bundesliga as a whole has managed a much greater degree of balance. During the 2011/12 season, revenue was generated in the following proportions; advertising 26.6 per cent, media rights 26.2 per cent, matchday revenues 21.2 per cent, transfers 10.1 per cent, merchandising 4.5 per cent and miscellaneous 11.4 per cent. This better degree of balance makes the Bundesliga less reliant on one source of income and better able to weather any changes that occur; a lesson that English football has still failed to heed despite the omnishambles that was ITV Digital.

This impressive degree of balance is complemented by the individual financial performance of the clubs participating in the Bundesliga. The teams of the Premier League might collectively generate money by the bucketload but, as we saw in chapter two, they also like to spend it as well. The English Premier League is a loss-making division, filled with clubs that regularly fail to make profits and which are burdened by the accrual of debt to cover losses. In Germany by contrast, collectively, the Bundesliga made a post-tax profit of €55m in 2011/12. What's more, 14 of the 18 clubs that compete in the top flight also spent 2011/12 in the black.

'And I think that 50+1 plays a role in this, the fact that it's so difficult for one single person to gain influence at a club means that the chances of an individual taking over, which has happened on innumerable occasions in England, loading the club with debt, chasing glory but ultimately causing ruin are less,' argues Dr Richard Elliot, director of the Lawrie McMenemy Centre for Football Research.

The 50+1 system introduces manifold different voices into the decision-making process of a club too. This co-operative way of organising is in sharp contrast to that which exists in most countries, where a single owner or a limited handful of people in a consortium can do what they please as they often answer to themselves and no one else.

'In Germany, clubs govern by consensus as they are accountable to their members. These types of organisations tend to produce a more cautious approach to business,' thinks Richard.

You can see the effectiveness of 50+1 in action through the example of 1860 Munich. Back in 2011, Jordanian businessman Hasan Ismaik shelled out €13 million for roughly 60 per cent of the football company's shares, along with an additional €5.4 million to pay off debts. But although he's shelled out millions and bought a majority of the club's shares, many of these were of the non-voting variety. In reality, all Ismaik has really got for his investment was a 49 per cent stake in the voting rights of 1860.

'Despite being made aware of the league's rules, I'm not sure he believed that they would be enforced. His realisation that despite the investment and the majority shareholding he'd acquired, his voting power at the club was limited to that of a minority shareholder has resulted in some difficulties behind the scenes at the club,' says Uli Hesse.

Ismaik has since railed against 50+1, calling for the DFL to show him some flexibility on this issue, and attempted to rally supporters against those on the board who have been resolute in their efforts to limit the Jordanian's hopes to use his cash (and promises of more to come) to extend influence at the club.

'Without the protection of 50+1,' argues Uli, 'it is debatable whether a club like 1860 Munich could have resisted the approach of someone like Mr Ismaik. Had this been taking place in England then it's pretty much a guarantee that the Jordanian would now be the proud owner of the entire club. And while this could have produced a positive outcome, it is equally possible that it could have proven ruinous.'

But as effective and useful as 50+1 is, its success and continued appeal has been underwritten by the licensing system that has been in effect in Germany since the Bundesliga was established. Under this system, clubs are required to submit economic data for scrutiny by the football authority. For clubs to receive a licence to participate in the relevant Bundesliga they must be solvent and demonstrate sufficient liquidity to last the next season.

Richard Elliot says, 'The DFL will look at aspects of the club's business, such as assets, cash and bank balances, liabilities and loan commitments. This review is undertaken in the pre-season period. If a club is failing financially then they can still be provided with a conditional licence, which allows them to play but gives the football authorities the opportunity to pay close attention to that club.'

The DFL also has sanctions available to it to punish clubs who it deems are not taking financial sustainability seriously or continuing to trade in a reckless fashion. These include fines, points deductions, transfer embargoes and ultimately expulsion from the three-division national structure.

And this is a system that does have teeth. In the summer of 2013, MSV Duisburg had their licence to play in Bundesliga 2 denied because of the club's shaky finances. Despite finishing the campaign an underwhelming yet respectable and safe 11th, the club was told that it would play the following season in German football's third tier.

The combination of 50+1 and the licensing system within German football has created a culture where cost control is important. And nowhere is this more evident than on the issue of wages.

According to Deloitte's 2013 Annual Review of Football Finance, during the 2011/12 season Premier League clubs spent 70 per cent of their turnover on players' pay. Although high, this figure is actually outstripped by other European leagues, such as Serie A (75 per cent) and Ligue 1 (74 per cent). In Spain the picture is better with the turnover/revenue ratio standing at 60 per cent but even this can't beat the German level, which in the Bundesliga stands at just 51 per cent, representing the best of any major league in Europe.

But despite the oversight that exists and the punishments that are available to apply to clubs that break the rules, like many other countries, Germany has not been immune from moments of financial madness.

If you cast the net beyond the top flight, then according to Uli Hesse there are plenty of examples of clubs that have all come close to going out of business recently.

He says, 'In November 2012, VfB Lübeck [who play in the fourth tier] were declared insolvent for the second time in four years and stopped competing immediately. A few weeks later, Alemannia Aachen, from the third tier, went into receivership. In the spring of the year that followed, Wuppertal could no longer pay the bills and were automatically demoted from the fourth tier. Around the same time, Kickers Offenbach, who not long ago competed in Bundesliga 2, went into administration. I think this goes to show that German football today is not immune from financial problems.'

If you look a little further back in time you can even see instances of really big clubs, like Borussia Dortmund and FC Kaiserslautern, coming dangerously close to bankruptcy. In fact, back in 2003, Dortmund were in such a mess, following a period in which they blew millions on foreign imports and amassed huge debts, that were it not for a loan from arch-rivals

Bayern Munich it's debatable whether the club would still be in existence today.

'Football is football; it's unlike any other business. What matters to fans is success on the pitch, not always a balanced budget and financial sustainability. And so whether it's a Russian oligarch in charge or the members of a Verein, the temptation in the game to overstretch is always going to be there. The system in the Bundesliga, despite its many attractions, is not perfect. What I would say about German football is that at least it's the supporters making the decisions here and not some "Johnny-come-lately" who can come in and ruin the club,' argues Richard Elliot.

One long-standing criticism of the German system's emphasis on supporter ownership is that by limiting investment, preventing outside parties from taking full control of a club and trying to create a system that is conscious of cost control, the Bundesliga has been in danger of falling behind other major leagues.

This certainly appeared to be the case during the 1990s and well into the 2000s, if you judged success by doing well in European competitions. Between 1990 and 2010, German clubs only featured in a handful of Champions League finals. Of those that made it, Bayern Munich, Bayer Leverkusen and Borussia Dortmund, only Dortmund and Bayern managed to win the trophy. In response, clubs such as Hamburg and Werder Bremen attempted to persuade the DFL to allow them to abandon the Verein model completely and float on the stock exchange, thereby attracting the finance they believed necessary for German teams to compete against the European elite.

This argument has lost some of its allure in recent years as clubs such as Bayern Munich, Dortmund and Leverkusen have started to perform better in Europe, a trend that culminated in an all-German Champions League Final in 2013. Of course, this could be a blip and we might not see another German club do well in the Champions League for years, who knows? But, for the moment at least, the contention that 50+1 is holding the league back has less validity than it once did.

Doing well in the Champions League is also a very limited definition of success. Another measure would be how popular the game is domestically. Attendances in the Bundesliga massively outstrip those of comparable leagues elsewhere in Europe and did so even when German club football was considered behind that of somewhere like England.

Many fans also consider the fact that supporters are seen as part of the club in Germany as another mark of success. 'In the German game the fan is unquestionably king, which is how it should be in football,' argues Jens Wagner, Hamburg 96 representative of the German football supporters' group Unsere Kurve.

For Jens the reason for this is simple. He says, 'The AGM, attended by all shareholding fans, is the highest decision-making body at most clubs. Only the AGM can change the club statutes and only the AGM members can elect several boards (board of directors, supervisory board etc). They wield the power. It's no surprise then that the people who run clubs think about what the fans want. The experience the fans have is important in German football culture; they are an integral part of what makes the Bundesliga the Bundesliga.'

The impact of this is perfectly illustrated by the matchday experience of the average German supporter. Many clubs, including Borussia Dortmund, Schalke and Bayern Munich, limit the percentage of season tickets available in their grounds to ensure that they don't end up with the same faces attending each game. German stadiums also tend to be bigger on average than their English counterparts, and include limited standing areas, giving more fans a chance to watch the match.

The cost to get into a game is also much lower than in many other leagues. During the 2011/12 season, whereas the Premier League charged an average of £28.30 for the cheapest matchday ticket, the Bundesliga charged a comparable average of £10.33. Admittedly there is plenty of variation within the leagues. The cheapest season ticket at Borussia Dortmund will cost you £303, which is higher than the cheapest equivalent at Manchester City (£275). And there are also several clubs in both Spain and Italy who offer better prices for fans than their German rivals. But, on average, fans are still better off in Germany than they are in other comparable European leagues.

'The situation in Germany is a good one,' thinks Jens. 'Fans matter much more than they do in other countries. And to me, this makes sense. Football is a sport that would be nothing without the people who turn out every week to watch the game. That's why German football should be considered such a success.'

Although most strongly associated with it in the popular consciousness, Germany is not alone in establishing the rule of 50+1. Over in Sweden every football club, professional or not, adheres to the same ownership principles; something that is enforced by the Riksidrottsförbundet (Swedish Sports Confederation).

'This has always been an immensely popular system among the fans,' explains Tony Ernst, Swedish journalist and football campaigner. 'Supporters of Swedish teams like the fact that we have some control over our clubs, that they can't be sold from under us or ruined by some outside investor. The clubs are also accountable to the supporters, so our views have to be taken into consideration.'

During 2009, the depth of support for this model of ownership was revealed when the Swedish Sports Confederation (SSC) proposed that the rule should be altered to allow each different national sport federation (e.g. the Football Association, the Ice Hockey Association, the Basketball Association etc.) to decide for itself what it wanted its ownership structure to be.

'There's been a long discussion in Sweden about this over the years,' explains Tony, 'with those proposing change proffering reasons similar to that which you've heard put forward in Germany, all mainly boiling down to the same thing; that our system thwarts investment and stops clubs competing with the best. I think that after years of discussion, the SSC felt that with neo-liberalism rampant across Europe and the belief in the regulation of markets in retreat, they would have the majority of clubs and fans behind them if they made a move.'

In response to the plan, the fans of clubs across Sweden organised together to campaign for the model's survival. The primary aim of the campaign was to secure the support of 34 per cent of those eligible to vote on the measure at the SSC AGM. Under its statutes, any changes to 50+1 required a two-thirds majority so 34 per cent would be enough to scupper the proposal.

The campaign initially targeted the smaller sport federations who were already concerned that the change would affect their government funding.

'This was a huge success and pretty quickly we'd managed to get close to our target,' says Tony.

Those against the changes then launched an offensive within the football movement where they sent in motions and had votes at all the different AGMs that were taking place, the overwhelming majority of which voted to keep 50+1.

Tony happily says, 'On the back of this we also asked the SEF (the Swedish equivalent to the Football League) for a vote on the proposed change, which we won. When it was time to vote in May at the SCC AGM they didn't even have to count the votes because it was so clear that we'd got a majority.'

What happened in Sweden provides an interesting perspective on how you define success in football. In the modern game, few Swedish teams have ever performed well on the European stage. Of those that have, it's been rare for them to progress to the latter stages of either the Champions League or the Europa League. Here was an example then where the promise of the potential investment that could be raised via privatisation should have been appealing to fans.

'Although there's quite a few supporters (generally those who don't go that often to watch matches in the Allsvenskan) who long for the successes of the Premier League, I think the campaign illustrated that the interested fan who watches most of their club's games understands that sustainability and supporter democracy are more important than conventional definitions of "success" (e.g. the obsession with winning European trophies that exists in some countries),' argues Tony.

What is evident from this is that across Europe supporter ownership has the capacity to not just succeed at the very highest levels but also to deliver fan satisfaction even at clubs where the possibility of European success is remote. But then culturally England is different to Germany, Sweden and Spain. And so, what works over there might not necessarily work over here.

'In many places in Europe there is a certainly a cultural tradition of community ownership in sport. And so for us to think less like customers and more like stakeholders is probably easier than it is for an English football fan,' thinks Tony.

'But,' he adds, 'perhaps as supporter ownership spreads and the idea becomes more embedded this will start to change. The concept of fans being in control is relatively new in England and so maybe it's just going to take time before it becomes as accepted over there as it is over here.'

11

Let's Hear it for the Board: The Owners Getting it Right

I N the long history of professional football, the private model of ownership has unquestionably thrown up more than a few crap owners and shifty chairmen.

There is George Reynolds at Darlington who saddled the club with massive debts after building a 27,000-seater stadium for a side with an average attendance of just a few thousand (a rattling millstone that contributed to their descent into administration). Or how about Darren Brown at Chesterfield, a man who emptied the coffers and left the club in near ruin, actions that led to him being given a four-year prison sentence?

And most delightfully of all we have got Ken Richardson, the charmer who arrived as Doncaster's saviour in 1995. Richardson took control at Doncaster Rovers with one thing on his mind, a new stadium. When his plans were given the knock-back by the local authority, Ken hatched a plan. Two local scallies were hired by Richardson to burn down the club's existing ground, Belle Vue, with an aim to claim on the insurance and sell the land to property developers for a tidy profit. The only glitch in this plan, at least from the owner's perspective, was the fact that one of the arsonists dropped their mobile at the scene. South Yorkshire police eventually linked the crime back to the club's owner, who was later sentenced to four years behind bars.

But it would be wrong and unfair to just focus on the bad. Despite what some fans might say about the men and women in charge after a few bevvies, the overwhelming majority come into the game to try and do some good and not simply to make a few quid.

Vic Marley, chairman of Crawley Town between 2007 and 2013, says, 'You get involved because you think you can have a positive influence. Before I became part of the set-up at Crawley I had been vice-president at Wimbledon FC, so I had the experience and the connections. Crawley were my local club and when they were in trouble I thought I could do something to help out.

'In the end, as chairman, I helped steer the club through a real "backs to the wall" crisis, one that could have seen them fold. It was an exhausting and time-consuming job that only a fool would do for financial reasons. I did it because I wanted this club, which is an important part of the community, to do well. I think that's something that motivates a lot of people who get involved in the non-playing side of the game.'

While there is also probably a degree of ego-stroking at work, most owners have good intentions when they arrive at a club. Although many are fans in the first place, such as Bill Kenwright at Everton, Peter Coates at Stoke City and Steve Gibson at Middlesbrough, this isn't always the case. Some are simply local businessmen who are concerned about an ailing community enterprise, others people who believe that their success in one sector should be easily transferable to the world of football.

But whether they're a fan or not the problem for many owners is that all too often their good intentions don't translate into success. Too many, specifically in recent years, have run their clubs badly, that all-important business savvy deserting them the minute they enter the boardroom.

The problem, at least according to Sean Hamil, former director with Supporters Direct and current lecturer in management at the Birkbeck University Sports Business Centre, is that the system that they work within often thwarts their lofty motives.

He says, 'Football, and this has been said many times, is not a conventional business. Generally in business, profit maximisation is paramount. If football was run along these lines then every club would balance the budget and where you finished in the league would perhaps be a secondary consideration. But football isn't normal. In football, balancing a budget only makes sense if everyone else agrees to do the same. But the temptation is always there for others to spend more than they've got in order to steal a jump on any club that is balancing the accounts. This means that a situation is created where a sustainable approach to business almost doesn't make sense because the danger of operating like this can lead to an increased chance of relegation.

'And this is why so many owners who come into the game with nothing but good intentions end up floundering. The harsh reality that all new owners learn is that most clubs aren't good businesses. Although they're welcome to run a club sustainably, there is every chance that by doing so, the club could well flirt with relegation.'

Despite this, there are examples of responsible owners, men and women who have managed to put their egos aside, ignored the short-term pressures endemic within English football and created clubs run in the spirit of sustainability.

The Majestic Madejski

One common criticism (however unfounded) levelled at owners by supporters is that they're not real fans. Without getting into a deep and lengthy investigation into what it means to be a 'fan' (something that could probably fill an entire book), it's fair to assume that what supporters mean by this is that owners are not like them, that they lack the same deep emotional attachment to a club, which for many comes close to Shankly's opinion that football, and by extension the following of a team, is indeed more important than life or death.

But should this really matter? Surely what is more important is the owner's motivation for involvement, whether he or she is a genuine fan or not. A desire to help a club, to bring their business expertise and financial clout to the table need not be predicated on a lifelong dedication to the team. And if proof be needed for this, then look no further than the example of Sir John Madejski at Reading, an owner who has managed to earn the respect of the fans without once ever claiming to share their levels of devotion to the club.

Madejski is a classic example of a 'local boy made good'. From relatively humble origins, he made his fortune during the 1970s and 1980s through his founding of *Auto Trader* magazine. In 1998, after decades in the publishing industry, he sold his company Hurst Publishing for £174m. Although not averse to the finer things in life (Madejski is the owner of two Rolls-Royces, two Bentleys, four Jaguars and two Ferraris) he is also well known for his philanthropy, specifically in his home town of Reading. And, according to Sir John, it was this philanthropic nature that initially brought him into contact with the local football club.

He says, 'Back in 1990, Reading FC were in a lot of trouble financially. I think they were losing about £20,000 per week, had amassed considerable debts and were facing the very real prospect of going under. They were on the lookout for a rich sucker to bail them out and as a local rich sucker I was obviously approached. To be honest, I was never a "fan" of the club as such. But I did see Reading FC for what it was; an extremely important part of our community. Football is the ambrosia of the masses, and the local stadium the place where people come on a Saturday afternoon to forget about their worries for 90 minutes and be entertained. The club, and the games that were played at Elm Park, were important to my community and because of this I felt motivated to get involved.'

Madejski was able to secure a controlling stake from the previous owner Roger Smee and begin the process of rebuilding the club. The new owner arrived at Elm Park with a big promise, namely to get Reading into the Premier League. Considering that they were mired in the Third Division, running at a loss and poorly supported this seemed fairly optimistic.

He says, 'From my point of view, coming in as someone with a business background, I saw that the key to sustained success in the future was to get out of Elm Park. It might have been a "traditional" ground and loved by the fans but the place was knackered. The corporate hospitality for example, vital to generating revenue, comprised of wooden boxes mounted on scaffolding at the back of the Main Stand. The stadium was also in the wrong part of town and hemmed in on all sides by roads and houses. I saw it as absolutely essential that this club needed a new, purpose-built stadium to play in. With the right facilities I thought that this could sustain our finances in the long term.'

It would take eight years for Madejski's plans to come to fruition. In the meantime, he ensured that the club operated on a more secure financial footing and began paying off Reading's debts. This improved financial performance also coincided with an upturn on the playing side. Reading managed to climb back up the football pyramid and in 1995 even made it to the First Division play-off final, narrowly losing to Bolton in extra time. Although disappointed at the time, in retrospect Sir John thinks that not going up might have been right for the club.

He says, 'Although football is all about success and getting into the Premier League would have been a wonderful achievement, I don't think we were ready. Elm Park was in no state to host top-flight matches. With our limited capacity and rather basic facilities, we would have been a joke.'

A few years later, at the beginning of the 1998/99 season, Reading took residency at the newly-opened, 24,000-seater Madejski Stadium, beating Luton Town 3-0 there on the opening day of the campaign. For many fans of the club, like Dan Wimbush, editor of the Reading FC blog The Tilehurst End, despite a lingering affection for Elm Park, the new ground was recognised as an important development.

He says, 'We were among the first group of new grounds that began to spring up in the late 1990s and the shiny and ultra-modern Madejski Stadium was a big lure for players to come to Reading. You're always going to get a small minority who want to cling on to the past but as much as we all loved Elm Park it was a crumbling wreck of a ground that wasn't suitable for a club with higher ambitions. There was no way we could have redeveloped the old ground and so moving was our only option. Some still grumble about the stadium's location but at least it's a bit more local than many other new stadia.'

Along with the commercial revenue that the stadium generates (augmented via a ground-share with the London Irish rugby union side), the club also benefits from Sir John's decision to incorporate a hotel into the complex, which supplies Reading with an additional income of around £5m per year. According to Sir John, this diversification of income streams is illustrative of his long-term vision for the club, which has always been about sustainability.

He adds, 'It would be the easiest thing in the world to arrive at a club, throw some money at it and chase short-term success. But what would be the point? I guarantee that even if you do succeed, in time the coffers will run dry, the debts will mount and before you know it the club is in administration. I wanted to build this club up brick by brick by investing in its infrastructure. We needed to have a decent ground to draw in support from the area and maximise our ability to generate revenue. We needed decent training facilities to ensure that our players can succeed and that young talent wants to come to the club.

'And lastly we needed a way for the club to make money beyond football, which is where the hotel came in. Over the last few decades we've had ups and downs, profits and losses but fundamentally we have been heading in the right direction and today Reading are a club that can hold their own financially.'

They are also a club that in 2006 managed to make it into the Premier League, finally delivering on the promise that Sir John made all those years ago. Although this dalliance with the top flight only lasted a couple of seasons, Reading were back among the big boys by 2012, proving that the club's earlier success was not an aberration.

What is telling about Reading's approach to the game during the Madejski era is that although there have been times of spending, there has been little evidence of over-reach. Whether chasing promotion from the Third Division, striving for the title in the Championship or fighting for survival in the Premier League, the guiding philosophy has been one of relative restraint. For Sir John, this degree of self-control at club level has been one of the most difficult parts of his job.

He says, 'The demand to spend and spend and then spend some more in the game is relentless. And it's got worse since I first became involved in football as wage rates and transfer fees have developed into a market that is simply absurd. Although at times we have splashed out on players and as the club has progressed begun to spend much more than we used to on wages and transfers, I have always tried to cut our coat according to our cloth.

'Within reason, the club has attempted to live within its means and if that meant relegation from the Premier League then that's just the way it has to be. I think I owed it to the fans to ensure that what we started to build back in 1990 wasn't derailed by some mad dash for success or some ill-advised splurge to fight relegation.'

After over two decades in charge of the Reading project, in May 2012 Sir John relinquished control of the club after he sold a 51 per cent controlling stake (with an option on the remaining 49 per cent) to Thames Sports Investments, which is backed by the Russian billionaire Anton Zingarevich. Although Sir John is to remain as chairman until 2014 and has the offer to become life president when he steps down, the sale effectively brings to an end his era with the club. For the fans, it's an era that they will always be grateful for.

Dan Wimbush says, 'It's safe to say that Reading Football Club wouldn't have spent the last decade in the top two tiers were it not for Sir John, while it's also reasonable to argue we wouldn't have a football club at all were it not for the former owner of *Auto Trader*. Sir John has often said that he only took over the club to stop it going out of business and during a time that saw sides including Newport, Maidstone and Aldershot go bust, there's no reason that a club like Reading couldn't have gone with them. Sure there's been the odd frustrating moment but by and large Sir John Madejski has been brilliant. To be sitting here talking of a new stadium, Premier League stints and multi-million-pound transfers is the sort of stuff you'd have been laughed at back when Madejski took over in 1990. He'll be remembered as one of, if not the greatest chairman in the club's history.'

What Sir John has done proves that the private model of ownership can produce amazing results without the club getting into all kinds of trouble. But although greatly valued by the modern fan, prudent finances are not enough on their own. What supporters increasingly want today is an owner who not only looks after the club's finances but who also listens to them too.

For a long time in English football this idea was alien. But this was not necessarily because owners were pig-headed (although many were). It was a view held with equal conviction by the millions who turned up to watch their clubs each season.

'Because of this,' argues Andy Burnham, 'you can probably forgive owners for being slow to come around to what has been a revolution in how fans see themselves. Football operated in a certain way for many years. Supporters' trusts and the concept of fans being more political are still relatively new developments in the game and so it's not a surprise that owners have been slow to accept them.'

But according to Andy this is changing. He adds, 'It's not universal and it's certainly not evident at every club but you are getting more examples of owners willing to listen to the fans and engage with them on certain issues. You will always get owners that are stubborn and want nothing to do with supporters' groups. But just as fans have changed the way they view themselves over the past 30 years, you're also getting a shift in how owners view their relationship with the supporters.'

If you travel down to the south coast to Brighton (or Brighton and Hove as nobody calls it) there's a perfect example of such an owner, a man with a hugely progressive approach to the relationship between club and fan. His name is Dick Knight and in short, he is the man who saved the Albion.

Brighton: A White Knight to the Rescue

For those of a certain age, it's hard to mention Brighton & Hove Albion without bringing to mind their heroic FA Cup run of the early 1980s. Everyone likes an underdog and when Albion came up against the might of Manchester United (even if they were still back then not what they are now), it's safe to assume that most people were rooting for the Seagulls. And this wasn't just because they had been relegated from the old First Division that season, although that helped. It was also because this was the first (and subsequently only) time that Albion had made it all the way to the final.

In the end the Seagulls came very close to a huge upset. In the dying seconds of extra time, with the score at 2-2, Brighton's Gordon Smith was put clear on goal with only the goalkeeper to beat. Rather than hit it first time, a decision that would probably have seen the ball safely into the back of the net, Smith took one touch too many and ended up having his shot smothered by the body of the advancing United keeper. The replay a few days later wasn't anywhere near as close, and United battered their opponents 4-0. But the scale of the defeat combined with the memory of how close Brighton had come to claiming the Cup only served to endear the club to neutrals that bit more.

That run and time in the top flight would turn out to be a high for the fans of the Albion. Their relegation marked the beginnings of a decline that wouldn't show signs of abating until the early years of the new millennium. In the 20 years that followed the drop the Seagulls would endure relegations, false dawns, successive bouts of financial crisis and, perhaps worst of all, the loss of their stadium.

For those who regard a football stadium as something more than bricks and mortar, the site of the Goldstone Ground today would be sure to depress. The Goldstone Retail Park, which now stands in place of Brighton's former spiritual home, is a great place for anyone who wants to buy a washing machine, do a bit of DIY and then top their shopping trip off with a flaccid burger. But it's not so good for anyone who thinks that football stadiums should be permanent, a physical link with a club's history.

The announcement that Brighton were upping sticks, flogging their stadium and entering a ground-share with Portsmouth was broken to supporters in the summer of 1995.

'It came as a real shock, a huge bolt out of the blue,' says Liz Costa, vice-chairman of the Brighton Supporters' Club.

A few years earlier two directors at the club, Greg Stanley and Bill Archer, had taken over, stepping in to rescue the Seagulls from a winding-up order (with Archer installed as chairman).

'The new regime had apparently invested £800,000 and promised to turn things around. Although at the time we saw precious little sign of things improving, there was still a feeling that the club wasn't in too bad a shape. That's part of the reason why it came as such a shock when the sale of the stadium was announced,' stresses Liz.

It was claimed by the owners, principally through their mouthpiece at the club, CEO David Bellotti, that Albion needed to sell the Goldstone because there was too much debt, a figure that they said stood at around £6m. To placate the fans, alongside the announcement concerning the sale, the club also revealed their long-term plans to build a new 30,000 all-seater stadium in the west of the city.

But the devil, as least for fans, was in the detail. As more was revealed about the sale and planned move, much of it dug up by the supporters themselves, it became clear that not all was how it seemed.

To begin with, it was discovered that far from arriving and saving the club with fresh investment, the new owners had in fact merely restructured Albion's finances and taken on an £800,000 bank loan to do so, a move that hardly helped the club's long-term financial position. The reality was that the new owners had probably put less into the club than some supporters. Archer, for example, had acquired his 56 per cent holding in Brighton for the princely sum of just £56.

Although no malicious intent was ever established, the owners hardly endeared themselves to the fans when it was also discovered that the Articles of Association of the club's holding company, Foray 585, had been altered to remove the prohibition against owners profiting from the sale of club assets, such as the stadium (in direct defiance of the FA's Rule 34). Although the articles were later corrected, the affair left a bad taste in the mouth for many fans.

There was also a sense that the owners were not being frank about future plans for a new stadium. Not only had no one explained how a club that was near bankrupt could afford to build a brand new ground, on successive occasions it was discovered that the owners' much-trumpeted plans (several of which appeared during their tenure at the club) had either been rebuffed by the local authority or were completely impractical from a planning perspective.

'So what you had,' explains Liz Costa, 'was a regime in charge at the club that no one believed was capable of telling the truth and which appeared to have no real plans to turn the club around and build strong foundations for the future. It was a recipe for conflict.'

And that's exactly what happened. During the 1996/97 campaign, the last that Albion played at the Goldstone, the fans undertook a season of protest against the board. The various demonstrations (which admirably never turned violent) took place all over the country and included a protest outside Archer's Lancashire home, marches through Brighton and London, petitions to the FA and a rally outside of the Crewe HQ of Focus DIY, Archer's company. There were also regular demonstrations inside the Goldstone on matchdays, one of the most heartening being the Fans United day.

Despite the protests, media hostility and support from across the game, the board remained defiant and the final game at the Goldstone took place on 26 April 1997, a 1-0 victory over Doncaster Rovers. Once the final whistle had blown, the home fans ransacked the stadium, many of them in tears. Most supporters, especially those who have endured an experience similar to that meted out to the Brighton faithful, can probably appreciate this need to claim a piece of what was being taken away from them. The Goldstone was later demolished in 1998, making way for the shoppers' paradise that stands there today.

But not all hope was lost, as Liz explains: 'Although we'd just become homeless, the fans had received some welcome news towards the end of the season when it was announced that Archer had lost control of the club.'

Since the spring of 1996 a consortium, put together and fronted by local businessman and lifelong Brighton supporter Dick Knight, had been attempting to remove the owners and put a new regime in place.

'Like a lot of fans,' explains Dick, 'I was horrified by what was going on at Brighton. I'd been a supporter for many years and could still clearly recall the excitement I'd felt when I'd been taken to my first game by my dad aged eight. The Albion were my club and it just saddened me to see them in such a mess.'

Knight was approached to get involved in efforts to oust Archer by Brighton's former manager, Liam Brady, who retained a soft spot for the club and a desire to rid the Albion of his old paymaster.

'Through all the years of support that followed, in my wildest dreams I'd not once ever pictured myself as chairman,' says Dick. 'It honestly hadn't crossed my mind. But then my brother-in-law, who knew Liam, suggested that I be sounded out about maybe getting involved in Liam's plans. I talked over his ideas with him and he really got me thinking about things.

'It was clear that someone had to confront Archer head-on and that someone had to be a fan, somebody who understood what this club meant to the people who followed it. It was also clear that Liam needed someone working with him, to show some leadership to get an effective group of people together, people who could take on the odious regime. So when Liam finally asked me the question, whether I was in or out, there was no other response than to say "yes". As a fan, it was my duty to do what I could.'

The consortium's efforts to take control at the club were fiercely resisted by Archer, who seemed inured to the increasing hostility of the crowd.

'I think he actually wanted to bait the fans. That's the only reason I can think of to explain the way he acted,' argues Dick. 'At the time Archer was building up his DIY empire and every instance of conflict raised his profile that bit more, so possibly that was the motivation behind his attitude towards the supporters, which at times was simply inflammatory.'

The problem for the club was the stark divide that existed during negotiations, with Archer determined to remain in control and the Knight consortium loath to accept anything less than 100 per cent ownership of the club.

'Although Archer only owned 56 per cent of the business, he effectively controlled the rest of it. And the nature of the business meant that if he didn't want to sell then there was nothing we could do about it. In fact, he didn't even have to talk to us, and for a long time that's just what happened,' explains Dick.

Dismayed at the impasse, the FA, which had been pretty ineffectual until that point, employed the Centre for Dispute Resolution to try and mediate between both sides. Against expectations, they secured an agreement for the future of the club. While Archer retained a shareholding, Knight's consortium gained *de facto* control, with Knight appointed chairman. To the fans' delight, David Bellotti was dismissed as part of the deal. Although Archer managed to hang around until 2002, when he was eventually bought out, his role and influence was greatly diminished and the supporters very quickly came to realise that their chief tormentor had been defeated.

Liz Costa says, 'Although Archer was still involved with the Albion and the Goldstone seemed lost (which it eventually was), the supporters felt that the club had turned a corner. We had faith in the new owners. Dick Knight was a totally different kind of man to Archer. He was communicative, honest and a man who carried through on his promises. But perhaps more than that, he was also a fan. Essentially, he was one of us.'

Dick adds, 'It had taken 18 months and plenty of hard work but finally we'd triumphed. I felt that the club could now start to rebuild and also repair the relationship with the supporters. At no time in the history of this club could I recall such a breakdown in relations between the fans and the board. Archer had gone out of his way to create this situation and it was now up to us, as real fans, to put it right. But before any of that could be done we had one very important task to achieve, and that was to make sure that Brighton would be playing in the Football League come the following campaign.'

During the season, the team's form had deteriorated markedly and for much of the campaign Brighton had struggled at the wrong end of the table. The victory over Doncaster during that final day at the Goldstone had thrown the club a lifeline, lifting them off the bottom of the Third Division and setting up a tantalising head-to-head against Hereford United the following weekend, where a point would prevent relegation to the Conference.

To add a little extra jeopardy to proceedings, the fixture that would decide Brighton's fate had neatly pitted the two candidates for the drop against each other on the final Saturday of the season. Most of the media attention had been focused firmly on Brighton, their loss of stadium and the fact that they had once been a top-flight side exercising the minds of most journalists. But Hereford's decline, although not as dramatic, was still a surprise for most with an interest in the lower leagues.

The previous campaign had seen the Bulls challenging for a play-off place and during the early part of the season that followed it appeared that their good form would continue. But a disastrous reversal of fortunes towards the end of the season had dragged them into the relegation zone and this nail-biting head-to-head.

Around 4,000 Brighton fans made the trip west and for the first 45 minutes they must have wondered why they bothered. The away side were overrun from the off, a tentative midfield capitulating under the advancing Hereford horde. When the home side scored in the 21st minute there was an air of inevitability about it, even if the goal was a horribly scrappy affair that ultimately went in off a Brighton defender. The away side went in at half-time despondent, knowing that if things continued in this way after the break then relegation was a certainty.

In his recently published autobiography *Madman*, Dick Knight recalls what happened next: 'The second half began. Immediately we were more positive, putting pressure on the fairly fragile Hereford defence, who sat further and further back and encouraged us to come forward. And the Albion fans roared them on… And then in the 63rd minute, we scored: Craig Maskell collected a weak clearance, took the ball on his knee and hit a left-foot volley past the keeper, Andy De Bont, which came back from his left-hand post across the goal. And Robbie Reinelt [only just on as a substitute] went for the rebound. I just had a feeling, when he was sprinting forward, that he was going to win the race with the defenders to the ball and bury it. And he did.'

Brighton spent the rest of the game dug in, thwarting everything that Hereford threw at them. When the final whistle blew the score remained 1-1 and with that the visitors were safe and the home side consigned to spend the following season in the Conference.

'We were all on a high after that game. But despite that, the reality was that the situation was still pretty dire,' admits Dick.

The club were now homeless and the only ground-share available to them was at Gillingham's Priestfield Stadium. For anyone who doesn't know this part of the south-east, the ground-share represented a 150-mile round trip for Brighton fans, a huge journey to undertake every fortnight.

Dick says, 'Not only that, but the club would be facing rental costs and a huge loss of earnings. But even this only represented part of our problems. We also had a squad of players that were not the best. Even our first XI was pretty poor. It's telling that during the following season we actually accrued 13 points less than the previous campaign, the one that had seen the club nearly drop out of the Football League. The only reason we managed to survive despite this dismal points tally was because there were other sides that were even worse.'

During their time at Priestfield, Brighton were also compelled to pay a £500,000 bond to the Football League or face expulsion from the league system – levied in response to the financial crisis at the club and the loss of their ground.

'That was money we could have really done without losing,' admits Dick. 'Every penny mattered back then and to have the

League punish the club and the fans for something that was in essence solely the fault of the previous regime was simply unfair.'

Hamstrung by the ground-share, with the club's finances in a parlous state and the fans facing a lengthy commute to watch home games, a return to Brighton in some capacity became of paramount importance to the new regime. The city wasn't blessed with many suitable sites but eventually the new board managed to arrange one.

During the 1999/2000 season the club took residency at the Withdean Stadium, an athletics and county league football arena just outside the city centre. If you're being kind then you could describe Withdean as 'cosy'. Another, more accurate description would be 'knackered'. The stadium has the dubious honour of being voted the fourth worst in English league football by *The Observer*. And that was after Brighton redeveloped it.

Despite this, the team's homecoming could still be seen as a triumph. With a little investment the run-down athletics arena was transformed into a workable 6,000-capacity football stadium, albeit one with a running track, a small covered North Stand and a large, open South Stand, a pretty dodgy pitch and some unappealing toilets.

'It was great to be back in Brighton,' says Liz. 'Withdean might not have been an ideal stadium but at least we were home again. Dick Knight had promised a return and been true to his word.'

The club's choice of Withdean hadn't been universally popular in Brighton, specifically among nearby residents. To win over public opinion and get the local authority behind them, the club and the fans worked closely together through the 'Bring Home the Albion' campaign. This close connection between supporters and the board was all part of Knight's philosophy about how clubs should operate, as Liz Costa recalls, 'The contrast between Dick Knight and Archer could not have been starker. Dick had been in communication with the fans throughout the fight to keep the Goldstone. Once he gained control of the club, this collaborative approach never once diminished. All the supporters' groups who had been involved in the protests against Archer were communicated with.

'Dick was also happy to listen to ideas from the supporters and always willing to give you half an hour of his time if requested. How many football chairmen are willing to talk to a fan who has telephoned him on the off-chance of a chat? We had the sense that Dick had the good of the club paramount in his mind. He wasn't enormously rich and the consortium didn't bring huge amounts of cash, but it was communicated to us from the beginning that the new regime would create financial stability, keep us all in the loop and just as important for the fans, get the club back in Brighton and with our own ground.'

Over the following decade Brighton managed to put the bad old days behind them. While never spectacular, the finances of the club improved and Knight and his board sought whenever possible to run things in a prudent manner. On the football side, although the Albion's form was erratic, the club managed to fluctuate between the Championship and League 1; a huge improvement on what had occurred towards the latter end of the 1990s. At the same time, Dick Knight and the rest of the board were tirelessly working to complete the second part of their promise to the fans; the construction of a brand new ground.

The Falmer Stadium (or the American Express Community Stadium, as it's less appealingly known), is a 30,000-capacity ground that lies just outside the city, next to the small village of Falmer. From first seeking planning permission to the eventual opening of the stadium, this was a ten-year project. The site's proximity to the South Downs National Park ensured that a raft of different interest groups opposed its construction, a degree of opposition that led to two public inquiries on this issue.

Liz says, 'Dick Knight, the board and the supporters worked tirelessly to make the Falmer stadium a reality. We all pulled together to raise money, keep the issue alive in the press and get the support of the football authorities, other clubs and the various local councils involved. The stadium did not come easy and there were plenty of times when we thought it might not happen, but Dick led the way, inspiring us all and providing guidance and real leadership. And the end result is that we have a fantastic stadium, one that provides the club with the ability to generate the income that you need to compete at this level.'

In recent years, Knight has taken a less active role at Brighton. Back in 2009 he stepped down as chairman and left the board, his position being filled by Tony Bloom, the club's majority shareholder. Bloom's £93m investment in the Albion has enabled the building of the Amex, a level of finance required by the club after the credit crunch had undermined the board's existing plans to build the new stadium. Despite no longer being the man-in-charge, Knight was made president for life at the club, which, according to Liz, both she and many other fans feel is a position that is richly deserved.

She says, 'It's fair to say that were it not for Dick Knight there could very well be no Brighton & Hove Albion today. When he came along the club was in a mess and very likely to be heading for Conference football and the real possibility of one day folding. With the help of the fans, he has rebuilt this club from the bottom up, turning it from a Football League basket case into a club that has the potential to make it into the Premier League.

'We've been rebuilt through hard work and a sensible approach to the "football business". At the same time, the club that Dick rebuilt is one that created a template for how supporters and the board can work together. The new regime never excluded the fans and also always made sure that we felt part of the club, everyone working together for a common purpose. It's the reason why so many fans respect him and the reason why we will always be so grateful for what he did.'

And this respect works both ways. Knight remains grateful for the role that Brighton fans played in protesting against the Archer regime and the patience and support he received when attempting to find a new ground and build the club back up again. Unlike chairmen and owners of old, Knight has always been supportive of some degree of fan involvement in football, as illustrated by his constant communication with supporter groups from the moment his consortium first showed an interest in the club. Towards the end of last year, Brighton's former owner decided to make this backing for greater supporter involvement more concrete when he announced that he intended to pass on his remaining shares in the club to the fans.

He says, 'It's always been my view that without the fans there would be no Albion today. As much as I and others on the board worked to save the club, get us back to Brighton and get the new stadium built, were it not for the talent and hard work of the many fans who threw themselves into our various campaigns then it's very likely that the Seagulls could simply have disappeared. This respect for the people of Brighton is one of the reasons why the club created such an extensive community programme, arguably the finest in the Football League.

'I always wanted to put something back into the community. It was the club's way of saying thank you. And that's also what's partly motivating my decision to pass on these shares to the fans. It's another way of showing my gratitude for everything they've done in the past.'

Financial rules dictate that shares cannot be given away for free. So, to circumvent this, Knight has decided to sell each share for the nominal sum of £1. At the end of his autobiography, Albion's life president asked fans to send him an 'expression of interest' in a stake of his shareholding. Any interested party needed to provide a synopsis of their Albion-supporting history and convince him why they would have the best interests of the club at heart.

He says, 'When combined, the shares only represent nine per cent. Our current owner, Tony Bloom, owns the rest. So, in no way is this about precipitating some kind of supporter-led coup. That can't happen at Brighton. But what can happen, is for those who eventually get a stake to have the right to attend the AGM, where they can present the views of the fans and have them officially recorded. They can also ensure that the board know what the fans think. Nowadays, the Albion are a much slicker, more corporate organisation than they were in my day. Although that tends to be what's needed to advance in modern football, there is the danger that the fans get left behind. With a shareholding comes a voice. And with that voice there's less chance of the supporters becoming disconnected from the club.'

For much of the game's history, the division between the boardroom and the terraces was a stark one. Chairmen, sitting in their luxury seats set apart from the heaving masses of the great unwashed below, believed that they knew what was best for the club and the fans should keep their collective noses out. Knight is more progressive, an owner who believes that the supporters deserve to be communicated with and have a sense that they are contributing to how the club is being run; that sustainability needs to come hand in hand with a collective sense that the board and the fans are working together. It's a template for club governance that has begun to appear elsewhere in football, most recently a few miles up the road from Brighton at Crystal Palace.

CPFC 2010

When Crystal Palace took to the pitch against Tottenham Hotspur during the opening weekend of the 2013/14 Premier League season, it marked the culmination of a long journey for the club. The previous 15 years had been a tough time for Palace fans. Two administrations, almost permanent financial turmoil and a near miss with relegation to the Second Division had made life as an Eagle something to be endured rather than enjoyed at times.

Although you can never be sure in football, those dreadful days of the past seem to be behind the club. Today, Palace, who earned themselves promotion to the Premier League through the 2012/13 Championship play off final, are run by a consortium of fans, four men committed to the principles of financial sustainability and to ensuring the fans feel that they are part of the club.

The financial madness at Palace began in earnest towards the close of the 1990s. Back then, Mark Goldberg, a long-time fan, had gained control when he had purchased Ron Noades's stake in the club in 1998.

Goldberg's time at Palace was a classic example of Sean Hamil's assertion that owners chase results rather than profits, with the owner seemingly abandoning all his business acumen at the front door to Selhurst Park. Take the example of Serbian defender Gordan Petric, signed from Rangers in 1998. Although no one doubted the centre-half's credentials, Goldberg sanctioned the £300,000 purchase (and a £5,000-a-week contract) at a time when Palace's financial problems were beginning to emerge and when the club had at least nine other senior players who could play in the same position.

Most damningly of all though was the package put together for the brief appointment of Terry Venables as manager. To begin with Goldberg had to shell out a £135,000 fee just to enter into talks about the manager's job with El Tel. Once he had taken the position, Venables managed to get himself a reputed deal that included a £750,000-a-year salary after tax, an unsecured £500,000 interest-free loan, a house costing £650,000 (in which Venables would retain the equity interest), a Mercedes car, a ten per cent pension contribution and £20,000 relocation expenses. Considering how much Venables was costing the club it was probably just as well that he only hung around for ten months.

Escalating player and staff salaries and an inability to maximise revenues from Selhurst Park (which remained in the hands of Noades) conspired to eventually catch up with Goldberg. With debts mounting and the owner unable to accommodate them any longer, Palace entered administration in March 1999. For both parties, the relationship had been a disaster. Palace, one of the founder members of the Premier

League, spent the next few seasons operating on a shoestring and shedding their brightest and best. Goldberg meanwhile lost his entire fortune through the debacle and was declared bankrupt in 2000.

You would think that Mark Goldberg would stand as a cautionary tale for whoever succeeded him, clear evidence of how dangerous overreach can be. Clearly Simon Jordan hadn't been paying attention. The club's new owner had made his money from mobile phones, as one half of the duo behind the Pocket Phone Shop. Having sold his business for £73m to One2One, he then used part of his recently-acquired fortune to take control of the club that he had supported since childhood.

Despite going through managers faster than Roman Abramovich, Jordan's reign at Palace initially went well. The club, which had been outside the top flight since relegation in 1998, managed to barge back into the Premier League in 2004, courtesy of a 1-0 win over West Ham in that season's First Division play-off final.

'Sadly for us, it would prove to be a brief dalliance with the top level of English football. Within a season we were back down in the Championship and not long after, beginning to face the same kind of financial problems that had dogged us in the past,' says Chris Waters of the Crystal Palace Supporters' Trust (CPST).

In 2008 Jordan made a decision that would ultimately cost the club dearly. Life in the Championship had been a struggle for Palace. The decline in revenue following relegation, combined with the outgoings required to make a sustained challenge for the play-offs, was starting to stretch the finances of the club. By this point Jordan had already sunk in £35m and was reaching the red line area of his finances he had promised his family that he would not cross. In his search for external funding he was approached by the newly formed hedge fund Agilo, which specialised in high-risk investment. A deal was done with Agilo to lend the club around £5m at a hefty borrowing rate.

As many clubs have realised over the past 20 years, the more people you owe, the more hands there are clamouring for repayment. The problem for Palace was that the revenue simply wasn't there. The financial fundamentals at the club, excessive costs, falling attendances and the fact that Palace still didn't own their own stadium meant that not only were they not making enough money to cover daily expenses, they were also unable to service existing debts, such as those to HMRC and Agilo. On 27 January 2010, the hedge fund finally decided that enough was enough and in an attempt to recoup the money they were still owed called in the administrators.

The problem for Palace was that there appeared to be no one willing to step in and take over the ailing South London club, which is understandable when you consider that its previous two owners had each blown a fortune only for the realities of football to overwhelm them.

'None of us who eventually formed the consortium that took over the club ever had plans to become owners. We are just fans. On a personal level, ever since I started following Palace as a nine-year-old back in the late 1960s, all I've wanted to do on a Saturday afternoon is watch the team that I love play football. I never had dreams to become the big man in charge of the club, puffing on a cigar and calling the shots. Unfortunately, it became clear that Palace would fold unless someone could come in and rescue the club. With no one coming forward to do this, the four of us felt compelled to do something,' says current co-owner Stephen Browett.

The men behind CPFC 2010, as the consortium that took over the club is known, are local businessmen and lifelong Palace fans Browett, Steve Parish, Martin Long and Jeremy Hosking. Importantly for the club, not only were they able to bring Palace out of administration after agreeing a CVA with the club's creditors, in a separate deal they were also able to buy the freehold for Selhurst Park from Lloyds Bank (who had gained responsibility for the stadium when the previous owners, Selhurst Park Limited, had gone into administration).

This meant that for the first time since 1998, both the club and the stadium were united under the same company, relieving Palace of the rental costs and freeing the club to maximise the commercial revenues that it was possible to generate from Selhurst.

According to Browett, since their arrival at Palace, the new owners have been keen to avoid the mistakes that were made in the recent past.

He says, 'It's really easy in this game to get carried away. The desire to succeed among fans and owners is intense. But we all know where that can lead. On two separate occasions, Palace have come close to disappearing. Our mantra is sustainability. This club has to be able to pay its way. It would have been reckless in the extreme if we had just come in and then borrowed to gamble on promotion to the Premier League. That's what's happened in the past and it's only led to ruin.'

Happily for Palace, through a combination of shrewd purchases and the appointment of a great manager in Ian Holloway, they not only managed to become more sustainable but at the same time the club earned promotion into the Premier League at the end of the 2012/13 season. For Stephen though, this elevation in their league status changes nothing.

He says, 'The danger, and we've seen this in the behaviour of plenty of clubs down the years, is to spend and spend in an attempt to maintain top-flight status. We're not going to do that. We'd like to stay up and we're happy to bring in new faces but that's not going to come at the cost of the club's financial health. If we go down, we go down. As we all know too well, there are worse things that can happen than relegation.'

This sustainable approach is one that has already struck a resonance with the supporters. The CPST was founded back in 2000, when the club were going through the first period of administration. According to Chris Waters, many of the club's supporters are much happier that the new owners appear determined to make sustainability of paramount importance.

He says, 'A lot of people think that all that football fans care about is getting into the Premier League and winning things. And while there's obviously some truth in this, it's all meaningless if one day your club goes bust. Palace fans are happy that for the first time in years the club is being run properly. It's to the owners' credit that they have understood just how important this is.'

The new owners have also been keen to make the Palace supporters feel part of the club. Although both Goldberg and Jordan were fans, Chris Waters feels that the voices of both the supporters and the CPST were rarely taken into consideration, something that cannot be said of today's regime.

Chris says, 'From the moment CPFC 2010 began to approach the administrators about a buy-out, the CPST have been in communication with them. Both groups have maintained a constant dialogue and our views on a variety of issues since, such as changes to the stadium, season ticket prices and ticket availability have been taken into consideration. On a wider level, the owners regularly appear online on the CPFC fan forum, and they are always willing to engage with supporters on a variety of issues. That's not something that you got with Goldberg or Jordan.'

According to Chris, the clearest example of the new regime's desire to work with the fans was their decision to allow the CPST to explore the possibility of building and owning a new training facility for the club.

He adds, 'Our previous chairman sold our current training facilities a few years ago when the club was in trouble, leasing them back at market rate. Although the new owners understood why Simon had done this they thought that the situation shouldn't continue. Under the scheme that was devised between us and the club, the trust would build and own the training facility and then rent it back to Palace at a favourable rate. Crucially for the fans, this asset would have belonged to the trust and not the club. This would mean that it couldn't have been sold by Palace. The whole thing represented a way for the

CPST to support the club but at the same time ensure that a key asset was protected in perpetuity.'

When the recent opportunity arose for the club to buy their old training ground for a knock-down price, this scheme was placed on hiatus. Although disappointed, Chris understands the thinking behind the decision and CPST members remain confident that their close relationship with the club will continue in the future.

He says, 'The owners have confirmed that eventually a club with ambitions such as ours will need to move. After all, nearby clubs like Spurs and Arsenal have training facilities that are much larger than ours. So, we're confident, as are the owners, that there will be ongoing dialogue about the training ground and it's something we will continue to look into. In the meantime though, we continue to talk to the club on a range of issues and also carry on with our community work.'

The men featured here are just a handful of those who could be used to illustrate that the private model of football ownership is capable of producing owners who really do have the best interests of the club in mind, are able to run a club in a financially sustainable manner and who are able in some cases to make fans feel part of the club.

To look at them in isolation you would be forgiven for thinking that all was well in English football. But all too often, this isn't the case. Supporter ownership, whether total or partial, has become a necessary part of the game. Although most instances of punk football in action have arisen from financial catastrophes, more and more fans are now interested in becoming involved in the clubs they follow.

Polling undertaken by YouGov on behalf of Co-operatives UK on this topic in 2010, revealed that across the country 56 per cent of football supporters want a say in how their clubs are run.

At some clubs, such as Manchester United and Liverpool, the figure was even higher (83 per cent and 72 per cent respectively).

'But if that is ever going to happen on a large scale,' argues Dave Boyle, 'then the benefits of supporter ownership need to be more widely understood and changes will have to take place in the game. At the moment this method of owning and running clubs remains quite niche and survives in an industry that is organisationally hostile towards it. But this should give hope.

'Without being pushed by the football authorities and with so many factors stacked against it, punk football has still blossomed over the past decade. If that hostility can change and more and more fans also come to appreciate this model's numerous benefits, of how collectively they could actually come together to get a stake in the clubs they follow, then in a generation's time we could see far more instances of supporter ownership than there are today.'

12

What the Future Holds: Reform of Football and the Supporter Trust Movement

ALTHOUGH not always a success, many supporter trusts have shown that fans can know what is best for a club and if provided with the opportunity can also run the club just as well as, if not sometimes better than, the local big-wig. Many of those involved in punk football also believe that fan control brings with it some natural advantages over the private model of ownership too. For Tom Hall, former head of England and Wales at Supporters Direct, one of the strongest of these is the financial discipline it can provide.

He says, 'Many clubs in the lower leagues and in the Conference are technically bankrupt. The only reason that they survive is because of the support of a sugar daddy. Because these people exist it makes privately-owned clubs sloppy. There's no need to run these clubs in a sustainable manner, so they aren't. Fan-owned clubs by contrast have to run a tight ship because no one is going to bail them out. Of course, no system of ownership is perfect and as long as people are people there are going to be mistakes but several supporter-run clubs, like AFC Wimbledon, FC United of Manchester and Exeter City, are models of financial prudence.'

Along with the sustainability that can arise from a greater level of supporter involvement, research undertaken by Supporters Direct has also revealed that another benefit is the degree of trust that is built between the club and its fans.

Tom argues, 'At the most fundamental level the fans become more involved with the club and so the barrier that always existed between the board and the terraces is eroded. From our research we've found that at clubs where fans have a stake in the ownership, supporters feel that the future of their club is in their own hands, that they're not powerless in the way that they have traditionally been. This imbues the relationship between the board and the supporters, even with those who are not members of the IPS, with a level of trust that is rare to find elsewhere in football.'

This feeling of togetherness and shared common purpose is assisted by the rules that govern any community benefit society. All trusts have to publish annual accounts to be approved by members at their AGM. Along with the democratic election of board members, this provides a level of scrutiny and recourse for ordinary fans that is lacking at other football clubs in England.

Many supporter-owned clubs often voluntarily go further than these rules stipulate. At FC United of Manchester for example, the annual AGM is also accompanied by a formal General Meeting each year, where a 'warts and all' discussion of the club's finances takes place. In recent years, since FC United have been developing plans for their own ground, the club has also held one further additional meeting to keep members informed on its progress, undertaken several surveys of fans on this issue and continued to involve as many supporters as possible in the consultation process.

The development of a stronger sense of trust between fans and the board, allied to the fact that the club is no longer being run by a private individual, has, according to Sean Hamil, also changed the nature of what it means to be a 'fan' at supporter-owned clubs.

He says, 'Clubs like AFC Wimbledon, Exeter City, Chester FC and even Swansea City, don't chase success at any cost. For these clubs football is about something more than what happens on a Saturday afternoon. Because of this, the fans that turn up are gracing the game for the right reasons. You're not getting glory hunters who only demand instant success but rather individuals who have bought into the philosophy of supporter ownership, regardless of whether that means a club might not do as well as it could if backed by financial doping.'

And this 'buying in' to the punk football philosophy also extends to further involvement in the club. Because of their limited financial power, fan-owned clubs have become dependent upon the goodwill of their supporters, something most often expressed through volunteering. AFC Wimbledon regularly receive voluntary support, with around 300 volunteers contributing their time to the club annually. This can include anything from sweeping the terraces, to staffing the turnstiles, to designing a new stadium. Even the chief executive of the club, Erik Samuelson, is a volunteer, albeit one who is paid one guinea a year.

'When you're supporter-owned there is a big difference in the way that fans view the club,' thinks Erik. 'We all feel part of something special, something that we have a very real stake in. We're not a football club in the traditional sense, one that's run privately and driven by one individual's vision. This is a community asset, run by the fans in the interest of the fans and the wider community. Because of this, engagement tends to go well beyond simply turning up at the game and paying your money to get in. People will give their time in a way that would never happen at a "normal" football club.'

At Exeter City, the level of volunteering prior to the supporters' trust taking over the club was negligible. Since then, the amount of jobs undertaken by ordinary supporters, whether members of the trust or not, has grown exponentially, to the point where Laurence Overend feels that the club could not survive without it.

He says, 'We owe so much of our success over the past decade to that vast, previously untapped resource that has suddenly become available to us. Without our army of volunteers we would have found it really difficult to keep our costs down. They've ensured that Exeter City's experiment in supporter ownership has been given the opportunity to flourish.'

If you stopped reading here then you would probably go away with the impression that punk football is amazing and that all clubs should rush out tomorrow and adopt it. After all, you would have to be mad to want to say no to financial sustainability, high levels of supporter engagement and an army of highly-motivated, free labour. But in the same way that the private model comes with plenty of pros and cons, so too does the one where it's the fans who call the shots. And probably the most telling drawback of supporter ownership is the potential for the clubs involved to fall behind their peers.

Dave Boyle says, 'A good way of thinking of this problem is to picture a supporter-owned club as being the only sane man in a world filled with lunatics. Clubs like AFC Wimbledon, FC United of Manchester and Exeter City all play by the rules. They don't borrow massive amounts to run the club, they maximise commercial revenue and they control costs. This would be great if the leagues they competed in possessed a level playing field. But this is never the case.

'Their peers, and by this I mean the overwhelming majority of league and non-league clubs in England, spend to win, regardless of the fact that this means accruing unsustainable levels of debt. And they do this because history has shown that some mug will normally be on hand to bail them out should matters take a turn for the worse. The effect of this madness creates a situation where sustainably run clubs are constantly finding it difficult to maintain their league standing, let alone begin edging their way upwards.'

Steve Beck adds, 'When you take over a club, as the York City Supporters' Trust did, you start to realise just how hard this game is and how many things are stacked against you as ordinary fans. You're trying as hard as you can just to keep your head above water and to field the best team that you can and all of that effort can just be blown out the water by Mr Moneybags at another club who has deep pockets and an open cheque book. When supporters get involved in ownership, as their stake increases this inevitably means that the opportunities for financially doping the club will decrease proportionally. This is why several trusts have had such a difficult time running clubs once they've assumed majority control.'

Where supporters' trusts have either sold up or surrendered most of their shareholding it is often because of the inequity inherent in modern football. This was certainly the case at York City and Brentford and also contributed to the failure at Stockport County. Donald Kerr of Bees United feels that unless this is resolved then fan ownership will remain a model potentially unpalatable for many.

He says, 'Football is about winning. No one goes to the game in the hope of defeat. Although I remain a huge fan of it, the problem with supporter ownership, certainly in the absence of comprehensive and far-reaching reforms to how clubs are financed, is that it is exactly the reality that some fans will face. It's what we faced at Brentford, the reality that our supporter-owned club simply did not have the finances to compete at our previous level and so was pretty certain to enter a downward spiral on the pitch that would see us tumble out of the Football League and possibly even out of the Conference too. Is this a price worth paying for the right to say that you own the club you support and that this club is run sustainably? I'm not sure too many fans will think that it is.'

For many of the clubs that have been taken over by supporters, their ability to compete financially and on the pitch has further been hampered by a legacy of debt. In the short history of punk football, it's rare to find many examples of trusts gaining any percentage of control in the good times. Far more common instead are instances of supporters emerging as 'owners of last resort', the only group the club have been able to turn to after the situation has become so dire that no business person, not even a rapacious asset stripper, has the appetite to become involved in a business so mired in money worries.

Almost all of the trusts that have become involved with existing clubs featured in this book have done so at times of extreme crisis. These trusts never start with a clean slate but rather have to spend the early years of their existence painstakingly paying for the mistakes of the previous regime. The CVA and a long road to recovery tend to be the birthing pool from which most supporter-owned clubs emerge.

'I often speculate how different our experience would have been if we'd taken control in happier times, or at least at a time when the club wasn't so indebted that it was nearing extinction,' muses Steve Beck. 'The YCST's time in charge was always hampered by the excesses of the past. We never really got a chance to get ahead of ourselves.'

Although money tends be the most important problem facing trusts, another issue highlighted by many of those interviewed for this book is the maintenance of support for the project among the fans. Paradoxically, despite the fact that periods of turmoil are horrible for fans to endure, nothing tends to bring supporters together like being up the creek. Cup runs and league titles are all well and good, but if you really want to unite fans and get them behind the club then there's nothing better than fear and anger; that's what really gets people motivated.

The examples in this book prove that. To save clubs like Exeter or Swansea or to establish clubs like AFC Wimbledon and FC United of Manchester, ordinary fans have dug deep into their pockets, given up their free time and in the process transformed what it means to be a 'supporter'. They have done things that most fans would never do in more benign times.

Ivor Heller says, 'I think that most football supporters simply want to go and watch a game. Getting political and agitating probably only really appeals to a small minority. That was certainly our experience at Wimbledon FC. But a crisis changes things. That small minority grows as more and more people get sucked into the various campaigns to save clubs, oppose takeovers, save grounds, take over clubs or start brand new ones. Fear of losing something you love or anger towards damage being perpetrated against something you cherish can be a great motivator.'

But what happens when the fear or anger dissipates? What happens when the crisis is resolved? The thing about trusts is that they need two factors without which they cannot function. The first one is the presence of members. A trust with two or three members is never going to get off the ground. Most of those that have become successful tend to begin with a few hundred and then numbers subsequently escalate from there. The more members a trust has the more money it can raise through membership fees and calls for donations (which most trusts do on a regular basis). A large number of members also provide trusts with a standing army to use for volunteering, campaigning and running the organisation.

Laurence Overend feels that the problem for any trust is that as time passes the memory of the crisis fades and with it the sense of fear that was generated.

He says, 'In some ways trusts then become a victim of their own success. The whole point of a trust takeover or the establishment of a new club is to provide a remedy to a problem. And several have achieved that when given the opportunity. But by doing so they remove their strongest recruiting tool.

Supporters can become complacent and over time start to question why they should be forking out an annual membership fee when things seem to be going OK. Membership could then fall and with that the trust's ability to run the club effectively.'

One antidote to this problem is success. Swansea City, AFC Wimbledon and to a certain extent, Exeter City are all examples of clubs where their trusts haven't had a problem maintaining membership levels. The reason for this is simple – at these clubs supporter control and success on the pitch have proven to be compatible. Think of AFC Wimbledon rising from the Combined Counties to League 2 or Swansea City storming into the Premier League and winning the League Cup. It has given the supporters the feeling that what's happening at the club makes sense and is having a positive impact; something that has helped retain members and attract new adherents to the cause.

But not all trusts have enjoyed this level of success. At York City and Brentford, the supporters did little better in charge than the previous owners. The trusts involved simply never had that all-important burst of success to really expand the project.

Allied to membership, the second factor is legitimacy among the fans. When trusts are involved with the ownership of a club they need the backing of the wider fan base, those supporters who are sympathetic to the trust's aim but have chosen to not commit via membership. Like any owner, the support of the fans is important. Without it there is an absence of legitimacy, something that can undermine the authority of any regime at a football club.

Steve Beck says, 'When a trust takes over a club, a mixture of goodwill towards you as supporters, anger towards the previous owners and, more than likely, the memory of a recent crisis means that the fans are initially very patient. You're given a chance to show them what you can do and probably more of a chance than a regular, private owner. But if it becomes clear, as it has on several occasions when trusts have been in control, that the club aren't going to be challenging for promotion or doing well in cups and that maybe the trust can even take the team down, then at some point the fans are going to start questioning whether the trust is the right organisation to be running the club, undermining legitimacy in the process.'

For many trusts success is tricky because of the uneven nature of English football. Simply maintaining league status is difficult so the draining of legitimacy and the loss of membership is something that is always going to be a problem unless the game is reformed.

One area that agitates many of those interested in competitiveness in football is the distribution of television money.

Rob Wilson explains, 'It's no coincidence that the problems of excessive debt, escalating wages and clubs spiralling into financial calamity coincide with the arrival of Sky. Although the game in this country was never a paragon of fairness, since 1992 the sheer volume of money that has been pumped into football has changed it irrevocably, in some ways not for the better. As it stands today, most of the money heads to the Premier League, causing a financial bubble that everyone is trying to keep up with.'

The recent deal agreed between the Premier League and both BT and Sky costs the broadcasters just over £3bn collectively for the rights to show Premier League games over the next three seasons. Overseas rights are then expected to push the amount of money the Premier League will generate over this period to £5bn. From this around 15 per cent is given to clubs in the Football League.

But although this sounds relatively generous, the lion's share of this money will be given in the form of parachute payments to those clubs relegated from the top flight. The rest of the clubs in the Football League will then have to pick over what's left with Championship members receiving £2.3m each, League 1 clubs £360,000 and League 2 participants £240,000.

'When you look at these figures,' argues Sean Hamil, 'you can see that there is definitely room for improvement. A more equitable distribution would take some of the steam out of the impact that the TV money has and at the same time provide smaller clubs with much-needed additional income. But, although welcome, better distribution would not be a panacea.

'Sugar daddies would still exist, the temptation to spend too much on wages and transfers would still be there and any alteration would do little to create a much more level playing field. For that to occur, we need fundamental change to how football clubs are financially regulated and this does finally seem to be happening.'

Although slow to act, moving at a pace that would embarrass some glaciers, in recent years the football authorities (domestically and in Europe) have begun to tackle some of the systemic financial problems that have dogged the modern game. The first example of this was undertaken by the Football League in 2004 when the Salary Cost Management Protocol (SCMP) was introduced into League 2.

The SCMP broadly limits spending on players' wages as a percentage of turnover, with clubs providing budgetary information to the Football League at the beginning of the season that is then updated as the campaign progresses. At the moment, League 2 clubs have their ratio capped at 55 per cent and League 1 clubs at 60 per cent. Any club that is in breach of the rules can find themselves at the wrong end of a transfer embargo, a sanction that was administered to Swindon Town during 2012 when the club narrowly exceeded League 1's cap.

Below League 2, in the world of the Football Conference (comprising the Skrill Premier, North and South) new, tougher financial rules were introduced for clubs in 2009. The Financial Reporting Initiative (FRI) was brought in as a response to a growing sense of crisis within the non-league game, where in the immediate years prior to its introduction several clubs had been subject to winding up orders and a handful, such as Farsley Celtic, Rushden & Diamonds and Chester City, had gone out of business.

Under the FRI, clubs are required to submit quarterly financial reports to the league authority. Failure to comply brings financial penalties, a possible transfer embargo and the possibility of a points deduction. There have already been instances where clubs have been punished for breaking the rules, such as Welling United who were found guilty of misleading the Football Conference by submitting false information relating to HMRC debt. The club were deducted five points and fined £5,000 (suspended for two years).

If we travel a little higher up the pyramid, the Football League has recently introduced a Financial Fair Play (FFP) system into the Championship. Phased in over a number of seasons, FFP aims for clubs, more or less, to break even in the long term. Every December, each club competing in the league is required to submit accounts from the previous campaign to the authorities. Within these accounts, during the 2011/12 reporting period a club was allowed to have a total acceptable deviation from the break-even requirement of £12m (or just £4m in the absence of an equity injection by the owner). By the 2015/16 reporting period the total acceptable deviation allowed by the league will be reduced to £5m (£2m in the absence of an equity injection).

As the new regulations are primarily aimed at controlling exorbitant wage and transfer payments, certain costs, such as those incurred from investment in youth development, stadium and training facility improvements and community projects, are exempt from the FFP calculation. Failure to adhere to the rules will result in sanctions, which consist of either a fine or a transfer embargo. The former can be quite hefty if a club breaches the rules and is then promoted to the Premier League. Should this happen then the transgressor in question becomes liable for a 'Fair Play Tax', which ranges from one per cent of any excess between £1 and £100,000 and up to 100 per cent of any excess over £10m.

But the daddy of all the various financial regulations currently affecting English football is the one that was hatched a few years ago by UEFA. Its version of FFP, from which the Football League took its inspiration, seeks to tame the massive seasonal losses regularly accrued by the biggest clubs in Europe.

This version of FFP is a comprehensive set of regulations that apply to any club that wishes to seek a licence to participate in either the Europa League or the Champions League. By applying for the licence clubs agree to play by the rules or face UEFA's sanctions. The rules covering FFP run to 90 pages long and cover a wide array of financial regulations but the headline statute, and the one that has created plenty of column inches, is the stipulation that clubs will have to break even if they want to participate in European competition.

Like the Football League, UEFA has made allowances for clubs to adapt to the new regime and so FFP has been phased in over a number of years and until 2018 licence holders will be allowed to make an acceptable deviation from the break-even requirement. Over the course of this implementation phase, UEFA has split the seasons into monitoring periods during which clubs are permitted to make losses. In the first monitoring period, which covered two years (2011/12 and 2012/13), clubs were permitted to lose as much as €45m. By the 2017/18 monitoring period, which covers three years between 2014 and 2017, this figure will fall to a maximum of €30m.

During the entire phasing-in period, these acceptable deviations are only permissible if funded by an equity injection by the club owner(s). If an owner(s) does not put any money in by way of cash for shares, each club's acceptable deviation is restricted to a mere €5m over each monitoring period. Like the Football League's version of FFP, UEFA has also allowed some exclusions from the calculations, such as costs related to infrastructure investment and youth and community development.

In 2012 UEFA published the list of eight punishments that the Club Financial Control Body (established to adjudge whether a club has broken the rules and what punishment they will receive) is permitted to mete out. These range from a slap on the wrist, through the deduction of points and ultimately, for the worst transgressors, exclusion from future competition. Despite its infancy, it is clear that FFP has teeth. Several clubs, such as Rubin Kazan, CSKA Sofia and Dinamo Bucharest, have had revenue withheld for breaking the rules and one club, Malaga CF, even received a one-season suspension from European competition for failing to pay their bills on time, losing their Europa League place in the process.

In England, the majority of clubs in the Premier League begin each season with an eye on a possible place in a European competition, whether through their position in the league or via victory in one of the domestic cup competitions. Because of this, for some time the Premier League contended that there was no need to introduce a domestic version of FFP for the top flight as UEFA's system would be sufficient to introduce a dollop of financial realism into the league.

But according to Daniel Geey, sports lawyer and the man behind The Final Score on Football Law, a blog that aims to demystify the numerous financial regulations currently affecting the game, the Premier League has shifted this stance in recent years in response to concerns from the big clubs that UEFA's FFP model was potentially handing smaller teams a financial advantage in the domestic league.

He says, 'The possibility could have arisen for some of the smaller clubs, who are less likely to be qualifying for Europe, of attracting a sugar daddy, taking on debt and storming the league. Although they might have been prohibited from playing in Europe if they finished in the top five it still would have upset the traditional Premier League hierarchy. There has therefore been more pressure in recent years from the big clubs for the Premier League to act and ensure that some degree of budget and wage control exists to cover all 20 clubs. As a result, the Premier League introduced additional costs and sustainability provisions last year.'

The rules, like those established by UEFA and the Football League, encourage clubs to aim towards breaking even. Starting in the 2013/14 season, over the course of the following three campaigns top-flight clubs will be permitted to make a cumulative loss of £105m if evidence of secure funding from the owner(s) is provided. If not, then a cumulative loss of £15m over this period will be the maximum permitted.

In keeping with other 'break even' models, the usual suspects are exempt, such as investment in infrastructure and youth development. But unlike the models established by UEFA and the Football League, the one created by the Premier League also aims to introduce a direct form of wage control.

During the 2013/14 season, spending on player wages should not exceed more than £52m, a figure that is then permitted to increase by £4m per season, reaching a maximum of £60m by 2015/16. Any club that breaks these limits must be able to illustrate that the overspend is attributable to contracts signed pre-2013 or can be covered by either their own increased commercial revenues that season or profits from player transfers. Clubs who breach the Premier League's FFP rules will be subject to a hearing before an independent panel. At this stage, the Premier League has not publicly discussed the range of sanctions available but they are intended to have real and relevant consequences for clubs who do transgress.

To those who have long argued that English football needs a massive injection of financial realism, the various models that have appeared over the past decade at least illustrate that the game has finally woken up to the twin horrors of debt and excessive wage costs that have plagued it for so long. But, as they currently stand, will these various attempts at financial regulation do any good?

Daniel Geey says, 'There are certainly some "loopholes/reliefs" that have caused concern. To take what's happening in the Championship as an example, there is nothing stopping a club from taking large losses in an attempt to get into the Premier League. Although they'll receive a fine from the Football League if they do this, the potential revenue upside might make the gamble worthwhile. Of course, if they fail to gain promotion then they'll be subject to a transfer embargo, which can be a very effective punishment.'

Sponsorship is another area where it is feared that some of the richer clubs might seek ways around the rules, by for example signing over-generous deals with their owners. A few years ago Manchester City announced a £400m, ten-year deal with Etihad Airways, the national airline of Abu Dhabi, coincidently the home emirate of City owner Sheikh Mansour. And then last season, Paris Saint-Germain, owned by the Qatar Investment Authority, signed a €200m-a-year, four-year deal with, surprise, surprise, the Qatar Tourism Authority.

'Overall though, I think the various authorities involved are now aware of the need for sensible financial regulation, which is positive,' concludes Daniel.

There are certainly some problems with these various pieces of financial regulation and only time will tell whether they will work as well as hoped. But considering that football has for many years been a game where the football authorities didn't appear to give a toss about how clubs ran themselves or the losses they incurred, the fact that something is being done should be seen as enormously positive.

At least now English football seems to be on the right path, one that might lead eventually to a time when clubs are on a more level playing field and where the days of benefactors coming in and unsettling the competitive balance of a league are a thing of the past. But will this help the cause of supporter ownership?

Dave Boyle is one person who thinks it will, and says, 'Despite the great examples of Swansea City, AFC Wimbledon and Exeter City, I'm still not sure the supporters in general think that if they owned the club that they could compete against their privately-owned rivals because the playing field has long been so uneven. I think that the more sustainable the game becomes financially and the fewer opportunities owners have of "doping" their clubs with soft loans, the better able existing supporter-owned clubs will be to compete. For the future, this will mean that fans might be more confident in uniting to invest in their club because the possibility of on-the-field success under a supporter ownership model, partial or total, will become that much greater.'

Most of the people who I have interviewed for this book have stressed that the future of punk football depends upon two factors; the creation of a more level playing field, something that seems to be happening, and the creation of a more benign environment for fan control to flourish, something that hasn't occurred yet. For many supporters of punk football, like Sean Hamil, responsibility for this creation of such an environment should lie with the football establishment.

He says, 'The FA and the various league authorities have it within their power to change the game as they see fit. If they wanted to promote a better relationship between supporter and club then they could. If they wanted to further the cause of fan ownership then they could do that too.'

To date there has been little movement in this area from any football authority. In fact, the only development of any note so far has been the introduction of supporter liaison officers (SLOs). Initially endorsed by UEFA as part of its club licensing and FFP regulations, the establishment of permanent SLOs across both the Premier League and the Football League has since been encouraged by the football authorities.

SLOs are employees of the club, whose responsibility it is for building bridges between the club and its fans. A perfect summing up of what a SLO should be was provided by UEFA when the role was first created. UEFA said that an SLO should be 'an advocate of both sides, representing the interests of the club (or national association/league) **and** those of the supporters'. The emphasis on '**and**' is UEFA's and highlights that a successful SLO should be more than a club employee who just protects his or her employers from the ire of the fans.

Although a step forward, the creation of SLOs is hardly the same as making supporter-elected directors mandatory or forcing clubs to be partially owned by the fans. To date, no football authority in England has shown any inclination to advance supporter representation within the domestic game.

'The problem,' thinks Sean Hamil, 'certainly from my experience of working with Supporters Direct, is that the FA, the Football League and the Premier League are simply unconvinced that the supporter ownership model offers any advantages over the private ownership model that would warrant any special regime measures to assist its development. Therefore they're unwilling to do anything.

'I don't believe they are hostile to the idea of supporter ownership; there are enough positive examples, particularly in the lower divisions, to demonstrate to the football authorities that supporter ownership is a viable model, particularly for clubs either facing, or emerging from, bankruptcy. It's just that they're not really that interested in it. The reality is that there is still a lot of work to be done by the supporters' trust movement to sell the benefits to the football authorities.'

One of the simplest ways that the football authorities could promote the cause of supporter ownership would be through the introduction of a club licensing system. In Germany, the 36 professional clubs that make up the Bundesliga's two tiers have to meet a variety of sporting, administrative, legal and financial obligations to acquire a licence that enables them to participate in league football. Failure to adhere to the league's standards can result in anything as minor as a fine or as major as expulsion from the Bundesliga, depending on the severity of the transgression.

Although the German system has primarily been used to ensure financial sustainability in the league, something that could also be intrinsic to any English model, the template established by the DFL could also be applied to other aspects of the game, such as supporter involvement in the club.

Within an English context, should a similar model be introduced then along with the various financial stipulations needed for the securing of a licence, a league authority could, for example, also include certain provisos that had to be met concerning the relationship that exists between the club and its fans. Tom Hall has a few suggestions as to what these provisos should be.

He says, 'At a basic level a league authority could stipulate that new owners had to provide full evidence of the source of their funds to the supporters' organisation. That organisation could also be provided with a veto over the sale of any fixed assets owned by the club or mortgages taken out against those assets. At a more sophisticated level, acquiring a licence could also be dependent upon an owner allowing a supporters' trust to have a representative on the board, first refusal on any shares made available or ownership rights over club assets, such as the club name and crest.'

Will this ever happen? To date there hasn't been any evidence that it will.

'The desire to act simply isn't there,' argues Dave Boyle. 'And the harsh truth is that there's no way for fans to change this as things stand; the act of getting 40 people elected to the FA Council to initiate change for example, is the work of generations.'

But the football authorities are not the only bodies with responsibility for the game. Government has a role too and since 2010, the House of Commons Culture, Media and Sport Committee (CMSC) has been looking into the issue of football governance, with part of their investigation covering the issue of ownership.

Experts from across the industry have given evidence to the committee, much of which contributed to the CMSC's report into this issue that was published in 2011. The report came out in favour of greater levels of supporter involvement in the ownership of football clubs, regarding the model as 'one of the positive developments in English football'.

It also proposed some ways that the government could intervene to assist, such as reducing the legal and bureaucratic hurdles that trusts face in raising finance. So far, none of the measures recommended have come into law and for many people involved in punk football, such as Dave Boyle, the Football Governance Inquiry has been both a disappointment and a lost opportunity.

Dave says, 'The inquiry has done what a lot of inquiries do, which is just kick the problem further down the line. Little of concrete has emerged from it but, from a PR perspective, at least the government has been seen to be making the right noises. What the sport needed was radical action and that's not what's happened. Part of the problem with football in this country, certainly compared to somewhere like Germany, is that it doesn't really exist in law. There is no legal framework for the game and because of this our Sports Minister has no power. In other countries the Sports Minister can intervene in football and dictate standards and regulations to the various authorities because his power is established via a Sports Law. This is what the committee should be recommending and what the government should be thinking about introducing.'

The creation of a Sports Law could be one of the most straightforward ways for the cause of punk football to be advanced. Any such law would be able to set its own parameters, redefining the ownership structure of English football in the process. This could be as conservative as enshrining supporter representation on the board in law or providing supporters' trusts with the first refusal to takeover a club when it has gone into administration.

If it was aiming to be more radical then the law could even create a new legal form of sports club, a bit like a German e.V, in which a minimum degree of supporter ownership is compulsory. Although the UK tends to be a more 'hands off' sort of country when it comes to intervening in sport, in the area of football there are precedents for a stronger role for government. On several occasions, specifically to tackle the issue of crowd behaviour, various pieces of legislation have been introduced over the past 35 years, such as the Football Spectators Act (1989), the Football (Offences) Act (1991) and the Football Disorder Act (2000).

Despite these precedents, Dave is unsure whether we will ever see the UK government go as far as to mirror what has happened in countries like Germany and Sweden. He says, 'I think the introduction of a Sports Law would require a huge culture change in government. Even back when intervention was in fashion during the 1950s, 1960s and 1970s, this country was still loath to intervene in football. Sport is viewed differently in the UK and the *laissez-faire* mentality still prevails.

'Although that's not to say that it's impossible that something could change. If a high-profile club goes into administration and we get a Labour government more committed to intervention than the last lot, then maybe a window of opportunity will present itself. But in the short term, I remain sceptical.'

Even in the absence of a Sports Law, there can still be a role for the government. Chapter seven highlighted the provisions in the Localism Bill that have enabled supporter organisations, such as the Manchester United Supporters' Trust, the Blues Trust and the Spirit of Shankly to register their club's stadiums as assets of community value. The guiding principle that has underpinned the Localism Act is that community groups should have the right to own and run local assets as they are best placed to value and protect them. But as yet, all the Act really provides supporter groups with is the right to bid for an asset. Trusts are not seen as preferential bidders and nor are they provided with first refusal on the sale of the asset.

'There's no reason why this can't be changed,' argues Tom Hall. 'The Localism Bill could, at the very least, give trusts the opportunity to have the first chance to bid on a stadium that's being sold or, if its breadth was extended, take over a club that has gone into administration. This could also include having first refusal on any majority stakes in clubs that come up for sale. This would mean making the community benefit of a stadium or a club more important in the decision-making process than its monetary value, but then that's what "localism" is meant to be about.'

The principles of localism could then also be assisted by the potential role of Big Society Capital. The Big Society might not generate the headlines that it once did but as a concept, it's still knocking about. One of the few tangible outcomes of David Cameron's ham-fisted attempt to repackage the idea of people being nice to each other was this government-backed social investment institution. The aim of the bank is to provide social enterprises with capital.

A recent research paper published by Supporters Direct, entitled *Developing Public Policy to Encourage Supporter Community Ownership*, suggested that the bank could assist trusts in three ways; by providing match-funding for a community share issue, by underwriting a community share issue and by giving short-term loan finance to bridge any gaps in subscription investment offers.

'Financially speaking there are also other things that the government can do too, specifically in the area of tax,' says Tom. *Developing Public Policy to Encourage Supporter Community Ownership in Football* outlined what this could involve. It suggested that one area where the government could help would be via the development of a new form of tax relief, similar in scope to the Enterprise Investment Scheme (EIS), which already exists to provide investors in social enterprises with the opportunity to set 30 per cent of the cost of their investment against income tax.

'As this is meant for new start-ups, supporters' trust takeovers don't always fall under the parameters of this scheme,' explains Tom. 'So, what we would need is the development of a new form of relief that could provide the same benefits to investors. This would be a long-term project and one that would have to take European law into consideration. But we think that supporters' trusts would be deserving recipients of some form of assistance.'

Another area where the government could help would be in protecting trusts from the compulsory purchase of minority stakes. Under UK company law, if an investor attempting to take over a company manages to amass a 90 per cent stake they are permitted to undertake a compulsory purchase and buy out the remaining shareholders.

In the world of football this has already happened on several occasions, such as when Malcolm Glazer took control of Manchester United. Minority shareholding trusts remain in a precarious position in the absence of any protection of their holding. Although action on this issue was recommended by the CMSC and supported by the Sports Minister at the time, so far the government has done nothing to remedy the problem.

So despite plenty of talk and some positive noises it doesn't look like the cause of supporter ownership will be getting much help from the football authorities or the government any time soon. But despite this, the future could still be bright. After all, look how far punk football has come since it first started. Back in 1992, few could have predicted how much of an impact this fledgling model created at Northampton Town would have on football.

But in the past 20 years supporters' trusts have blossomed across the game. Without them, it's likely that the English professional game would look very different today. Trusts have been instrumental in putting forward the views of fans and saved several clubs that might otherwise have disappeared completely.

With a potentially more level playing field in the future, punk football has the capacity to grow. In the absence of any further assistance from the football authorities or the government, what would really help is another AFC Wimbledon, but this time on a larger scale. The arrival of a big fan-owned club, powering up the leagues, taking on and beating privately-owned rivals would do the movement a power of good.

And it just so happens that this could become a reality. A few years ago, down on the south coast, a former Premier League 'big boy' got into a heap of trouble and were it not for the fans then it's likely that the club would have gone out of business. They might reside in League 2 today but with their 20,000 fans and a trust that has majority control, Portsmouth are a club that many of those involved with punk football thinks could become the standard bearer in the coming years.

Epilogue

AFC Wimbledon v Portsmouth, 16 November 2013

TO the casual observer this is just a game, a League 2 tussle little different to any other taking place on this cold November afternoon. It is probably one that won't make your list of the top ten games of all time. But there's more to this fixture at Kingsmeadow than meets the eye.

On one side you have AFC Wimbledon, one of the clubs most closely identified with the concept of punk football, a club that showed everyone just how powerful a force ordinary fans could be and one that has proven that supporter ownership and success on the field can live hand in hand.

On the other you have Portsmouth FC, the first and only Premier League club to have entered administration, a club that have become a byword for financial mismanagement and lately, the largest community-owned football club in the English game. What you have here in essence, are the elder statesmen (in supporter ownership terms) pitted against the movement's great hope for the future.

Being a Pompey fan has not been easy in recent years. Portsmouth have endured one of the most dramatic and demoralising falls from grace ever seen in the modern game. This is a team that finished eighth in the Premier League in 2008, that won the FA Cup in the same year and which fielded players of the calibre of Glen Johnson, Jermain Defoe and Kevin-Prince Boateng. As I'm writing this, Pompey are currently languishing mid-table in League 2. Their descent down the pyramid was rapid and eventful, a journey characterised by two periods of administration, an owner who was wanted by the police and another owner who might not even have existed at all.

What happened isn't unique. The story of over-reach, over-spend and financial collapse is one common to English football. The only difference is the scale. Portsmouth are a big club. They had their snouts in the Premier League's trough, gobbling up millions in TV money. Like everyone else in the big league they bought and sold high-value players, paid them top-flight wages and created sides that could compete with the best. But like every tale of over-reach that has appeared in this book, the foundations upon which Portsmouth's charge for glory were based were shaky to say the least.

Fratton Park, home to Pompey since 1898, is a 'proper' ground, an anachronistic treasure. It is everything the DW Stadium, the Reebok Stadium and Amex aren't. Rectangular, tired and a throwback to the pre-Taylor era, it's the kind of place where you could imagine Bovril still being served, rattles shaken and a trip to the toilets a fairly unpleasant experience.

With a capacity of just 20,000 and little in the way of corporate hospitality, it is also exactly the wrong kind of place for a club to inhabit if they have hopes of becoming part of the Premier League's elite. In harsh terms, it's the kind of ground more suited to a team resigned to life yo-yoing between the top tier and the second. And this would have been fine if Portsmouth had tailored their spending accordingly, sensibly shelling out only what the club could reasonably expect to make from its ground and through player sales. But they didn't.

Under the management of Harry Redknapp and ownership of French businessman Alexandre Gaydamak between 2006 and 2009, the club spent cash like it was going out of fashion. Players were brought in such as Peter Crouch (£11m from Liverpool), Glen Johnson (£4m from Chelsea), Younes Kaboul (£6m from Spurs) and Sulley Muntari (£7m from Udinese), all on wages consummate with a team that was aiming high. This overspend was funded with loans from Gaydamak and the bank, the kind of approach to the football business that rarely ends happily.

When the recession started to bite in 2008 it hit Portsmouth hard. Not only did Gaydamak's business interests suffer but the banks began to ask for their money back. With debts rising, an inevitable consequence of such an aggressive and expansionary attempt to challenge for European football, Gaydamak decided that he could no longer fund the club and opted to sell up.

The 2007/08 season would prove to be Portsmouth's high watermark. Over the following two seasons, they would lose Harry Redknapp, sell much of the talent that he had recruited and ultimately face the humiliation of relegation. Their ownership and finances would also descend into something approaching a farce, a process that began in the late summer of 2009 when, after a protracted takeover process, it was announced that the club had been sold to the United Arab Emirates businessman Sulaiman Al-Fahim.

Keen to extricate himself from Pompey, Gaydamak had sold the club for £1, extracting a promise at the same time from Al-Fahim that the new owner would inject a further £5m into the club (with more to follow at a later date). But this money was never forthcoming. What occurred instead was one of the briefest tenures of any owner in the history of the modern game. Unable to raise the finance to maintain repayments on bank loans owed by Portsmouth, just six weeks after he had taken control, Al-Fahim announced that he was selling his 90 per cent stake to Falcondrone, a company registered in the British Virgin Islands and owned by the Saudi businessman Ali al-Faraj.

There is debate as to whether al-Faraj ever actually existed. After the takeover was completed it was revealed to the press that al-Faraj had never met any of the club's directors, league officials or demonstrated that he had the cash to support his takeover. An investigation by the *Spectator Business* magazine failed to find anyone who had in fact ever met al-Faraj, leading them to claim that the football authorities had seriously failed in their responsibility to fully scrutinise the background of the new owner.

But even if the existence of al-Faraj was in doubt, what was clear pretty quickly was that Falcondrone didn't have anywhere near enough cash to support a business as indebted as Portsmouth. To compensate for this lack of actual capital, the aim had been to borrow around £30m from the private bank EFG, a plan that failed to pan out. Instead, they managed to borrow £17m from the Hong Kong-based businessman Balram Chainrai. In return, his company Portpin was granted a mortgage over Fratton Park and other assets of the club.

Despite this injection of cash, Portsmouth remained in a financial hole. Along with a wage bill that stood at around 90 per cent of turnover, they also owed too many people too much money. Clubs like Chelsea and Liverpool were still due transfer fees for players that had arrived at Fratton Park several seasons earlier and the taxman, a creditor that many clubs seem to ignore at their peril, was owed millions.

The 2009/10 season turned out to be a miserable one. The financial turmoil at the club, which previously had been a 'behind the scenes' affair, started to make itself felt on the pitch. On a number of occasions during the first half of the season the club failed to pay the players. This contributed to a period of poor form, something that could not be rectified in the transfer market as the Premier League had placed Pompey under an embargo in response to their financial chicanery. This sanction was later increased to a nine-point penalty when, in February 2010, Portsmouth entered administration with reported debts of £135m.

Chainrai, who had (from his perspective) reluctantly gained control of the club a few weeks earlier when Falcondrone had failed to meet a scheduled loan repayment, undertook this move to, in his words 'protect the club from liquidation'.

The nine-point penalty only confirmed what had been apparent for some time; that Portsmouth were destined for the drop. The club would go on to finish the season in 20th position. To add insult to injury, despite reaching the final of that year's FA Cup, Pompey lost 1-0 to Chelsea, capping off a wretched season.

'As a fan, that was a terrible time. Our success had unravelled so quickly and so comprehensively that it was sometimes difficult to believe what has happening,' says Colin Farmery, one-time spokesperson for the Pompey Supporters' Trust (PST) and now the club's PR consultant.

But according to Colin, even after relegation there was still an optimistic belief that Pompey could turn things around.

He says, 'After all, we'd been in administration back in 1998 and had come out of that to go on to secure promotion to the top flight and win the Cup. But any optimism turned out to be seriously misplaced. What occurred after our relegation was a period so dire it has to rank as the worst in the club's history.'

Although Portsmouth managed to emerge from administration in the summer of 2010, following a decision by creditors to endorse a CVA, they remained hamstrung. Not only did the club have to repay a percentage of the debts they had accrued, in Balram Chainrai they also had an owner who was unwilling to invest.

At their lowest ebb, a sliver of hope suddenly appeared in the form of Convers Sports Initiatives (CSI), owned by the Russian banker Vladimir Antonov. In June 2011 it was announced that CSI had bought the club from Chainrai for the price of £17m and that, along with the development of a new stadium, CSI would also be providing finance for transfers. This latter promise was manna from heaven for a club that at the beginning of the 2010/11 season had been forced to release ten players because of the worsening financial picture at Fratton Park.

'Taking into account the problems that we had endured with owners, most fans greeted the arrival of Antonov cautiously. And we were right to, because within four months this supposed white knight had a Europe-wide arrest warrant issued against him and the club was once again facing the prospect of financial oblivion,' says Colin, angrily.

The warrant had been issued by Lithuanian prosecutors as part of an investigation into asset-stripping at the Lithuanian bank, Bankas Snoras, in which Antonov was the majority shareholder and chairman. After his eventual arrest the Russian's assets were seized, a move that had serious implications for Portsmouth. Despite claiming that it would be 'business as usual', so dependent was it on Antonov's money, that CSI was soon placed into administration, leading the Russian to resign as chairman of the club. With no owner and no cashflow, Portsmouth were thrown into turmoil once more.

In February 2012, administration arrived again, earning Pompey a ten-point deduction. For a club that was already performing poorly in the league, this was a massive blow. Facing the real prospect of liquidation, the appointed administrator Trevor Birch initiated a severe cost-cutting process that resulted in many of the team's best players being sent off on loan in an attempt to reduce the business's untenable wage bill.

With a weakened side taking to the pitch and a ten-point penalty to contend with, it was little surprise to many that Pompey ended the season in 22nd position, condemning them to life in League 1; the first time in 30 years that they had played at that level.

For most fans, pre-season is an exciting time. New signings arrive, optimism (however misplaced) is in the air and the prospect of the season to come is something to look forward to. But for Portsmouth fans like Colin, the summer of 2012 was as bleak as it's possible to imagine.

He says, 'It's difficult to know what was worse, the fact that we were starting the season on minus-ten points because of our ongoing administration, the fact that we remained in administration with apparently no hope of exiting it or the fact that in the summer the entire professional playing squad left the club because we could no longer afford them. It was the worst way you could imagine any team starting a campaign. The low point was losing 4-0 in a pre-season friendly to Gibraltar, as the then manager Michael Appleton tried to cobble together a coherent squad with no guarantee there would even be a club next week.'

Portsmouth were one of the favourites for relegation from the off and as the season progressed those early predictions were spot-on, with the 2012/13 season turning out to be a dismal one. Under the stewardship of caretaker manager Guy Whittingham (who took over from Appleton in November), Portsmouth went on a record winless run that stretched from October 2012 to February 2013, covering 23 matches. Even without the ten-point penalty, with this kind of form they would have struggled to avoid relegation. As it was, the campaign ended with Portsmouth bottom of the league and one of four condemned to life in the bottom tier the following season.

The only positive to emerge from this disastrous campaign was the resolution of the club's ownership issues. After a period of 14 months in administration, on 10 April 2013 Portsmouth emerged from this straitjacket when it was announced that the Pompey Supporters' Trust had agreed a deal with the administrators to take ownership of the club.

Formed a few years earlier, the PST had faced a difficult challenge in its attempts to take control, as Colin explains, 'On the one hand we had to motivate people to get involved with the trust and pledge money to help us in our bid. Considering that we had to raise millions and that most fans are ordinary, working people, this was a big ask. And on the other, we realised early on that the PST alone probably wouldn't have the financial power to take full ownership of the club, so we also had to find local people who had both the money to support our bid and who were sympathetic to the philosophy of supporter ownership.'

Through pledges and fundraising, the PST was eventually able to raise £2.5m, a considerable sum by supporter trust standards. This was then complemented by the cash provided by several local businessmen and long-time Pompey fans, who each invested a minimum of £50,000 in the bid. The money given by these 'presidents', as the PST has termed them, was external to that provided by the trust and designed to make them shareholders in the club and not the PST. 'Combined,' says Colin, 'it gave us enough cash to approach the administrators with a bid.'

The only stumbling block was the attitude of Balram Chainrai, who had taken out a secured charge against Fratton Park in the event of default by CSI. When that happened it made him, in practical terms, the quasi-owner of the stadium, even if the nominal title remained with the club. Chainrai placed a valuation of around £12m on Fratton Park, believed at the time to represent his way of recouping part of the £17m he claimed to still be owed to him by the club.

After months of legal wrangling and a trip to the High Court, an out-of-court settlement was eventually reached between the administrators, Portpin and the PST. Under the terms of the deal, the PST (along with its 'presidential' partners) agreed to pay Portpin £3m for Fratton Park and £450,000 for other assets. Two additional payments of £125,000 were then also agreed to, one at the end of the 2016/17 season and the other at the end of 2017/18. Should Pompey reach the Premier League at any point in the next ten years then Portpin would also be due one final payday, to the tune of £2m.

In late January, the bid by the PST and its partner presidents was very nearly gazumped. A proposed takeover led by the merchant banker Keith Harris and supported by his partners Alan Hitchens (a professional investor, and Kent-based vet) and Pascal Najadi (an investment banker) threatened to ruin everything that the club's fans had been working towards since Pompey had entered administration for the second time.

Fortunately for the fans, in the end the rival bid was scuppered, in part because the supporters' proposal remained the preferred choice of the administrators but also because the Football League threatened to expel Portsmouth if the supporters' bid did not go through, citing a League provision that no club can start two consecutive seasons in administration and that the lateness of the Harris bid was making this more of a reality in Pompey's case.

It turned out to be very fortunate for the club that Harris and his partners failed. Not long after Portsmouth's ownership issues were finally resolved it emerged that Najadi's father, Hussain, had been shot dead in Malaysia. Attributed by the police to a property deal that had gone sour, the outcome of this affair was Najadi's relocation to Moscow on the guidance of his security advisors. As a major backer of Harris's rival bid, his absence could have had serious implications for the club had the deal gone through, potentially plunging it once again into the midst of another crisis, one that Pompey might not have been able to emerge from.

The new owners of the club, Portsmouth Community Football Club Ltd (PCFC), are a consortium that's comprised of the PST and the 11 'presidents' that contributed to the bid. At the moment, the trust's shareholding is around 57 per cent and that of the presidents at 43 per cent. This holding provides the trust with three of the seven directors that currently sit on the club's board. It has been a long and difficult road to get to this point but according to Colin, this is just the first step on an even longer and more difficult path to come.

He says, 'We've inherited a football club that has been battered and pretty much hollowed out by previous regimes. I can't think of a club in England that has had such a dramatic fall from grace or one that has suffered so much financial turmoil. And in our modern game that really is saying something. In the future, not only do we have to keep paying for the mistakes that were made in the recent past but we also have to re-energise the supporter base, reconnect with our corporate partners and try to build a squad that can get the club back to where most of the fans think they belong, which is in the top two tiers. At the same time, we also have to make sure that the PST stays motivated and that our presidential partners continue to believe in this model of ownership. None of this is going to be easy.'

Not easy, but the potential to grow and succeed is there. So far this season, Pompey have been averaging crowds of around 15,000 at home, with a high of just over 18,000 for their campaign opener against Oxford. Their nearest league rival in terms of attendances is Plymouth, who only manage around 7,000 a game. In fact, Portsmouth's crowds dwarf the League 2 average, which stands at around just 4,500 per match. If you're looking for a more direct comparison for crowd size at Fratton Park, then it's best to cast your eyes much higher up the pyramid. Pompey's average gate of 15,000 is more in keeping with Championship sides such as Wigan Athletic, QPR and Watford.

This ability to generate income from the fans could be further enhanced if the club is one day able to redevelop Fratton Park or relocate to a new stadium. Although this seems unlikely in the short term, after all Pompey are still recovering from their financial meltdown, in the longer term if the club wants to progress up the football pyramid and do so sustainably, then greater capacity at their stadium, including the development of better corporate facilities, would be fundamental to this.

And in terms of supporters, there is every reason to believe that should the club start improving on their league position, the fans would be there to fill any extra capacity. Considering their fall from grace, Pompey's supporters have been amazingly loyal; 18,000 people for a League 2 clash with Oxford is illustrative of this. This could easily be improved if extra capacity and an improvement in form occurred. After all, Portsmouth is a city with a population of just over 200,000, with a wider catchment of around half a million people and which contains no rival club for them to compete against for attention.

If they could capitalise on this potential and really grow then many of those who have been involved with punk football feel that this would be inspirational.

Dave Boyle says, 'AFC Wimbledon gave the idea of fans owning clubs a real boost. But as inspirational as they have been, they're still a lower-league club and one that could never probably, in the short term at least, make it to the Premier League. What the idea now needs is a big community club to embrace supporter ownership and thrive with it and in doing so raise the profile of the model and prove that majority control and success are not mutually incompatible.

'What happened at Swansea has helped but their fans still only own a minority stake. Which is why what's going on at Portsmouth is so exciting. We've got a club here where the fans have majority control, which is pulling in Championship attendances in League 2 and which has massive potential to grow in the future. The impact on the reputation of supporter ownership should this club be successful could be massive.'

Sean Hamil adds, 'Prior to their rescue by the fans this was a club that embodied everything that is wrong with the modern game. Over-reach, over-spend, dodgy owners, labyrinth finances, debt, administration, the prospect of liquidation; they became shorthand for football's failures and in the process "doing a Portsmouth" entered the game's lexicon. But if that period of financial turmoil under the private model of ownership could be contrasted with a period of success and sustainability under a model where it's the fans that call the shots, it would provide a beautiful narrative wouldn't it?'

Tom Hall explains, 'There is a perspective that punk football is something more suited to small clubs and those competing in non-league football and the lower regions of the Football League. And of course, there is an element of truth in this. Over the past decade there have certainly been more opportunities for supporter-led takeovers in the lower regions of football.

The reality of the modern game is that as worthy as all clubs are, what tends to excite both those with an interest in football and people working in media is what happens at bigger clubs.

'They might be down in League 2, but Pompey are still a relatively big club. And they have the potential to be bigger. Their success could be one that the media latches on to, something that would do much to raise the profile of punk football.'

Of course, there's no saying what will happen to Portsmouth over the coming years. If the short history of supporter ownership has proven anything it's that failure is always a real possibility. Although Pompey could very well be the next AFC Wimbledon, they could also be the next Stockport County. Fans can be fickle and football remains a game where it's results that matter most. The club could stay true to its new model or in a decade they could be owned by another wealthy adventurer, whose deep pockets and big promises have wooed supporters keen to recapture the glory days when the club competed in the Premier League and featured in FA Cup finals.

At the moment the trust and 'presidents' have the goodwill of the fans, enormous potential and, courtesy of the various financial regulations being introduced into English football, the beginnings of a more benign environment within which to compete. But only time will tell whether any of this really amounts to much and whether the great hope for supporter ownership ever fulfil their potential.

Until then, those fans who want to see a greater role for supporters in the game will have to content themselves with spectacles like the one which unfolded here today at Kingsmeadow. Two teams that shouldn't really exist playing to a packed stadium filled with men and women who have bought a stake in the clubs they follow. Such a sight would have been inconceivable a generation ago; thousands of fans united not just in the ownership of their club but also in an idea, a belief that supporters together can challenge the status quo in English football and provide a solution to the manifold problems affecting the sport.

But despite the shared affinity between both sets of fans, football remains a partisan game. They might be comrades, active under the banner of punk football but when the whistle blows at kick-off any sense of brotherly love quickly dissipates. Although the Premier League gets all the attention, what happens down in League 2 can be just as compelling and today's game was a perfect example of this. The quality of football might not have the precision and technical craft that you see in the top flight but does that really matter? Both sides played with speed, passion and commitment. Yes, there was the occasional long ball (actually, more than occasional) and sporadic examples of extreme head tennis were evident, but even to the neutral observer what was on offer at Kingstonian was entertaining.

For those with an emotional investment in what was happening, who let's face it matter more than some uninvolved Evertonian, it's the home fans who would have been happier come the final whistle. They might be the great hope for the future but on today's evidence, Pompey still have a long way to go to fulfil those dreams. AFC Wimbledon, the elder statesmen of punk football, gave the movement's new boys a lesson in how to play. The final scoreline of 4-0 flattered Portsmouth. It could have, and for the want of some better finishing should have been more.

Ten years ago, on the same weekend that this game took place, AFC Wimbledon played Cobham FC in the Combined Counties Premier Division and beat them 4-0. At the same time, in the Premier League (nine levels up the pyramid) Portsmouth took on Leeds United and battered them 6-1. Since then both sides have enjoyed and endured an extraordinary reversal in fortunes, one benefiting under the ownership of the fans and the other nearly being destroyed by private hands. Their stories since then can tell us a lot about the many problems facing our national game.

But more than anything, these divergent tales should offer a sense of hope. Supporters are not powerless. The days of fans meekly accepting their lot and kowtowing to the board are a thing of the past. Working together supporters can achieve something remarkable. They can save clubs from extinction, bring new clubs to life and ensure that those in charge are always held to account. Punk football has changed what it means to be a fan in England today. Stakeholders with a right to be heard. Customers no more.

Bibliography

Books

Mel Nurse, *Mr Swansea* (YLolfa Cyf 2009)

Adam Brown and Andy Walsh, *Not For Sale: Manchester United, Murdoch and the Defeat of BSkyB* (Mainstream Publishing 1999)

Steven North and Paul Hodson, *Build a Bonfire: How Football Fans United to Save Brighton & Hove Albion* (Mainstream Publishing 1997)

Neil Carter, *The Football Manager, A History* (Routledge 2006)

Jimmy Burns, *La Roja: A Journey through Spanish Football* (Simon & Schuster 2012)

Kirk Blows and Ben Sharratt, *Bring Me the Head of Trevor Brooking: Three Decades of East End Soap Opera at West Ham United* (Mainstream Publishing 2010)

Andrew Ward and John Williams, *Football Nation: Sixty Years of the Beautiful Game* (Bloomsbury 2010)

Brian Reade, *An Epic Swindle: 44 Months with a Pair of Cowboys* (Quercus 2012)

David Conn, *The Beautiful Game? Searching for the Soul of Football* (Yellow Jersey Press 2005)

Dick Knight, *Madman* (Vision Sports Publishing 2013)

David Conn, *The Football Business* (Mainstream Publishing 2002)

Stefan Szymanski & Simon Kuper, *Soccernomics: Why England Loses, Why Spain, Germany and Brazil Win, and Why the US, Japan, Australia, Turkey and even Iraq are Destined to Become Kings of the World's Most Popular Sport* (HarperSport 2012)

Paul Tomkins, Graeme Riley, Gary Fulcher, *Pay As You Play: The True Price of Success in the Premier League Era* (GPRF Publishing 2010)

Ian Ridley, *There's a Golden BSkyB: How Twenty Years of the Premier League Have Changed Football Forever* (Bloomsbury 2012)

Ulrich Hesse-Lichtenberger, *Tor! The Story of German Football* (WSC Books 2003)

Stephen Dobson and John Goddard, *The Economics of Football* (Cambridge University Press 2011)

Rogan Taylor, *Football and its Fans: Supporters and Their Relations with the Game, 1885-1985* (Leicester University Press 1992)

Percy Young, *History of British Football* (Stanley Paul & Co Ltd 1968)

James Walvin, *The People's Game: A Social History of British Football* (Allen Lane 1975)

James Walvin, *The Only Game: Football and Our Times* (Longman 2001)

Mike Lewis, *The Trains Don't Stop There Anymore* (Vertical Editions 2007)

Trevor Watkins, *Cherries in Red* (Headline Book Publishing 1999)

Paul Dempsey & Kevan Reilly, *Big Money Beautiful Game* (Nicholas Brealey Publishing Limited 1998)

Simon Inglis, *League Football and the Men who Made it* (Willow Books, Collins 1988)

Articles and Reports

Culture, Media and Sport Committee, *Seventh Report on Football Governance* (House of Commons 2011)

Dr Adam Brown, Kevin Jaquiss, Dr Mark James, Dr Annabel Kiernan & Prof. Guy Osborn, *Supporters Direct Briefing Paper No. 1, Developing Public Policy to Encourage Supporter Community Ownership in Football* (Substance 2011)

Dave Boyle, Dr Adam Brown, Tom Hall, Dr Mark James, Kevin Jaquiss, Partner, Dr Annabel Kiernan, and Prof. Guy Osborn, *Supporters Direct Briefing Paper No.2: Developing Football Regulation to Encourage Supporter Community Ownership in Football* (Substance 2011)

Dr Adam Brown, Fiona McGee, Kevin Jaquiss, Thea Longley, *Supporters Direct Briefing Paper No. 3: Financing Supporter Community Ownership* (Substance 2011)

Dr Adam Brown and Fiona McGee, *Supporters Direct Briefing Paper No. 4: The Business Case for Supporter Community Ownership* (Substance 2011)

Stefan Szymanski, *Insolvency in English professional football: Irrational Exuberance or Negative Shocks?* (http://www. soccernomics-agency.com/?p=1)

David Conn, *Follow the Money* (London Review of Books, Vol. 34 No. 16, August 2012 pages 25-26) (http://www.lrb. co.uk/v34/n16/david-conn/follow-the-money)

Charles P. Korr, *West Ham United Football Club and the Beginnings of Professional Football in East London, 1895-1914*

(Journal of Contemporary History, Vol. 13, pp. 211-232)
(http://history.msu.edu/hst455/files/2012/05/Korr-West-
Ham-1978.pdf)

Grant Thornton, *Focus on Football Finance 2012* (http://www.
grant-thornton.co.uk/pdf/Focus_on_football_finance.pdf)

Bundesliga Report 2013 (DFL Deutsche Fußball Liga GmbH
2013) (http://static.bundesliga.com/media/native/autosync/
report_2013_gb_72dpi.pdf)

Dave Boyle: *Football Mad: Are we Paying More for Less* (The
High Pay Centre 2012) (http://highpaycentre.org/files/
hpc_06_07.pdf)

Sara Ward, Thomas J. Scanlon and Tony Hines, *Mutuality
Ownership Form and Professional Sports: Football* (Nonprofit
and Voluntary Sector Quarterly, 4 (42), 763-780) (http://
www.hssr.mmu.ac.uk/mmufc/files/2013/05/Sara-Ward-
Journal-Article.pdf)

Paul Thomas, *Marching Altogether? Football Fans Taking
a Stand against Racism*. In: *Sport and Challenges to Racism. Global Culture and Sport Series* pp. 185-198 (Palgrave
Macmillan 2010)

Sir Norman Chester Centre for Football Research: *Fact Sheet
No.10, The New Football Economics* (http://www.furd.org/
resources/fs10.pdf)

Sir Norman Chester Centre for Football Research: *Fact Sheet
No. 7, Fan 'power' and Democracy in Football* (http://www.
furd.org/resources/fs7.pdf)

Sean Hamil, Geoff Walters and Lee Watson, *The Model of
Governance at FC Barcelona: Balancing Member Democracy,
Commercial Strategy, Corporate Social Responsibility and
Sporting Performance* (Soccer & Society Vol. 11, No. 4, July
2010, 475–504) (http://users.polisci.wisc.edu/schatzberg/
ps616/Hamil2010.pdf)

Share in Football's Community, FC United of Manchester Community Share Offer Document (http://www.fc-utd. co.uk/mcsf/FCUMComShares2011Full.pdf)

Videos

Michael Jackson's speech in Exeter
http://www.youtube.com/watch?v=EpgWEbuU5TY

Glen Mulcaire's first goal for AFC Wimbledon
http://www.youtube.com/watch?v=jUxSuHPDbK

Brighton & Hove Albion v Hereford United 3 May 1997
http://www.youtube.com/watch?v=-4SyMPHlwn8

BBC Panorama: *The Trillion-Dollar Con Man*
http://www.youtube.com/watch?v=FH-p0SLL-4vw&list=PL23F6755DE4750C72

Manchester United v Exeter City, FA Cup, 8 January 2005
http://www.youtube.com/watch?v=bzehqJF6Y9o

Manchester United v Brighton & Hove Albion, FA Cup Final 1983 (extra time highlights)
http://www.youtube.com/watch?v=-d4-lFjGnU-A&list=HL1385637638

Websites

The Football Task Force and the 'regulator debate'
http://www.bbk.ac.uk/management/mscmres/publications/seanpublications/footballinthedigitalage/FITDA-chapter32.shtml

Premier League finances: turnover, wages, debt and performance:
http://www.theguardian.com/news/datablog/2013/apr/18/premier-league-club-accounts-debt

Liverpool FC: Life under the control of Tom Hicks and
George Gillett
http://www.theguardian.com/football/2010/oct/06/
liverpool-takeover-hicks-gillett

Arsenal FC
http://www.arsenal.com

Premier League club accounts: how in debt are they?
http://www.theguardian.com/football/2012/may/23/
premier-league-accounts-profit-debt

Championship finances 2011/12 numbers:
http://swissramble.blogspot.co.uk/2013/08/championship-
finances-201112-numbers.html

Deloitte Money League
http://www.deloitte.com/view/en_GB/uk/industries/
sportsbusinessgroup/index.htm

Pay As You Play
http://transferpriceindex.com

Premier League annual net transfer spend 2002-2012
http://www.sportingintelligence.com/2011/08/24/sale-of-
nasri-makes-arsenal-a-net-selling-club-over-a-decade-24080/

Yet more uncertainty for Bradford City
http://twohundredpercent.net/?p=11980

Bourne again
http://www.wsc.co.uk/the-archive/30-Clubs/6431-bourne-
again

Guilty pleas close grim chapter in Grecian history
http://www.theguardian.com/football/2007/apr/25/
newsstory.sport5

Notts County and Munto Finance, the inquest begins
http://twohundredpercent.net/?p=4516

I bitterly regret Notts County sale says trust chief
http://www.theguardian.com/football/2009/dec/11/notts-county-john-armstrong-holmes

Clubs in Crisis
http://www.clubsincrisis.com

Stockport County, no one is innocent
http://twohundredpercent.net/?p=5102

Tangled Webb, Brentford are being destroyed by their own chief executive
http://www.wsc.co.uk/the-archive/30-Clubs/6288-tangled-webb

Atletico Madrid – it's a mad world
http://swissramble.blogspot.co.uk/2012/08/atletico-madrid-its-mad-world.html

The truth about debt at Barcelona and Real Madrid
http://swissramble.blogspot.co.uk/2012/04/truth-about-debt-at-barcelona-and-real.html

Reading FC – dear prudence
http://swissramble.blogspot.co.uk/2012/06/reading-fc-dear-prudence.html

Mark Goldberg: I am not embarrassed about my time at Crystal Palace
http://www.theguardian.com/football/2011/nov/11/mark-goldberg-crystal-palace

Venables' deal cost Palace
http://www.theguardian.com/football/1999/mar/06/newsstory.sport5

Football League clubs want more money from Premier League
http://www.bbc.co.uk/sport/0/football/22205419

How do ticket prices for the Premier League compare with Europe?

http://www.theguardian.com/news/datablog/2013/jan/17/
football-ticket-prices-premier-league-europe

The final score on football law
http://www.danielgeey.com/blog/

What's gone wrong at Portsmouth? Ten reasons for the
demise of a club
http://www.theguardian.com/football/2010/feb/05/
portsmouth-balram-chainrai-sacha-gaydamak

Compare the leagues
http://comparetheleagues.com

The Tilehurst End
http://thetilehurstend.sbnation.com/

FC United of Manchester
http://www.fc-utd.co.uk/home.php

Manchester United Supporters' Trust
http://www.joinmust.org/about/wsc.php

Pompey Supporters' Trust
http://www.pompeytrust.com

York City Supporters' Trust
http://www.ycst.org.uk

Spirit of Shankly
http://www.spiritofshankly.com

Trust Everton
http://www.trusteverton.com

Crystal Palace Supporters' Trust
http://palacetrust.org.uk

The Dons Trust
http://llocally.com/thedonstrust

AFC Wimbledon
http://www.afcwimbledon.co.uk

Swansea City Supporters' Trust
http://www.swanstrust.co.uk

Arsenal Supporters' Trust
http://www.arsenaltrust.org

Exeter City Supporters' Trust
http://www.ecfcst.org.uk

Bees United
http://www.beesunited.org.uk

Arsenal Fanshare
http://www.arsenalfanshare.com

The Blues Trust
http://www.bluestrust.org